Basil Ell

User Interfaces to the Web of Data based on Natural Language Generation

User Interfaces to the Web of Data based on Natural Language Generation

by
Basil Ell

KIT Scientific Publishing

Dissertation, Karlsruher Institut für Technologie
KIT-Fakultät für Wirtschaftswissenschaften, 2015

Tag der mündlichen Prüfung: 5. Mai 2015
Referenten: Prof. Dr. Rudi Studer, Prof. Dr. Philipp Cimiano

Impressum

KIT Scientific Publishing

Karlsruher Institut für Technologie (KIT)
KIT Scientific Publishing
Straße am Forum 2
D-76131 Karlsruhe

KIT Scientific Publishing is a registered trademark
of Karlsruhe Institute of Technology.
Reprint using the book cover is not allowed.

www.ksp.kit.edu

Print on Demand 2017 – Gedruckt auf FSC-zertifiziertem Papier

ISBN 978-3-7315-0462-7
DOI 10.5445/KSP/1000051072

Abstract

The core idea of the Semantic Web vision is the evolution from a Web of hyperlinked human-readable web pages, the Web of Documents, to a machine-interpretable Web of Data. Since natural language text is a suitable knowledge representation for humans and not for machines, the knowledge representation formalism RDF was developed and large amounts of RDF data are published. Now that machine-interpretable data is available, the fact that RDF data is not human-readable poses challenges for humans intending to interact with the data and to exploit the wealth of data. In this work, Natural Language Generation is applied to bridge the gap from machine-interpretable data to human-readable text to improve user interfaces to the Web of Data.

In the context of a concrete research practice, i.e., the qualitative and quantitative analysis of a large digital corpus of educational lexica, we[1] explore how Virtual Research Environments based on Semantic Web technologies support research interactions with RDF data in various stages of corpus-based analysis.

We analyze the human-readability of a large subset of the Web of Data in terms of the availability of human-readable labels of entities and propose label-related quality metrics. Since our analysis shows that labels are missing for a significant percentage of entities we explore an approach to derive labels from names of variables in queries formulated in SPARQL, which is an RDF query language.

In the context of search interfaces to RDF data a class of SPARQL query-generating systems exists where users signify their information needs in the form of keywords or (controlled) natural language questions. For the purpose of enabling a user to observe a potential discrepancy between an intended question and the system-generated query we created a method to verbalize SPARQL queries. Here, the meaning of a query encoded in SPARQL is conveyed to the user via English text.

The different syntaxes of RDF are not suitable for the presentation to casual users. We introduce a template-based approach to verbalize RDF graphs. Since manual creation of these templates is tedious work we developed a language-independent approach to induce RDF verbalization templates from a parallel corpus of text and data.

[1] I use the form *we* instead of *I*, since the work was published together with coauthors. In most publications, however, I provided the main contribution and was acknowledged as first author. Using the form *we* instead of *I* serves for the purpose of acknowledging my coauthors.

Acknowledgments

This thesis is the result of my work as a research assistant at the Intitute of Applied Informatics and Formal Description Methods (AIFB) under the guidance of Rudi Studer. I am deeply indebted to Rudi Studer for creating such a productive environment and letting me become a member of that environment, for his guidance, and in general for the inspiring calm and wise way he interacts with people and the freedom he provided which allowed me to explore topics on my own and to pursue my research interests.

I am also grateful to Philipp Cimiano for acting as a second reviewer of this work and to Andreas Oberweis and Bruno Neibecker for being part of the examination committee.

My time at AIFB was awesome and memorable due to many people to which I'd like to express my gratitude: Andreas Harth for being a great advisor, for asking the right questions and his special trait of being provocative in a productive way, for his attitude to work, for being approachable, all the discussion and the fun we had during dinner and Friday beers or the informal and spontaneous discussion on the weekend in coffee houses. Denny Vrandečić and Elena Simperl for their guidance during early stages of my Ph.D and the interesting environment they created via the projects they involved me in. Benedikt Kämpgen for all the late night rehearsal talks in hotel rooms in some remote locations, his thoughtfulness, and good nature. Maribel Acosta for all the jokes only we find funny and all the references only we understand. And for the squid, sort of. Michael Färber for the close collaboration and all the discussions about philosophical topics. Tobias Käfer for being an endless source of puns, cultural references, and bad jokes. Anees ul Mehdi for the many interesting discussions beyond semantic technologies, his hospitality and the great food at his home! Lei Zhang for always being kind and thoughtful. And for all the many others that I will miss, such as Achim Rettinger, Aditya Mogadala, Anja Hess, Beate Kühner, Daniel Herzig, Fabian Flöck, Gisela Schillinger, Ignacio Traverso Ribón, Julia Hoxha, Martin Junghans, Nadia Achmed, Patrick Philipp, Steffen Thoma, Tobias Weller, Verónica Rivera Pelayo, and Yongtao Ma.

I very much enjoyed to work with Christoph Schindler, Anne Hild, Anna Stisser, Cornelia Veja, and Marc Rittberger from the SMW-CorA project and for the many interesting and fruitful interdisciplinary discussions. And the great Korean food, Christoph!

Finally, I'd like to thank the Deutsche Forschungsgesellschaft (DFG) for funding the SMW-CorA project, the European Union for funding the ACTIVE project, and Thorsten Tüllmann from the Steinbuch Centre for Computing (SCC) for his excellent support as well as the SCC for their generously provided computing infrastructure.

Contents

1 Introduction

1.1 Motivation

The World Wide Web used to be merely a Web of Documents – it mostly consisted of documents created by humans and intended to be viewed or read by humans. On the Web, a vast source of humanity's knowledge is available in textual form. A human with a specific information need has to have tools available for the purpose of searching and retrieving relevant information. While machines can process large quantities of data and can scan billions of documents for specific terms, understanding the meaning of text would require a machine to be capable of performing Natural Language Understanding (NLU). NLU is a subtopic of artificial intelligence research that deals with machine reading comprehension [Ovc12] and is an active area of research.

Scanning documents for search terms has limitations. A relevant search term might not be explicitly mentioned in a document. Consider, for example, a document that describes how to prepare a biscuit roll but does not contain the phrase *cake recipe*. Finding that document using the search term *cake recipe* is difficult. While a human can derive that the document contains a cake recipe, deriving the same conclusion is a difficult task for machines. Besides detecting the topic of a document (here the topic is *cake recipe*), consider a user being interested in all affective statements about a product (this problem is known as opinion mining) from social media data or a user being interested in particular events from a set of news documents (known as event detection). These tasks require more than scanning documents for search terms.

NLU is difficult for several reasons. To mention just a few: Words may have multiple meanings (homonyms, e.g. *fluke*, which can mean a flatfish, a lucky stroke, or flat end of an arm of an anchor).[1] Words may be vague (e.g., red, tall, near, expensive). The capability to distinguish between literal and figurative meaning is relevant, for example, to understand the expression *Iraq is another Vietnam* [EP09]. Humans make use of their knowledge about the world when interpreting natural language expressions. While, for example, for a machine the two sentences *I like to eat pizza with mushrooms* and *I like to eat pizza with friends* are syntactically identical, having experiences in the real world helps humans understand that mushrooms are a topping, friends are companions, and toppings and companions are disjunct. Additionally, ambiguities

[1] Example taken from: *The Online Etymological Dictionary*. Retrieved 2014-07-21.

present in a sentence such as *The man sees the woman with the telescope*[2] need to be either resolved or preserved when converting that sentence into a formal knowledge representation. Finally, natural language utterances can be context-specific. "Bring me some water" uttered in the dining room could mean something different when uttered in the garden.

The vision of a Semantic Web is to publish machine-processable data on the Web, so that machines can support humans in information retrieval tasks without understanding natural language text. In traditional search on the Web, given a set of keywords a search engine scans an index of documents for the occurrence of these keyword (or synonyms of these keywords), ranks documents according to a relevance function, and presents the user a list of links to these documents. Machine-processable data enables more sophisticated search capabilities. For example, given a query language, an expert user could write a query to retrieve *flights this week-end from an airport near Karlsruhe for a price below 300 EUR to a sunny destination where cultural festivals take place*. Given that, typically, for such a complex information need no single page exists on the Web that answers this specific question and contains all keywords necessary so that the search engine would find that page, addressing this information need is unfeasible without the availability of machine-processable data. When searching on the Semantic Web, information from multiple data providers would be incorporated, such as from a provider of geographical information (to find airports near the city of Karlsruhe), the airlines (to find flights below 300 EUR and the travel destinations), weather data providers (to filter out non-sunny destinations), and event agencies (to find cultural festivals).

With RDF (Resource Description Framework) [CW14] a data model was created and standardized that enables machine-processable data to be published on the Web as *Linked Data* [HB11]. RDF represents information in the form of a graph built from unique identifiers of entities (e.g., unique identifiers for a city or an airport) and unique identifiers of relations (e.g., unique identifiers for the relations *is located near* or *has mean temperature*). In the last years, more and more data has been published in RDF and large quantities are available today, thus offering potential for interesting use-cases exploiting this wealth of machine-processable data.

While RDF is primarily machine-processable, RDF data should be related to natural language (e.g., English) for a couple of reasons:

- An expert user capable of writing queries in a formal query language needs to understand which entities and relations to use when formulating the query. For example, the user needs to know the unique identifier of the relation that expresses that something is located geographically near something else. Ideally, these entities and relations are explained in natural language.

[2] Is the man using the telescope to see the woman or does the man see the woman carrying the telescope?

- The majority of users of the Web are not experts in Semantic Web technologies and therefore not able to write formal queries. These users would communicate their information need to a *semantic search* [GMM03] interface for example as a set of keywords or as a natural language question. The interfaces then need to identify entities and relations related to these keywords for the purpose of creating a formal query. Furthermore, search interfaces trying to resolve ambiguities during interpretation of the user's information need may resolve ambiguities by engaging in a clarification dialog with a user and therefore need to have natural language expressions available so that the search interfaces can provide alternative options in natural language.
- Once a search interface has executed a query and retrieved results, the data needs to be communicated to the user. While some query results might be very simple such as *yes* or *no*, a telephone number, or a set of links to documents and can thus easily be displayed to the user, they can also be more complex, such as in the example above, where the resulting RDF graph would consist of information about airports, flights, dates, prices, destinations, events, and the relations between the entities.

Where RDF data is not related to natural language this constitutes a gap. A gap between RDF and natural language (be it English or any other natural language) would limit the applicability of the Web of Data and impede realization of systems supporting interesting use-cases. In this thesis we investigate which research interactions with RDF data need to be supported by a Virtual Research Environment in the context of a concrete research practice: the qualitative and quantitative analysis of a large digital corpus of educational lexica in the field of History of Education. Furthermore, we propose a set of metrics to study the gap between RDF and natural language. Given a large subset of the Web of Data we find that the gap exists and therefore propose reducing it via an approach that provides human-readable names for entities. We make the behavior of search interfaces transparent by verbalizing system-generated formal queries – queries formulated in the RDF query language SPARQL [PS08] – in English, introduce a template-based approach to verbalize RDF graphs, and provide a method that automatically induces RDF verbalization templates from example texts and data.

1.2 Research Questions

The principal research question of this thesis concerns **interfaces enabling human users to interact with the Web of Data**. This question is broken down into ten individual research questions which are briefly introduced.

Interaction with RDF data in a Virtual Research Environment
Research Question 1.1 *How can capabilities of researchers be enhanced by a semantically-enhanced Virtual Research Environment?*
In the context of a Virtual Research Environment (VRE) that is based on Semantic Web technologies and where research objects are described in RDF, certain interactions with research data in various stages of corpus-based analysis may be enabled or enhanced via Semantic Web technologies. We give an example of a concrete research practice: the qualitative and quantitative analysis of a large digital corpus of educational lexica in the field of History of Education.

Research Question 1.2 *How can research interactions be enabled by a semantically-enhanced Virtual Research Environment?*
Besides interactions between researchers and RDF data in the semantically-enhanced Virtual Research Environment, we investigate how socio-technical interactions between researchers and, for example, digital libraries can be enabled.

Labels in the Web of Data
Research Question 2.1 *Which properties are used for the purpose of labeling?*
Entities in the Web of Data need to have human-readable names, known as labels, so that labels can be shown to humans in user interfaces, labels can be searched for in search applications, and natural language can be generated from RDF data. The RDFS vocabulary provides the property `rdfs:label`. However, several other properties are in use for the same purpose and these properties are not always explicitly linked to the property `rdfs:label` thus they cannot be automatically identified as labeling properties.

Research Question 2.2 *Which metrics help study the properties of labeling within a dataset?*
The quality of an RDF dataset can be assessed in terms of the availability of labels. Besides the availability of labels, further criteria, such as the availability of labels in multiple languages, are also relevant. A set of label-related quality criteria and metrics is required when studying the state of labeling in a dataset of the Web of Data.

Research Question 2.3 *What is the state of labeling in the Web of Data according to these metrics?*
Once a set of label-related metrics is defined, the Web of Data (or a subset thereof) can be analyzed according to these metrics for the purpose of studying the state of labeling. Insights gained through these analyses can be relevant for dataset providers as well as developers of user interfaces to RDF datasets.

Analyzing SPARQL query logs
Research Question 3.1 *How can human-readable labels be derived from variable names in SPARQL queries?*
Our assessment of the state of labeling in the Web of Data showed that a large percentage of entities lack a label. Human authors of SPARQL queries (SPARQL is a query language for RDF data) may use meaningful variable names, thereby reflecting their knowledge about entities. From variable names labels can potentially be derived.

Research Question 3.2 *Which SPARQL graph patterns are common?*
Knowing about frequent common structures of SPARQL queries and their number of occurrence in a real dataset is valuable information for RDF database engine developers. Knowledge about frequent common structures can be helpful for designing indexing and caching strategies for the purpose of increasing the performance of query engines.

Verbalizing SPARQL queries
Research Question 4 *How can SPARQL queries be verbalized in a mostly schema-agnostic manner?*
Search interfaces to RDF datasets exist that generate SPARQL queries based on the interpretation of the user's information need where the user provides hints about the information need via keywords or a natural language question. For the purpose of enabling a user to observe a potential discrepancy between the information need and the system-generated query, the meaning of a SPARQL query needs to be communicated to the user. Verbalizing a query is the task of rendering its meaning in the form of text. Ideally, such an approach does not depend to a specific schema (e.g., specific entities or relations) but is schema-agnostic: being applicable on any RDF dataset independently of the entities and relations being used.

Verbalizing RDF graphs
Research Question 5.1 *How can RDF graphs be verbalized as a single sentence using a template?*
The different syntaxes of RDF are not suitable for presentation to casual users. However, information encoded in RDF can be of interest to users: e.g. when RDF data is returned by a search interface or a tool that extracts information from text, represents the information as RDF and presents the information to a human user. Verbalizing an

RDF data graph by verbalizing each triple individually, which is explored by related approaches, results in unnatural texts since sentences in natural language usually express multiple triples in a concise manner. Having templates where a template allows an RDF graph to be verbalized as a single sentence would enable the concise verbalization of RDF graphs.

Research Question 5.2 *How can RDF verbalization templates be learned from a parallel text-data corpus?*
Manual creation of RDF verbalization templates is tedious work. Templates are domain-specific and genre-specific – thus they cannot be reused for other domains and genres. Therefore, an approach that automatically induces templates from examples is desirable. From domain-specific and genre-specific examples it would automatically learn appropriate templates. A parallel text-data corpus consisting of texts where entities and their relations expressed in texts are also expressed formally as RDF data can potentially be used to learn how RDF graphs can be expressed in natural language. Resulting templates are as concise as the example sentences the templates are learned from, and they are natural since the example texts provide evidence for the naturalness of the extracted patterns. This is in contrast to the results of verbalization approaches that verbalize each triple individually.

1.3 Contribution of the Thesis

This thesis makes the following contributions:

- To address *RQ1.1 How can capabilities of researchers be enhanced by a semantically-enhanced Virtual Research Environment?* and *RQ1.2 How can research interactions be enabled by a semantically-enhanced Virtual Research Environment?* we engage with a concrete research community and identify and support a set of research tasks: *importing research data, enriching research data, linking to external data, data cleansing, exploring and analyzing*, and *export and sharing* and enable previously unsupported interactions between life-cycles. The research interactions are supported via a set of tools developed for this purpose as extensions to MediaWiki (*OfflineImport, SemanticImageAnnotator, SemanticTextAnnotator, SemanticWebBrowser* (co-developed), and *AnalysisTool*).
- For the purpose of addressing *RQ2.1 Which properties are used for the purpose of labeling?* we analyze the Billion Triples Challenge (BTC) corpus,[3] which is a large snapshot of the Web of Data. From a set of 3,167,799,445 quadruples we derive 36 properties (shown in Table 4.1, p. 53) as labeling properties. Most of these properties are not connected to `rdfs:label` in a way that would allow machines to automatically discover the alternative labeling property.
- We introduce four label-related metrics thus addressing *RQ2.2 Which metrics help study the properties of labeling within a dataset?*: *Completeness* is defined as the ratio of entities in a dataset that have a label; *efficient accessibility* is defined as the ratio of RDF terms in a dataset that have a label; *unambiguity* is defined as the ratio of entities that have more than one label; and *multilinguality* of a property is the number of languages for which labels are provided for entities in a dataset.
- To address *RQ2.3 What is the state of labeling in the Web of Data according to these metrics?* we analyze the BTC dataset and find that: regarding completeness, only 38.2% of all non-information resources have a label; regarding efficient accessibility, labels for non-vocabulary URIs are only provided within a dataset in 33.82% of cases; regarding unambiguity, most labels (98.0%) are unambiguous; and multilinguality is a strongly underexploited feature. Either no language tag is used, or few languages such as English, German, and French, dominate.
- We present and evaluate an approach to derive human-readable labels from variable names in SPARQL queries from a large set of SPARQL queries which we extracted from the DBpedia[4] and SWDF[5] query logs. The evaluation shows

[3]The Billion Triples Challenge (BTC) corpus is a dataset consisting of Linked Data crawled from the web. The 2014 crawl is available at http://km.aifb.kit.edu/projects/btc-2014/ (last accessed 2015-01-02)

[4]DBpedia is a dataset extracted from Wikipedia, see [Aue+07].

[5]SWDF is a dataset about people, conferences, and publications in the area of Semantic Web research, see [Möl+07].

that the approach is applicable for deriving human-readable labels, thus we address *RQ3.1 How can human-readable labels be derived from variable names in SPARQL queries?*

- For the purpose of addressing *RQ3.2 Which SPARQL graph patterns are common?* we analyze a large set of SPARQL queries extracted from the DBpedia and SWDF query logs. We develop a hypergraph-based visualization of the most frequently occurring graph patterns and apply it to visualize our measurement results in Figure 5.3 (p. 70) and Figure 5.4 (p. 71).
- We introduce a domain-independent SPARQL query verbalization approach based on domain-independent templates to address *RQ4 How can SPARQL queries be verbalized in a mostly schema-agnostic manner?* Being schema-independent renders the verbalization system potentially applicable in many domains. The approach is mostly schema-agnostic because, besides being tied to a set of properties known to be labeling properties (e.g., the property `rdfs:label`) and the property `rdf:type`, all other elements (properties, classes, and instances) are treated only based on linguistic cues found in their labels, their local name, or their fragment identifier. In a comparative evaluation our approach outperforms the state of the art approach SPARQL2NL by obtaining higher or equal accuracy (43 cases (37.72%) and 66 cases (57.89%) respectively); higher or equal syntactical correctness (52 cases (45.61%) and 45 cases (39.47%) respectively); and higher or equal understandability (74 cases (64.91%) and 16 cases (14.04%) respectively).

  In a non-comparative evaluation our system successfully verbalized 98.6% (287/291) of our query dataset built from queries from the QALD (Question Answering over Linked Data)[6] challenges. In 70 out of 120 cases the evaluators attested the best score for syntactical correctness (58.33%), in 47 out of 120 cases the evaluators attested the best understandability score (39.16%).
- To address *RQ5.1 How can RDF graphs be verbalized as a single sentence using a template?* we formally introduce RDF verbalization templates consisting of a sentence pattern which includes modifiers and a graph pattern of unrestricted size. These templates allow RDF data to be verbalized in sentences. Furthermore, to address *RQ5.2 How can RDF verbalization templates be learned from a parallel text-data corpus?* we devise an approach that automatically induces RDF verbalization templates from a parallel corpus. Automatic induction is relevant since manual creation of templates is tedious work. Furthermore, automatically inducing templates from examples has the benefit of generating sentences that are similar in style to those found in the example texts. The approach is based on the distant supervision principle: training data is generated automatically by aligning a database of facts with text; therefore, no hand-labeled data is required. The approach does not use language resources such as parsers or dictionaries and is

[6]See http://greententacle.techfak.uni-bielefeld.de/~cunger/qald/ (last accessed 2015-01-02)

thus language independent. Furthermore, it does not depend on a certain ontology. While the approach induces patterns that contain terms from the ontology used in the corpus, the approach does not require that a certain ontology is used.

We validate the feasibility of the approach for English and German given a large parallel text-data corpus consisting of texts from Wikipedia and data from DBpedia. We show that there are plenty of groups of sentences that share an equivalent sentence abstraction. The more such groups exist, the more templates can potentially be induced. In total, we derived 5066 templates. Evaluation of the coverage shows, that: 1) given this set of templates, a large part of the DBpedia data can be verbalized; and 2) most templates are applicable to a large number of subgraphs of DBpedia. Furthermore, verbalization results are mostly syntactically correct and understandable.

1.4 Published Results

The main material presented in this thesis has been published in the following publications (listed in reverse chronological order):

[EH14] Basil Ell and Andreas Harth. "A language-independent method for the extraction of RDF verbalization templates". In: *Proceedings of the 8th International Natural Language Generation Conference (INLG 2014)*. The Association for Computer Linguistics, June 2014, pp. 26–34

[EHS14] Basil Ell, Andreas Harth, and Elena Simperl. "SPARQL Query Verbalization for Explaining Semantic Search Engine Queries". In: *Proceedings of the 11th Extended Semantic Web Conference*. ESWC 2014. Heidelberg: Springer, 2014, pp. 426–441

[Sti+14] Anna Stisser, Anne Hild, Basil Ell, and Christoph Schindler. "Neue Forschungswerkzeuge in der Historischen Bildungsforschung. Die virtuelle Forschungsumgebung SMW-CorA für die kollaborative Analyse und Aus-wertung umfangreicher digitalisierter Quellen". In: *Jahrbuch für Historische Bildungsforschung 2013*. Vol. 19 Avantgarden. Bad Heilbrunn: Julius Klinkhardt, 2014, pp. 305–324. ISBN: 978-3-7815-1960-2

[ESR13] Basil Ell, Christoph Schindler, and Marc Rittberger. "Semantically Enhanced Interactions between Heterogeneous Data Life-Cycles. Analyzing Educational Lexica in a Virtual Research Environment". In: *Proceedings of the 7th Metadata and Semantics Research Conference (MTSR 2013)*. Ed. by Emmanouel Garoufallou and Jane Greenberg. Communications in Computer and Information Science Vol. 390. Thessaloniki: Springer, Nov. 2013, pp. 277–288

[SER13] Christoph Schindler, Basil Ell, and Marc Rittberger. "Virtual Research Environment SMW-CorA and its Capacities for Interaction in Social Science and Humanities Research – Using the Example of History of Education". In: *Informationswissenschaft zwischen virtueller Infrastruktur und materiellen Lebenswelten. Tagungsband des 13. Internationalen Symposiums der Informationswissenschaft*. Ed. by H.-C. Hobohm. Glückstadt: vwh, Mar. 2013, pp. 254–266

[SE13] Christoph Schindler and Basil Ell. "Kollaborative Analyse von historischen Netzwerken: Virtuelle Forschungsumgebung für die Historische Bildungsforschung". In: *Netzwerke in bildungshistorischer Perspektive*. Ed. by Andreas Hoffmann und Peter Metz Hans-Ulrich Grunder. Bad Heilbrunn: Verlag Julius Klinkhardt, Oct. 2013, pp. 142–148

[EVS15] Basil Ell, Denny Vrandečić, and Elena Simperl. "SPARTIQULATION: Verbalizing SPARQL queries". In: *The Semantic Web: ESWC 2012 Satellite Events*. Ed. by Elena Simperl, Barry Norton, Dunja Mladenic, Emanuele Della Valle, Irene Fundulaki, Alexandre Passant, et al. LNCS 7540. Springer, 2015, pp. 426–441 (This is an extended version of the ESWC 2012 ILD paper with the same title.)

[EVS12] Basil Ell, Denny Vrandečić, and Elena Simperl. "SPARTIQULATION: Verbalizing SPARQL queries". In: *Proceedings of the Interacting with Linked Data Workshop, co-located with the 9th Extended Semantic Web Conference*. Vol. 913. ILD 2012. Heraklion, Greece: CEUR-WS.org, May 2012, pp. 50–60

[SE12] Christoph Schindler and Basil Ell. *Semantic MediaWiki for Collaborative Corpora Analysis: Analyzing Educational Reference Books in a Virtual Research Environment*. Peer-reviewed abstract. ECER 2012. Sept. 2012

[SER12] Christoph Schindler, Basil Ell, and Marc Rittberger. "Intra-linking the Research Corpus: Using Semantic MediaWiki as a lightweight Virtual Research Environment". In: *Digital Humanities 2012*. Ed. by Jan Christoph Meister, Katrin Schönert, Bastian Lomsché, Wilhelm Schernus, Lena Schüch, and Meike Stegkemper. Hamburg: Hamburg University Press, 2012, pp. 359–362

[EVS11a] Basil Ell, Denny Vrandečić, and Elena Simperl. "Deriving Human-readable Labels from SPARQL Queries". In: *Proceedings of the 7th International Conference on Semantic Systems (I-SEMANTICS 2011)*. ACM, Sept. 2011, pp. 126–133

[EVS11b] Basil Ell, Denny Vrandečić, and Elena Simperl. "Labels in the Web of Data". In: *Proceedings of the 10th International Semantic Web Conference*. Ed. by Lora Aroyo, Chris Welty, Harith Alani, Jamie Taylor, Abraham Bernstein, Lalana Kagal, et al. ISWC 2011. Springer, Oct. 2011, pp. 162–176

The publications are related to the chapters of this thesis as follows (the main publication is set in bold):

Chapter 3 Semantic CorA
[ESR13], [SER13], [SER12], [Sti+14], [SE13], and [SE12]

Chapter 4 Labels in the Web of Data
[EVS11b]

Chapter 5 Deriving Human-Readable Labels from SPARQL Queries
[EVS11a]

Chapter 6 Verbalization of SPARQL Queries
[EHS14], [EVS15], and [EVS12]

Chapter 7 Induction of RDF Verbalization Patterns
[EH14]

1.5 Guide to the Reader

This thesis consists of eight chapters. Each core chapter (Chapter 3 - Chapter 7) i) declares a problem, ii) discusses related work, iii) presents an approach, iv) evaluates the approach or carries out experiments, v) draws conclusions, and vi) presents a list of contributions. The thesis ends with a summary of the main conclusions and provides an outlook in Chapter 8.

Chapter 1 The first chapter introduces this work, breaks down the principal research question into ten individual research questions, presents the main contributions, lists published results, and provides this guide to the reader.

Chapter 2 The second chapter reviews fundamentals in Semantic Web technologies, Semantic MediaWiki, and Natural Language Generation.

Chapter 3 The third chapter presents research interactions with RDF data enabled by a semantically-enhanced Virtual Research Environment and addresses the following research questions:

RQ1.1 *How can capabilities of researchers be enhanced by a semantically-enhanced Virtual Research Environment?*

RQ1.2 *How can research interactions be enabled by a semantically-enhanced Virtual Research Environment?*

Chapter 4 The fourth chapter studies the state of labeling in the Web of Data and addresses the following research questions:

RQ2.1 *Which properties are used for the purpose of labeling?*

RQ2.2 *Which metrics help study the properties of labeling within a dataset?*

RQ2.3 *What is the state of labeling in the Web of Data according to these metrics?*

Chapter 5 The fifth chapter presents a method to derive labels from variable names in SPARQL queries and addresses the following research questions:

RQ3.1 *How can human-readable labels be derived from variable names in SPARQL queries?*

RQ3.2 *Which SPARQL graph patterns are common?*

Chapter 6 The sixth chapter presents an approach to verbalize SPARQL queries and addresses the following research question:

RQ4 *How can SPARQL queries be verbalized in a mostly schema-agnostic manner?*

Chapter 7 The seventh chapter introduces RDF verbalization templates and presents an approach to induce these templates from example data. The following research questions are addressed:

RQ5.1 *How can RDF graphs be verbalized as a single sentence using a template?*

RQ5.2 *How can RDF verbalization templates be learned from a parallel text-data corpus?*

Chapter 8 The last chapter concludes the thesis with a summary, discusses the main conclusions, and provides an outlook on future work.

On the use of pronouns:

- In the content chapters (Chapter 3 - Chapter 7) I use the form *we* instead of *I*, since the work was published together with coauthors. In most publications, however, I provided the main contribution and was acknowledged as first author. Using the form *we* instead of *I* serves for the purpose of acknowledging my coauthors. These collaborations always involved fruitful discussions and the exchange of ideas. For those publications where I did not appear as first author I put a focus on my contributions.
- For the purpose of avoiding gender bias in writing, I try to avoid third-person personal pronouns such as *he* or *she*.

2 Foundations

This chapter briefly introduces Semantic Web technologies (RDF, LinkedData, and SPARQL), Semantic MediaWiki, and Natural Language Generation.

2.1 Semantic Web Technologies

The Semantic Web vision is to extend the Web of Documents with a Web of Data where information becomes processable for machines [BLHL+01]. For the purpose of realizing the Semantic Web vision, several technologies have been developed that make up the *semantic web stack*, depicted in Figure 2.1. Core parts have already been realized. Layers drawn with dashed lines still lack mature standards and tooling. In the context of this thesis, the relevant technologies are RDF and SPARQL, which are therefore introduced in the following sections. For a textbook-style introduction to Semantic Web standards see [HHS14] and [HKR09].

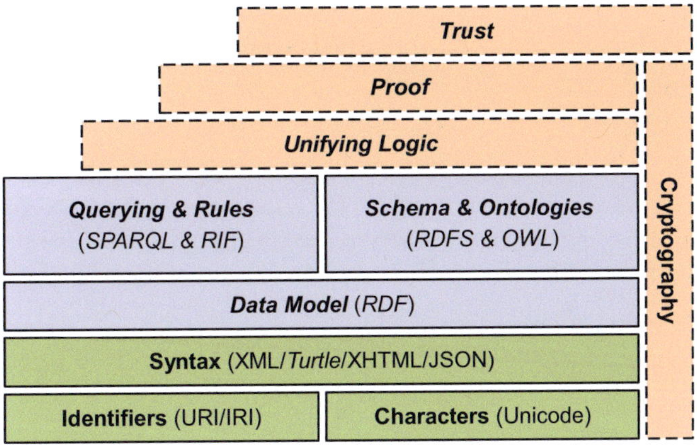

Figure 2.1: The Semantic Web technology stack. (Diagram from [HHS14], image courtesy of Aidan Hogan.)

2.1.1 RDF Data Model, Vocabulary, and Schema

RDF Data Model

RDF (Resource Description Framework) is the core data model of the Semantic Web. RDF allows statements about resources[1] to be made in the form of *RDF graphs* where an RDF graph consists of a set of *RDF triples*. An RDF triple (s, p, o) is an ordered set of three *RDF terms*: a *subject* $s \in \mathcal{U} \cup \mathcal{B}$, a *predicate* $p \in \mathcal{U}$, and an *object* $o \in \mathcal{U} \cup \mathcal{B} \cup \mathcal{L}$. An RDF term $t \in \mathcal{T}$ is either a *URI* $u \in \mathcal{U}$, a *blank node* $b \in \mathcal{B}$, or a *literal* $l \in \mathcal{L}$ where $\mathcal{T} = \mathcal{U} \cup \mathcal{B} \cup \mathcal{L}$ and $\mathcal{U}$, $\mathcal{B}$, and $\mathcal{L}$ are pairwise disjunct.

A *URI* (Uniform Resource Identifier) is a string of characters used to identify a resource. A resource might be anything from a person to an abstract idea to a simple document on the Web. For example, the URI `http://dbpedia.org/resource/Karlsruhe` is an identifier for the city of Karlsruhe in Germany. This URI (and per definition every URI) is a *unique identifier*, since the URI identifies exactly one resource.[2] Whereas terms in natural language may be ambiguous such as fluke, a URI enables referring unambiguously to a resource. The resource a URI refers to is either an *information resource* (IR) or a *non-information resource* (NIR). *Information resources* are resources that consist of information, such as a JPG file or an office document, and therefore all of their essential characteristics can be conveyed in a message and be transported over protocols such as HTTP. IRs can be copied from and downloaded via the Internet given their URIs – dereferencing (also called resolving) a URI means to send an HTTP request to the URI to obtain a representation of the resource that it identifies. Disjoint from the set of information resources is the set of *non-information resources* – resources that cannot be accessed and downloaded via the Internet – such as a person or a country. Nevertheless, non-information resources can be identified with URIs.

URIs with a hashmark (#) contain a *fragment identifier* after the hashmark. For example, the fragment identifier in the URI `http://www.example.com/about#bob` is `bob`. The *local name* is the string after the last slash (/) and before the hashmark, or, if the URI contains no hashmark, the end of the URI. The local name of the URI above is `about`.

A *literal* is a string of characters that is either language-tagged (a language-tagged literal) or typed (a typed literal).[3] For example, a country may have language-specific names (e.g., the Russian capital *Moscow* has the German name *Moskau*). Tagging each

[1] Within this thesis, the terms *resource* and *entity* are used synonymously. However, mostly the term *entity* is used.

[2] RDF does not have a *Unique Name Assumption*. If two URIs are different, they may refer to the same resource – there can be multiple unique identifiers that all refer to the same resource. For example, the URIs `http://dbpedia.org/resource/Karlsruhe` and `http://wikidata.org/entity/Q1040` both refer to the city of Karlsruhe.

[3] While in RDF 1.0 a literal could also be neither tagged nor typed (a plain literal), RDF 1.1 does not allow plain literals anymore.

name with the appropriate language allows applications to select and display names in a language understood by the application's current user. Just as values in programming languages can be typed (e.g., integer, float, boolean), literals can be typed.

A *blank node* represents a resource for which no URI or literal is given. Amongst other uses, blank nodes can be used when representing n-ary (with $n > 2$) relationships. For example, given that according to a certain cooking recipe a certain cake is made with 300g of butter, the ingredient relation is n-ary (with $n = 4$): the cake, the ingredient's type (butter), the ingredient's amount (gram), and the amount's value (300).[4]

RDF Syntaxes

RDF data can be represented in a variety of syntaxes, such as RDF/XML,[5] Turtle,[6] N-Triples,[7] N-Quads,[8] N3,[9] and JSON LD.[10] In this thesis the Turtle serialization is used since Turtle is the most concise and readable serialization format and it is similar to SPARQL – the RDF query language (see Section 2.1.3). Instead of formally introducing the syntax, and since not all language features are used within later chapters of this thesis, only a subset of the main characteristics is shown with an example of a small RDF graph serialized in Turtle in Listing 2.1.

```
@prefix dbpedia-owl: <http://dbpedia.org/ontology/> .
@prefix dbr: <http://dbpedia.org/resource/> .
@prefix rdf: <http://www.w3.org/1999/02/22-rdf-syntax-ns#> .
@prefix rdfs: <http://www.w3.org/2000/01/rdf-schema#> .
@prefix owl: <http://www.w3.org/2002/07/owl#> .
@prefix ex: <http://www.example.org/> .
@prefix xsd: <http://www.w3.org/2001/XMLSchema#> .

dbr:Karlsruhe rdf:type dbpedia-owl:Town .
dbr:Karlsruhe rdfs:label "Karlsruhe"@en .
dbr:Karlsruhe dbpedia-owl:populationTotal "288917"^^xsd:integer .
dbr:Karlsruhe owl:sameAs <http://wikidata.org/entity/Q1040> .
ex:MarbleCake ex:hasIngredient _:b1 .
_:b1 rdf:type ex:Butter .
_:b1 ex:hasAmount ex:Gram .
_:b1 ex:hasValue "300"^^xsd:integer .
```

Listing 2.1: A small RDF graph serialized in Turtle

[4] This example can be found in [Cim+13].
[5] See http://www.w3.org/TR/rdf-syntax-grammar/ (last accessed 2015-01-02)
[6] See http://www.w3.org/TR/turtle/ (last accessed 2015-01-02)
[7] See http://www.w3.org/TR/n-triples/ (last accessed 2015-01-02)
[8] See http://sw.deri.org/2008/07/n-quads/ (last accessed 2015-01-02)
[9] See http://www.w3.org/TeamSubmission/n3/ (last accessed 2015-01-02)
[10] See http://www.w3.org/TR/json-ld/ (last accessed 2015-01-02)

The first seven (1–7) lines are prefix definitions. These enable shortening URIs in the following lines. The lines 9–16 show triples. Each triple ends with a dot. Most URIs are shortened. For example, the URI `http://dbpedia.org/resource/Karlsruhe` is shortened to `dbr:Karlsruhe` given the prefix definition for `dbr` in line 2. Line 10 contains a language-tagged literal in the object position – the language tag `en` stands for the English language. The triple in line 11 contains a typed literal in the object position. The value of the literal is `288917` and the type is `xsd:integer`, which is the datatype's shortened URI. URIs that are not shortened, such as the one in the object position of the triple in line 12, are embraced in angle brackets (<...>). Line 13 contains a blank node in object position. This blank node appears in the subject position of the triples in lines 14 to 16.[11]

Occasionally in this thesis, for the case of brevity, the prefix is omitted in shortened URIs as in `:birthPlace` if the complete URI is not relevant for the purpose of explaining an issue by giving an example. Furthermore, occasionally in this thesis the trailing dot is omitted if the triple appears within text.

RDF Vocabulary and RDF Schema

Besides defining the data model, the RDF specification defines a set of RDF terms which form the *RDF vocabulary*. The most prominent term is `rdf:type`. Other terms support features such as RDF containers and reification. The *RDF Schema* vocabulary extends the RDF vocabulary and allows the semantics[12] of classes and properties to be defined. The most prominent terms of the RDF Schema vocabulary are `rdfs:subClassOf`, `rdfs:subPropertyOf`, `rdfs:domain`, and `rdfs:range`.

`rdfs:subClassOf` The property `rdfs:subClassOf` enables a class hierarchy to be defined, as in `ex:Human rdfs:subClassOf ex:Mammal` ("Every human is a mammal").

`rdfs:subPropertyOf` The property `rdfs:subPropertyOf` enables one property to be defined as sub-property of another property, which means that all entities related via the sub-property are also related with the super-property. For example, given the sub-property definition `foaf:name rdfs:subProperyOf rdfs:label`, from the statement `dbr:Karlsruhe foaf:name "Karlsruhe"@en` the statement `dbr:Karlsruhe rdfs:label "Karlsruhe"@en` can be inferred.[13]

[11] Turtle allows the triples in lines 13–16 to be expressed as `ex:MarbleCake ex:hasIngredient [ rdf:type ex:Butter ; ex:hasAmount ex:Gram ; ex:hasValue "300"^^xsd:integer ] .` This notation is not introduced here since it is not used in later chapters of this thesis.

[12] More semantics can be specified using the OWL (Web Ontology Language) vocabulary. For example, in OWL it is possible to specify, amongst other things, that a property is transitive and that a person can have at most one age. See http://www.w3.org/TR/2012/REC-owl2-syntax-20121211/ (last accessed 2015-01-02)

[13] RDFS entailment patterns specify formally how to infer statements from other statements. See http://www.w3.org/TR/2014/REC-rdf11-mt-20140225/#rdfs-entailment (last accessed 2015-01-02)

rdfs:domain, rdfs:range Using the properties rdfs:domain and rdfs:range, the domain and range of a property can be specified, as in foaf:based_near rdfs:domain geo:SpatialThing . foaf:based_near rdfs:range geo:SpatialThing . Given these domain and range statements, from a statement ex:Karlsruhe foaf:based_near ex:Stuttgart it follows that ex:Karlsruhe and ex:Stuttgart are both instances of the class geo:SpatialThing.

2.1.2 Further Relevant Concepts

Linked Data The term Linked Data refers to a set of best practices[14] for publishing and connecting structured data on the Web.[15] The Linked Data principles [BL06] are defined by Berners-Lee as follows:

1. *Use URIs as names for things.*
2. *Use HTTP URIs so that people can look up those names.*
3. *When someone looks up a URI, provide useful information, using the standards (RDF*, SPARQL).*
4. *Include links to other URIs. so that they can discover more things.*

LOD Linked Open Data is Linked Data which is open – *open data and content can be freely used, modified, and shared by anyone for any purpose.*[16]

The Linking Open Data community project[17] aims to publish open datasets as RDF on the Web and interlinking these datasets.

Quad & Context While the RDF definition does not define the notion of context, applications may need to add contextual information to a triple, such as the triple's origin, and treat a triple based on its origin, for example, to distinguish triples from trusted sources from triples from untrusted sources. Harth and Decker [HD05] thus extend triples (s, p, o) to quads (s, p, o, c) with $c \in \mathcal{U} \cup \mathcal{B}$.

[14] See http://www.w3.org/TR/ld-bp/ (last accessed 2015-01-02)
[15] See http://linkeddata.org/faq (last accessed 2015-01-02)
[16] See http://opendefinition.org/ (last accessed 2015-01-02)
[17] See http://www.w3.org/wiki/SweoIG/TaskForces/CommunityProjects/LinkingOpenData (last accessed 2015-01-02)

2.1.3 SPARQL

SPARQL is the W3C Recommendation [HS10] for querying and accessing RDF data.[18] A SPARQL query consists of up to five parts:

Prefix Declarations As in Turtle, the definition of prefixes allows shortened URIs to be used.

Dataset Clause In cases where a triple store hosts multiple datasets, those datasets to be incorporated in the query can be specified in the dataset clause. Moreover, datasets can be dereferenced.

Result Clause The result clause specifies the query form (`SELECT`, `ASK`, `CONSTRUCT`, or `DESCRIBE`) as well as the projection variables.

Query Clause Within the query clause the query patterns are specified. Query patterns are matched against the data graphs resulting in variable bindings.

Solution Modifiers Query results can be ordered, sliced, and paginated.

`SELECT` queries result in a list of mappings from variables to RDF terms, `ASK` queries return true if there is a match for the pattern defined the query clause, `CONSTRUCT` allows to query data and to return RDF by defining an RDF template with which query results are formatted, and `DESCRIBE` requests RDF descriptions about an RDF term.

Figure 2.2[19] gives an example of a simple SPARQL SELECT query. Prefixes are declared in the first two lines. The dataset clause is omitted – the default dataset is queried. The query form is `SELECT`, as specified in line three, as part of the result clause. Moreover specified in the SELECT clause are the two projection variables `?label` and `?lang` where `?lang` is the result of applying the `lang` operator to the value of the variable `?label`. The `lang` operator returns the language tag of the literal it is applied to. The query clause consists of a triple pattern in line four and a filter expression in line five. An RDF graph pattern is a set of triple patterns and an RDF triple pattern (s,p,o) consists of a *subject* $s \in \mathcal{T} \cup \mathcal{V}$, a *predicate* $p \in \mathcal{U} \cup \mathcal{V}$, and an *object* $o \in \mathcal{T} \cup \mathcal{V}$ where $\mathcal{V}$ is a set of variables. The filter expression removes all results where the language tag of the value bound to `?label` is equal to `en`. The solution modifier in line six specifies that the results are ordered according to the values of `?lang` and that only up to ten results are selected. In one sentence, what the query does is to query for up to ten non-English labels for the city of Karlsruhe and sorts them by the name of the languages. Visualizing the results in tabular form results in a table with two columns with labels in the first column and corresponding languages in the second column.

[18] See also [PAG08] for the semantics of SPARQL.

[19] This query can be executed on the public DBpedia endpoint at http://dbpedia.org/sparql (last accessed 2015-01-02).

Figure 2.2 shows the result of executing the SPARQL query from Listing 2.2 on the DBpedia endpoint.[20]

```
PREFIX dbr: <http://dbpedia.org/resource/>
PREFIX rdfs: <http://www.w3.org/2000/01/rdf-schema#>
SELECT ?label (lang(?label) AS ?lang) WHERE {
   dbr:Karlsruhe rdfs:label ?label .
   FILTER(!lang(?label)="en")
} ORDER BY ?lang LIMIT 10
```

Listing 2.2: *An example of a SPARQL SELECT query*

label	lang
"كارلسروه"@ar	ar
"Karlsruhe"@de	de
"Karlsruhe"@es	es
"Karlsruhe"@fr	fr
"Karlsruhe"@it	it
"カールスルーエ"@ja	ja
"Karlsruhe (stad)"@nl	nl
"Karlsruhe"@pl	pl
"Karlsruhe"@pt	pt
"Карлсруэ"@ru	ru

Figure 2.2: Result of executing the SPARQL query from Listing 2.2 on the DBpedia endpoint.

Further language constructs relevant in the context of this thesis are `DISTINCT`, `COUNT`, `OPTIONAL`, and `UNION`:

DISTINCT This solution modifier eliminates duplicate solutions from the result set. Consider, for example, the following query which retrieves up to ten names of persons:

```
PREFIX rdf: <http://www.w3.org/1999/02/22-rdf-syntax-ns#>
PREFIX dbpedia-owl: <http://dbpedia.org/ontology/>
PREFIX foaf: <http://xmlns.com/foaf/0.1/>
SELECT DISTINCT ?name WHERE {
  ?person rdf:type dbpedia-owl:Person .
  ?person foaf:givenName ?name .
} LIMIT 10
```

[20] The DBpedia endpoint can be accessed at http://dbpedia.org/sparql. The query was executed on 2015 January 12.

Without the DISTINCT modifier the result set contains duplicate values since the result set is a set of tuples (?person, ?name) where only the names are displayed.

COUNT COUNT is an aggregate function and aggregates are defined in version 1.1 of SPARQL. For example, it enables the quantification of a result set, as in the following query which retrieves the number of persons known to DBpedia:

```
PREFIX rdf: <http://www.w3.org/1999/02/22-rdf-syntax-ns#>
PREFIX dbpedia-owl: <http://dbpedia.org/ontology/>
SELECT COUNT(*) WHERE {
  ?person rdf:type dbpedia-owl:Person .
}
```

COUNT can be combined with DISTINCT as in COUNT(DISTINCT ?name)). * is a shorthand notation for selecting all query variables as projection variables.

OPTIONAL Optional parts of a query can be specified with the OPTIONAL keyword. For example when querying DBpedia for persons and their gender, as shown in the following query, not for every person the gender needs to be known. Since the gender is optional, the query will also retrieve identifiers of persons for which no gender is known.

```
PREFIX rdf: <http://www.w3.org/1999/02/22-rdf-syntax-ns#>
PREFIX dbpedia-owl: <http://dbpedia.org/ontology/>
SELECT * WHERE {
  ?person rdf:type dbpedia-owl:Person .
  OPTIONAL {
    ?person dbpedia-owl:gender ?gender .
  }
} LIMIT 10
```

UNION Alternatives can be specified using the UNION keyword. For example, DBpedia provides several properties that relate a person to the person's place of birth. The following query retrieves the places of birth for Ryuichi Sakamoto where at least one of the two properties relates the subject to the object, thus realizing a logical disjunction.

```
PREFIX dbr: <http://dbpedia.org/resource/>
PREFIX dbpedia-owl: <http://dbpedia.org/ontology/>
PREFIX dbpprop: http://dbpedia.org/property/>
SELECT * WHERE {
  { dbr:Ryuichi_Sakamoto dbpedia-owl:birthPlace ?place . }
  UNION
  { dbr:Ryuichi_Sakamoto dbpprop:placeOfBirth ?place . }
}
```

2.2 Semantic MediaWiki

A wiki is a collaboratively edited website. A well-known wiki is Wikipedia[21] – an online encyclopedia. The wiki software underlying Wikipedia is *MediaWiki*.[22] MediaWiki provides a markup syntax so that editors, besides working with content, can also format the content, for example, to change the font style, link pages, create paragraphs and tables, and categorize pages.

The functionality of MediaWiki can be extended by installing what are known as extensions. *Semantic MediaWiki*[23] (SMW) is an extension that brings ideas from the Semantic Web to MediaWiki by allowing content to be annotated, queried, and exported as RDF data. For example, imagine the sentence

```
Karlsruhe is a city in Germany with a population of 299,103.
[[Category:City]]
```

in the article about Karlsruhe. Wiki markup allows links to be added to the content of the page as in the following sentence:

```
Karlsruhe is a city in [[Germany]] with a population of
299,103. [[Category:City]]
```

The brackets embracing Germany turn that string into a link to the wiki page with the name Germany. While for a human that understands English it is clear from this sentence that the sentence expresses the `located_in` relation between Karlsruhe and Germany, for a machine not capable of Natural Language Understanding it is only known that Karlsruhe and Germany are related via a link. Semantic MediaWiki extends the link syntax

[21] http://www.wikipedia.org/
[22] Available at http://www.mediawiki.org/wiki/MediaWiki (last accessed 2015-01-02)
[23] Available at http://semantic-mediawiki.org/ (last accessed 2015-01-02)

for the purpose of explicitly naming the relation, as in `[[located_in::Germany]]`. Now, a machine can derive the triple

```
ex:Karlsruhe ex:located_in ex:Germany .
```

where `ex:Karlsruhe`, `ex:located_in`, and `ex:Germany` are unique identifiers. Furthermore, the extended syntax allows values to be annotated, such as the population value:

```
Karlsruhe is a city in [[located_in::Germany]] with a
population of [[population::299,103]].  [[Category:City]]
```

As in RDF where properties are either object properties (the property's domain is a set of entities) or datatype properties (the property's domain is a datatype), this distinction can be made in SMW. Therefore, each property can have its own wiki page where the property's type is declared. In this example, declaring the type of the population property as `integer` and the type of the `located_in` property as `page` has the effect that in the example sentence, Germany is displayed as a link whereas the population value is not displayed as a link.

The benefit of typing links, annotating values, and declaring properties comes with the query and export functionalities provided by SMW. An example of a query that exploits the properties introduced above is shown below:

```
{{#ask: [[Category:City]] [[located in::Germany]]
 | ?population
 | format=table
}}
```

The query retrieves from the wiki all entities that are categorized as city and that are located in Germany. The query results in a table where the entity (here: the name of the city) is shown in the first column and the population value, where available, is shown in the second column. These queries, known as *inline queries*, can be added to wiki pages and can thus be altered by wiki editors. The inline query functionality is added to the wiki syntax as a *parser function* (here, the name of the parser function is `#ask`).

Further MediaWiki extensions related to SMW add further result formats.[24] Instead of simple result formats such as table and list, query results can be visualized using bar charts, on a map, on a timeline, as a graph etc.

[24] Available at http://www.mediawiki.org/wiki/Extension:Semantic_Result_Formats (last accessed 2015-01-02)

Template pages are special wiki pages where the template's content can be transcluded into other pages. For example, if the page about every person were to show a timeline visualizing the person's achievements, then the query and visualization code could be stored in a template. Each person page that calls this template will have the template's content transcluded. Variables can be passed to templates, so that, for example, within the template, data can be stored in properties or inline queries can query for a person's data. Further parser functions such as `#if`[25] allow, for example, reaction according to a variable's value or according to the result of a query. Templates can also be used as result printers of inline queries, thereby enabling custom query result presentations.

SMW allows the user to import vocabularies[26] and to bind properties defined within the wiki to properties of the imported vocabulary. The RDF export functionality of SMW enables export of a wiki's structured data to RDF. For a wiki property that is bound to a property from an imported vocabulary, the imported property's unique identifier is used within the RDF export instead of the property's wiki-specific identifier. This functionality increases the ease of reuse of exported RDF data.

The extension *Semantic Forms*[27] adds an important feature to a wiki, since it allows the user to add forms to the wiki that enables wiki pages to be created and a wiki page's structured data to be edited without a user seeing or editing wiki syntax. Thus, Semantic Forms constitutes a low technological barrier for novice users to contribute content.

2.3 Natural Language Generation

Natural Language Generation (NLG) is "*a subfield of artificial intelligence and computational linguistics that focuses on computer systems that can produce understandable texts in English or other human languages*" [RD00] in order "*to meet specified communicative goals*" [McD92].

A natural language generation system may generate outputs directly for end users (*computer as author*) or is used as an *authoring aid* where the generated text is subsequently refined by a human.

2.3.1 Examples

Examples of NLG systems are *WeatherReporter* (*computer as author*), *FoG* (*authoring aid*), *ModelExplainer* (*computer as author*), *PEBA* (*computer as author*), and *Inquire* (*computer as author*):

[25] See http://www.mediawiki.org/wiki/Help:Extension:ParserFunctions#.23if (last accessed 2015-01-02)
[26] See https://semantic-mediawiki.org/wiki/Help:Import_vocabulary (last accessed 2015-01-02)
[27] See http://www.mediawiki.org/wiki/Extension:Semantic_Forms (last accessed 2015-01-02)

- *WeatherReporter* [RD00] analyzes data from meteorological devices and produces texts that retrospectively report about the weather in one calendar month. For example, it may generate the following output:
  The month was cooler and drier than average, with the average number of rainy days. The total rain for the year so far is well below average. There was rain on every day for eight days from the 11th to the 18th.

- The Forecast Generator *FoG* [GDK94] is a bilingual (English and French) report generator that produces routine and special-purpose forecasts from graphical weather depictions. It creates outputs indistinguishable from texts written by human forecasters, for example:
  WINDS NORTHWEST 15 DIMINISHING TO LIGHT MONDAY AFTERNOON. CLOUDY WITH OCCASIONAL LIGHT SNOW. FOG PATCHES. VISIBILITIES 2 TO 5 NM IN SNOW.
  FoG serves as an authoring aid and helps weather meteorologists compose forecasts.

- *ModelExplainer* [LRR00] generates textual descriptions from object-oriented models, which are typically depicted graphically. For the purpose of maximizing communicative efficiency – experiments have shown that a graphical representation is not suitable for certain user groups –, graphics are complemented by natural language descriptions. The system generates hypertext. Underlined parts are links to the description of the respective entity, as in the following example:
  A Section must be taught by exactly one Professor and may belong to zero or more Courses. It must be taken by one or more Students and may have at most one TA.

- *PEBA* [MTD96] is an intelligent encyclopedia about animals which generates hypertext pages. Content and style of the generated pages depend on whether the user is an expert or novice and what material the user has seen before. Moreover, it allows comparisons of entities to be generated.

- A more recent NLG system is *Inquire*.[28] Inquire is an interactive intelligent biology textbook *that answers students' questions, engages their interest, and improves their understanding* [Cha+13].

2.3.2 Input

According to Reiter and Dale [RD00], input to an NLG system is a four-tuple (k, c, u, d) where k is the knowledge source to be used, c is the communicative goal to be achieved, u is a user model, and d is a discourse history. In the case of *WeatherReporter*, the knowledge source is a database of numerical sensor measurements made at meteorological stations. The communicative goal is the purpose of the generated text, such

[28] See http://www.inquireproject.com/ (last accessed 2015-01-02)

as to communicate information about a certain month. A user model may capture characteristics of the intended audience and may, for example, capture which terms the target audience understands and which terms are too technical for casual users. In multi-interaction scenarios, which is the case for PEBA and Inquire, the dialog history captures which information has already been communicated and which entities have already been introduced, so that the system can avoid repetition and create output tailored toward user and situation.

2.3.3 Tasks

According to Reiter and Dale [RD00], the NLG process can be thought of as consisting of seven tasks:

Content Determination is the task of deciding which information to communicate.

For the purpose of summarizing the weather in a given month, *WeatherReporter* operates on raw tabular data and structures it in the form of a collection of daily weather records. From this data it creates messages – informational elements that are deemed to be considered for inclusion in the generated text. For example, a particular message might cover the fact that heavy rain fell on a particular day or, as a more complex message (consisting of less complex messages), a message could represent that a sunny day followed a day with heavy rainfall.

Document Structuring is the task of constructing messages from the input data and of deciding for their order and structure.

Document Structuring can be realized in a bottom-up strategy by aggregating messages to more complex messages. Complex messages define relations between simple messages. A top-level message could, for example, provide slots for messages that provide introductory information, such as the average weather in a month, followed by messages about unusual events.

Lexicalization is the task of deciding which specific words and syntactic constructs to use for expressing the content.

For example, a choice in this task could result, in the end, in two different output sentences: *It rained for seven days from the 20th to the 26th*, or *It rained during Thanksgiving week.*

Referring expression generation is the task of deciding how to refer to an entity that has already been introduced.

Always explicitly referring to an entity in text adds an unnatural feel to the text. Consider the two sentences *The Eifel tower was built in 1889. The Eifel tower is an iron lattice tower.* Since the entity is already introduced in the first sentence, the second sentence can be modified to `It is an iron-lattice tower.`

Aggregation is the task of deciding how to map messages onto linguistic structures such as sentences and paragraphs.

Imagine one message representing the fact that the Eifel tower was built in 1889 and another message representing that it is an iron-lattice tower. Aggregation of these two messages for the purpose of communicating them in a single sentence could, for example, result in the sentence *The Eifel tower, an iron-lattice tower, was built in 1889.*

Linguistic Realization is the task of converting abstract representations of sentences into real text. For example, care needs to be taken to correctly realize noun pluralization, to correctly introduce negations into sentences, or to generate sentences in active or passive voice.

Structure Realization is the task of adding markup to the generated text in order to be interpreted by the presentation system, such as a web browser. For example, hyperlinks and paragraphs can be added, or the font style can be modified.

2.3.4 NLG in the Semantic Web

In the context of the Semantic Web, approaches exist that verbalize from data represented using a Semantic Web format. For example, approaches exist that verbalize OWL ontologies [ALG13; AOK07; Bao+09; Bon05; BA+11; FKV10; Gal+09; GA07; GNS10; KF07; PT10; Sch09; Ste+11; TWP11; Wil11], that verbalize from RDF data [Fur+10; Pic+11b; SM07; SM06; WJ03; Wil03], or that verbalize SPARQL queries [NN+13]. Besides approaches to generating text from a Semantic Web format, works exist that induce ontology lexica [WUC13] or lexically ground ontologies [Cim+07; Bui+09]. With *lemon*[29] a model exists that enables lexical information to be provided in the Semantic Web which can be applied to NLG. A good overview of Natural Language Generation in the context of the Semantic Web is provided by Bouayad-Agha et al. [BACW14].

[29] See http://lemon-model.net/ (last accessed: 2015-01-02)

3 Semantic CorA

3.1 Introduction

In recent years, Virtual Research Environments (VREs) emerged as a topic referring to the established research field in the digital humanities: enabling research practices with digital tools. First projects in this area are realized and discussed by the community [CR10; Dun09; Neu+09]. In the humanities, researchers point out that the *data deluge* [HT03], which has influenced several national and supranational information policy agendas in the sciences, does not cover the full range of aspects of research practices in the humanities. While digital libraries and archives offer a new plurality of research resources in the humanities, the *complexity deluge* [Dun09] formulates an opposite agenda addressing the sometimes fuzzy, interfering and dispersed practices of humanities research. A similar field of tension is articulated for the sciences as *science friction* [Edw+11] by addressing the problems of different disciplines working on the same phenomena and trying to interoperate. Another aspect is sharing of research data, which is an intricate and difficult problem (*conundrum*) in science in general [Bor12].

A large-scale study on Virtual Research Environments points out the necessarily closely involvement of researchers in the development process, that this process needs to be executed iteratively with constant feedback from researchers [CR10], and that a VRE needs to be conceptualized as a community building project rather than a technology project. Borgman [Bor12] also stresses the point that close engagement with a specific research community and an analysis of how data are handled is necessary. Thus, requirements need to be articulated within research communities.

Based on these discussions, for the purpose of supporting actual research practice we focus research data and the necessary interaction capabilities with research objects. The development of a Virtual Research Environment is based on articulated needs in the research community *history of education*. The articulated concrete need is to study educational lexica from a discourse analytical perspective and to carry out qualitative and quantitative analyses. Due to our close cooperation with the Research Library for the History of Education (BBF – Bibliothek für Bildungsgeschichtliche Forschung) [Rit03] we were able to access their holdings of digitized lexica and to import more than 20,000 lemmata (articles of lexica) as a starting point for interacting with the community. Aside from data made available by the BBF, more and more digital libraries such as the

Europeana[1] or services of the German National Library[2] are being established and are making their content available using Semantic Web standards, thus they are publishing RDF in the Web of Data. Thereby, new opportunities arise for research projects to exploit these resources offering new capacities for research which can be addressed by Virtual Research Environments offering a variety of methods and tools [Fra05; VP09].

In this chapter we answer the following research questions:

RQ1.1 *How can capabilities of researchers be enhanced by a semantically-enhanced Virtual Research Environment?*

RQ1.2 *How can research interactions be enabled by a semantically-enhanced Virtual Research Environment?*

The remainder of this chapter is structured as follows. Section 3.2 provides information about the research project from which our results were obtained. Section 3.3 provides an overview of related work and Section 3.4 presents our participatory design approach. We argue that Semantic MediaWiki is a suitable platform in Section 3.5 and present the research data lifecycle, explain how it is supported within the VRE, and how Semantic Web technologies can be applied to enable new socio-technical interactions in Section 3.6. We discuss the role of Semantic Web technologies in Section 3.7, draw conclusions in Section 3.8, and highlight our main contributions in Section 3.9.

3.2 The SMW-Cora Project

Results presented in this chapter were obtained in the context of the project *Entwicklung einer Virtuellen Forschungsumgebung für die Historische Bildungsforschung mit Semantischer Wiki-Technologie – Semantic MediaWiki for Collaborative Corpora Analysis* (duration: 1/2011 – 10/2014).[3] The project targets the development of a Virtual Research Environment (VRE) based on Semantic MediaWiki (SMW) for a collaborative analysis of comprehensive digitized text corpora and an exemplified sustained nesting into the professional community of researchers in the History of Education. Moreover, the project aims to provide for a possible further use of the enrichment and analysis works carried out by the researchers and in the long term, an infrastructural distribution of the VRE (Semantic CorA) to other disciplines with community building.

The project was funded by the German Research Foundation (DFG) in the domain of *Scientific Library Services and Information Systems* (LIS) and was realized in a cooperation between the German Institute for International Educational Research (DIPF), the Karlsruhe Institute of Technology (KIT), the Library for Research on Educational

[1] See http://www.europeana.eu (last accessed 2015-01-02)

[2] See http://www.dnb.de/EN/Service/DigitaleDienste/LinkedData/linkeddata_node.html (last acc. 2015-01-02)

[3] See http://www.semantic-cora.org/ about the VRE *Semantic CorA*.

History (BBF), and historical educational researchers mainly of the Georg-August-University Göttingen.

3.3 Related Work

Today, Virtual Research Environments (VREs) aim to enhance research by using the capabilities of networked technologies, distributed resources and computational power.[4] While, up to now, the facilitation of research in the fields of science and technology has been focussed, the World Wide Web is beginning to impact on the fields of Humanities and Social Sciences, addressing and enforcing collaboration of researchers in projects and beyond. Some VREs have started to use Semantic Web technologies in order to enhance research practices. *MyExperiment* is one example which allows users to create, share and publish the workflows of scientists [DRGS09]. Accordingly, resources are described using RDF. Furthermore, the VRE *ourSpaces* [Edw+12] uses an ontological framework for provenance [Mor+08], semantic policy reasoning for access management of resources [Şen+10], and a user interface to create metadata. While the library community addresses the potential of VREs as a driving force for change [BS07] there is still a lack of VREs that offer semantically-enhanced interactions on the research data level: to interact with RDF data or interactions enabled by RDF data. Our VRE *Semantic CorA* allows users to interact in various ways with research data encoded as RDF for which the import process and the formal annotation are described in [Sch+11; SE12; SE13].[5] In comparison to other VREs, SMW-CorA integrates the research data itself in a semantic environment and enables researchers to carry out research directly on a semantic level: underlying research data as well as data created via research interactions are represented as RDF whereas in previous approaches an additional translation process was necessary.

In the domain of Semantic Web, Auer et al. [Aue+12] describe a life-cycle of Linked Data. Beyond the scope of this work by Auer et al. we would like to emphasize the possible intersections and overlappings of various life-cycles, which we address in a research environment and its interactions with a digital library in a concrete field of Humanities and Social Sciences. The background is that data practices in research and the prospects of data sharing are identified as a conundrum, a problem which has to be addressed for particular research communities and their concrete interactions in research practice [Bor12].

[4] Some VREs are listed at http://misc.jisc.ac.uk/vre/projects (last accessed 2015-01-02)

[5] Further realizations of SMW as a VRE are Docupedia (http://www.docupedia.de) which is a reference work in the area of historical research, [Huv12] as an archaeological infrastructure, [LS10] as an archaeological corpus, http://wiki.digitalclassicist.org, and [Huv08] in the context of archives. The webpage http://smw.referata.com/wiki/Special:BrowseData/Sites?Data_type=Science (last accessed 2015-01-02) lists further examples.

The field of corpora centered research in the digital humanities offers interesting insights into the design of VREs. In the early 1990s, Biber pointed out the main aspects of corpus design by problematizing a priori determinations of its boundaries and formal specifications. He recommends the selection of relevant objects and the formal description to be realized as a cyclic or iterative process of corpus work [Bib93]. While a linguistic approach mainly aims at a statistical 'representation' in relation to a target population, qualitative corpus research, which is the focus here, pursues a so called qualitative selection, i.e., a typification of yet unknown properties in research [ABG00]. We argue that this indeterminacy of entities and properties in qualitative research emphasizes the affordance of a VRE to enable researchers to intra-link the corpus – it means giving them the ongoing capabilities to create, modify and re-arrange entities and properties while doing research, thus interacting with RDF data. This topic of qualitative corpus research addresses the research and design desideratum of qualitative annotations [Juo08] and a demanded shift to further capabilities for the researcher to control the data [SHR08].

3.4 Design and Method

A recent large international survey of social media indicates that Web technology offers great capacities to enhance research and data practices. The study shows that social media are already used *at all points of the research life-cycle, from identifying research opportunities to disseminating findings at the end* [Row+11]. Nevertheless, the challenge is raised, especially in the humanities, that requirements should be articulated by the scholars themselves [Bor09] and the solutions should be aligned to specific research communities [Bor12].

Therefore, a specific approach is used for designing concrete capacities of interaction in research practice: a participatory design approach with agile development has been taken, as required for Virtual Research Environments [CR10; VP09]. Apart from researchers, staff members working with a digital library (Research Library for the History of Education, BBF) were involved as active participants in the requirement elicitation and realization process. For establishing ongoing feedback loops we organized several on-site meetings and continued to hold online team meetings in the course of the project. Furthermore, the iterative development, the requirement elicitation as well as the testing of the realized functionalities, relied on two researchers in the field of History of Education who are carrying out their research in the VRE. Based on these interactions a set of functionalities, for example, regarding data integration, annotation, analysis and data export, were collaboratively articulated and realized. The requirements were either confirmed or continuously differentiated and rearticulated. After introducing the VRE, in particular the features, the syntaxes of MediaWiki, and Semantic MediaWiki to the researchers, the researchers learned to carry out their research within this environment, to explore the data by writing queries, and to adjust the VRE while being assisted when necessary by the developers. For two years the two Ph.D projects integrated more than 60 lexica and performed more than 17,700 edits.

3.5 Semantic MediaWiki as a Modular Platform

MediaWiki (MW) is the technological platform of the well-known online encyclopedia Wikipedia. Realizing a Virtual Research Environment using MediaWiki, and its extension Semantic MediaWiki (SMW, see Section 2.2) has the benefit, that this platform is supported by an active community, the user interface is well-known, and a number of extensions are readily available. Moreover, crucial for the decision to use (Semantic) MediaWiki as a platform were two factors:

1) MediaWiki, as a modular platform, can easily be adjusted, which is especially relevant for the Humanities and Social Sciences research due to the heterogeneous research data and flexible research processes. Compared to a content management system (CMS), Semantic Mediawiki, as a technological platform, allows functionalities to be added to the research environment that support specific research interactions such as the creation of queries and automatic metadata creation. These functionalities can be realized using Wikisyntax and are stored on Wiki pages. Thus, they can be edited by users, which represents a lower technological barrier. This leads to an adaptable research environment which facilitates the researchers' modification of their research environment.
2) Furthermore, SMW allows interacting with the Web of Data since it allows importing vocabularies and exporting data in RDF format.

3.6 The Research Data Life-Cycle and its Interactions

Data providers may adhere to a data life-cycle model such as the DCC Curation Lifecycle Model [Hig08]. While this model covers actions such as the access to the data by designated users and reusers and the action of receiving data in accordance with documented collecting policies, this model focuses on the curators' perspective to research data and needed interactions. Given a landscape with multiple data collections maintained by diverse initiatives where overlap exists regarding the digital objects and databases they are centered around, interactions not foreseen by the DCC model can take place. Data consumers, e.g., researchers who perform research on data retrieved from a digital library, may add new levels of data, enrich it with further information, add missing pieces, create abstractions and aggregations, complement it with new data, add new perspectives or identify and correct errors in the data. The main interactions, described in more detail in subsequent sections, in our realization of a heterogeneous life-cycle model are as follows:

Importing research data: Research data such as historical lexica that are hosted by a source such as a digital library and that are relevant for a particular research project carried out within the VRE are imported.

Enriching research data: Research data imported into the VRE or created within the VRE are enriched with further information, missing pieces are added, abstractions and aggregations are created, they are complemented with new data, and perspectives are added.

Linking to external data: Corresponding entities in external data sets are identified; links to these external entities are added to the VRE.

Data cleansing: Errors in the data are identified and corrected.

Exploring and analyzing: Unstructured and structured content can be explored; structured content can be analyzed qualitatively and quantitatively.

Export and sharing: Content can be selected and exported to allow for reuse by third parties.

Note that these interactions need not be executed in any specific sequence. They can be carried out at any time, in parallel, in any order and an arbitrary number of times. Moreover, they are dependent on and enabled by semantic metadata. In the following sections each of these interactions is discussed. Beyond performing interactions with the digital library, the research projects carried out within the VRE may interact due to overlap in lexica relevant to their projects, as well as with life-cycles of data outside the VRE but within the Semantic Web in general.

3.6.1 Importing Research Data

As mentioned above, the research data of the example realization of the VRE are historical lexica. Lexica that are of interest here are mainly available at the digital library Scripta Paedagogica Online (SPO),[6] hosted by the Research Library for the History of Education (BBF)[7] which has indexed the lexica and rendered them accessible online as image files as part of their library life-cycle. The corpus contains a total amount of nearly 22,000 articles and more than 25 lexica. Each lexicon is bibliographically described as a collected edition in the library database allegro-C and the digital library environment Goobi.[8]

[6] The lexica are available at http://bbf.dipf.de/digitale-bbf/scripta-paedagogica-online/digitalisierte-nachschlagewerke (last accessed 2015-01-02).

[7] Bibliothek für Bildungsgeschichtliche Forschung: http://bbf.dipf.de/en

[8] See http://www.allegro-c.de/ and http://www.goobi.org

The data consists of images of scanned pages and pertinent metadata. Therein, four levels of entities, their properties and relations are formalized (lexicon, volume, lemma, and image). The collection is accessible via an OAI interface.[9] A custom-made application of the VRE communicates with the interface, creates representations reflecting the levels of entities within the VRE, and imports the scanned images [Sch+11]. How this tool creates representations of the data within the VRE can be specified using XSLT[10] (Extensible Stylesheet Language Transformations) documents. The development of custom import tools is necessary if the data to be imported are not available via OAI.

Several Semantic Web vocabularies were imported into the VRE to represent the available metadata. These are: FOAF, PRISM, BIBO, SKOS, and DC.[11] Using these well-known vocabularies has benefits since this simplifies the reusability of exported data by third parties as discussed in Section 3.6.6.

In addition to the life-cycle of the digital library, the researchers themselves have their own life-cycles of creating and using research data. Thereby, they define the scope of relevant lexica in respect to their research question which is iteratively adjusted while getting new insights in the research process. To offer these capacities of integrating lexica which are not digitized and available at the digital library SPO, the *OfflineImport*[12] feature was developed. This feature allows creating pages for lexica, volumes, lemmata, and images given a minimal set of metadata with minimal effort for the researcher. Researchers can annotate the pages of these lexica and perform their analysis in the same way as with the automatically integrated lexica. Thus, the data life-cycles of the digital library and the research carried out within the VRE are interacting. This interaction offers feedback in an additional direction: digital libraries can be informed about potential consumers of relevant research data, they can set priorities in their digitization activities, and inform the researchers once the requested content has been digitized.[13]

3.6.2 Enriching Research Data

Research data such as the imported lemmata need to be annotated to facilitate analysis. In the Social Sciences this process of annotating segments of text is referred to as *coding* where annotation facilitates qualitative and quantitative analysis of the content. Since the research data, the historical lexica, are integrated as images from scanned pages, parts of images are annotated instead of parts of texts. Therefore, we developed and published

[9] An OAI interface implements the Protocol for Metadata Harvesting (OAI-PMH) defined by the Open Archives Initiative (http://www.openarchives.org/).

[10] See http://www.w3.org/standards/xml/transformation

[11] FOAF (Friend of a Friend ontology) [BM05], PRISM (Publishing Requirements for Industry Standard Metadata) [IDE12], BIBO (The Bibliographic Ontology) [DG09], SKOS (Simple Knowledge Organization System) [MB09], and DC (DCMI Metadata Term) [Boa12].

[12] The extension is available at: http://www.mediawiki.org/wiki/Extension:OfflineImportLexicon.

[13] While these interactions are in principle possible and are technologically already realized within our VRE, the processes are yet to be established with the BBF.

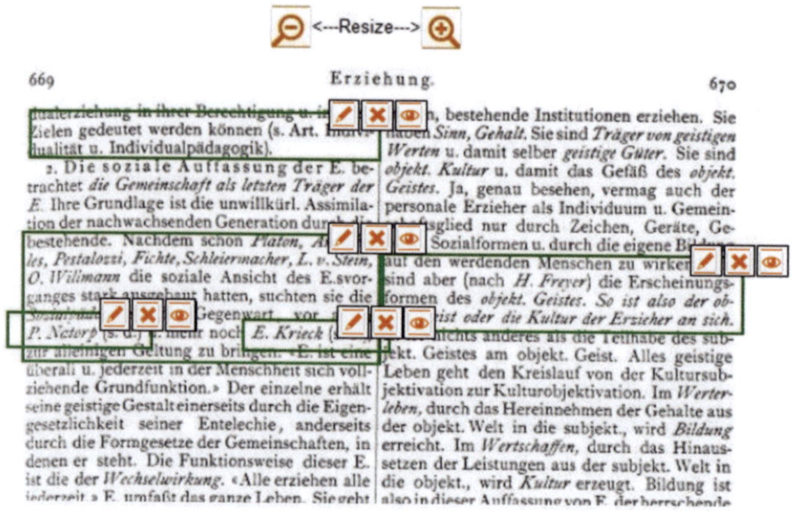

Figure 3.1: Example of an image in *annotation display mode* with five annotations.

the *SemanticImageAnnotator* (SIA) as an extension of MediaWiki. This extension allows rectangular areas on images to be selected and annotated (either with free annotations or existing thesauri or classification systems).[14] Figure 3.1[15] shows an example of an annotated image in *annotation display mode*: annotated rectangular areas are highlighted and icons to edit, delete, and view an annotation are shown. Buttons enabling zooming in and out are displayed above the image.

Although within the research projects currently carried out in our VRE the research objects mainly consist of images (scanned pages of lexica), we developed a tool which is similar to the SemanticImageAnnotator but allows texts instead of images to be annotated: the *SemanticTextAnnotator* (STA).[16] The STA extension prepares the VRE to be suitable for carrying out future research projects where research resources are texts. Figure 3.2[17] shows a screenshot of the STA. The vertical band on the left shows the

[14]This technique can be applied in further use cases of qualitative Social Sciences and Humanities projects where images have to be coded (annotated). Further uses for the SIA tool are the annotation of technical diagrams (construction plans, floor plans), pieces of visual art, photos where people and objects need to be annotated, and the like. The extension is available at: http://www.mediawiki.org/wiki/Extension:Semantic_Image_Annotator.

[15]The full picture has the identifier `urn:nbn:de:0111-bbf-spo-13890627`, is available online at http://goobiweb.bbf.dipf.de/viewer/content/12268009x/800/0/00000350.jpg, and is part of the digitization carried out by BBF (Bibliothek für Bildungsgeschichtliche Forschung) of the lexicon `1930-32 Spieler`.

[16]The extension is available at: http://www.mediawiki.org/wiki/Extension:Semantic_Text_Annotator.

[17]The text is an excerpt from the speech *I Have a Dream* by Martin Luther King, Jr., delivered 28 August 1963, at the Lincoln Memorial, Washington D.C.

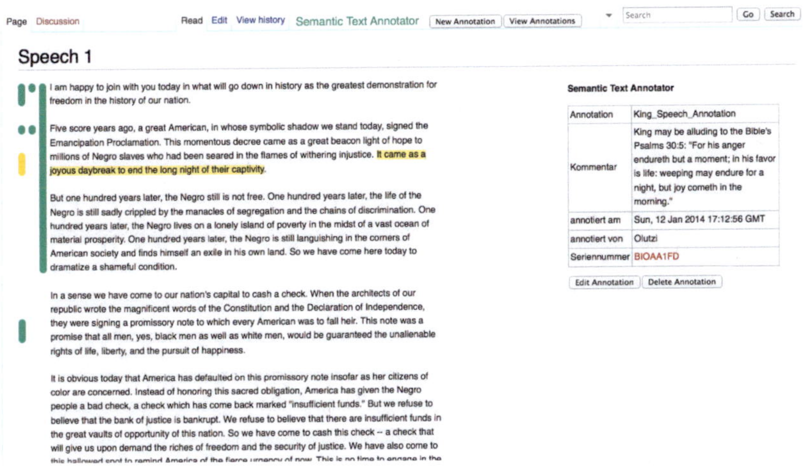

Figure 3.2: Example of a text which is annotated using the *SemanticTextAnnotator*.

vertical extent of the annotations. Clicking on one of them causes the annotated text area to be highlighted and the annotation's metadata to be displayed in the box on the right. The differences between annotations created with the STA and the usual SMW annotations are: the properties of an annotation are stored on the annotation's own wiki page. Only begin and end markers are added to the annotated text. The benefits of this approach are that an annotation itself can be annotated and that annotated sections in a text may overlap.

Existing computer-based qualitative analysis tools provided guidance for the development of an annotation tool. Compared to the prevalent tools Atlas.ti,[18] NVivo,[19] and MaxQDA[20] which are popular in the social sciences and humanities, we identified, realized and confirmed further requirements:

1. A combined editing and query capability of bibliographic data, properties, classifications and annotations;
2. Collaboration facilities in a Web-based environment;
3. Import and export capabilities with standard metadata vocabularies.[21]

As an example of an annotated part of an image, a section of an article of a lexicon can be annotated with i) the type of argument used by the author, such as a moral or

[18] See http://atlasti.com/

[19] See http://www.qsrinternational.com/products_nvivo.aspx

[20] See http://www.maxqda.com/

[21] This capability has recently be described as a key desideratum of existing software solutions within the community of qualitative social science [CG11].

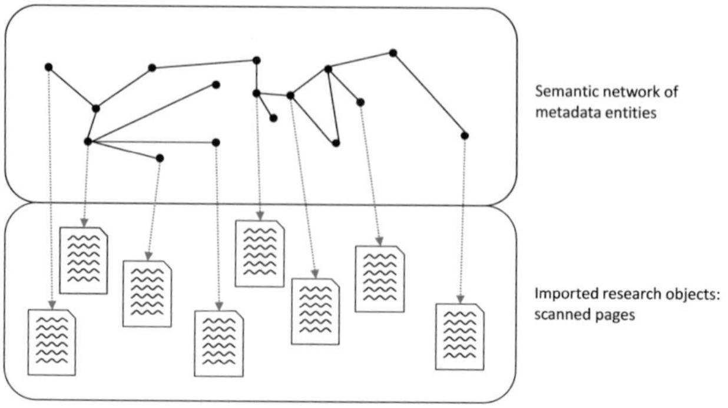

Figure 3.3: The layers of research data and the semantic network.

ideological argument, ii) the topic that is subject of the argument, and iii) the position taken by the author towards this topic. Furthermore, the affiliation of the author, such as the affiliation to a religious institution, can be stored on the author's page. Thus, by annotating and linking the imported and created research data, a semantic network of relevant entities is created by the researchers. Each annotation is stored as an object that links to the image and has semantic properties such as the coordinates on the image, categories, tags, and any other property the researcher wishes to assign. This network can then be subject to qualitative and quantitative analysis (as discussed in Section 3.6.5) where this network serves the purpose of a surrogate for the underlying research data which is not computer-processable.

The semantic network (depicted in Figure 3.3) consists of two layers. The bottom layer consists of the imported images which are not computer-processable. The layer above consists of the semantic network where research data are represented as nodes that are linked with further nodes depicting the imported metadata (lexicon, volume, lemma, etc.) as well as entities created within the VRE. Data in both levels can be maintained by multiple life-cycles, thereby establishing interactions between digital libraries, research projects and further initiatives and data sources. When referring to entities during the annotation process, these entities do not need to exist and can be created automatically.

To give an example of an analysis that exploits this network, imagine the following situation: The concept of *Affenliebe* (infatuation) is mentioned in three articles A1, A2 and A3 which are authored by three people P1, P2, and P3 who are affiliated to the institutions I1, I2, and I3, respectively. The term is negatively connotated in A1 and A2 but positively connotated in A3 thus the set of institutions can be divided into two groups regarding the attitude towards this concept: {I1, I2} and {I3}. Furthermore, for I3 it is known that, contrary to the institutions I1 and I2, articles authored by members of I3 are usually characterized by a religious perspective. This distinction may serve as a basis for explaining the individual connotations.

Besides linking research data via annotations and linking created entities with other created entities, entities can also be linked to entities outside of the VRE. For this purpose we co-developed the *SemanticWebBrowser*[22] extension. On an entity's page, further URIs referring to this entity can be stored. For example, on the page representing an author of an article, the author's unique identifier[23] as used by the authority file of the German National Library (DNB) can be stored. At the bottom of each page a fact box displays all property and value pairs, such as `Profession:Tutor`, that are stored within the local page. The *SemanticWebBrowser* extends this list by adding external facts – property and value pairs retrieved from RDF data available when dereferencing the URI. For example, the property and value pair `Date of birth:1900` can be retrieved from data provided by the DNB. Therefore, researchers can become aware of externally available data and decide to manually import this data.[24]

3.6.3 Linking to External Data

Apart from the description of entities created within the VRE, other data sets such as provided by a digital library may also contain useful information about entities described within the VRE. For instance, the researchers currently using the VRE are collecting data about individual people which had to be completed with data available from the German National Library. Manually looking up hundreds of records in an external dataset and entering this data into the VRE would be a tedious task. Identification of corresponding entity pairs which represent the same real world object is known as the Entity Matching (EM) problem [New+59; FS69]. EM is and has been a subject of various scientific disciplines and numerous different approaches to solve EM have been developed. Avoiding redundancies is an example for an application in database systems where EM is called *deduplication*. The diversity of EM tools is also a consequence of the different domains they were developed for.
Taking advantage of these tools and frameworks, we developed an extension which integrates these into the VRE which allow links between entities within the VRE and entities in the Web of Data [Böh+12; Vol+09] to be generated.

3.6.4 Data Cleansing

Data imported from external sources such as a digital library may contain errors. Further possible sources of error are the import process or the work of researchers within the VRE. Since these errors can distort results of analyses, researchers need to be able to correct errors or to mark errors and ask for help or engage in clarifying discussions.

[22] Available at http://www.mediawiki.org/wiki/Extension:Semantic_Web_Browser.

[23] For example for Josef Spieler: http://d-nb.info/gnd/117483885/about/rdf (last accessed 2015-01-02)

[24] A remaining issue of the beta version of the SemanticWebBrowser is to enable the users to select which externally available facts to import. Currently, externally available data is displayed only and not imported.

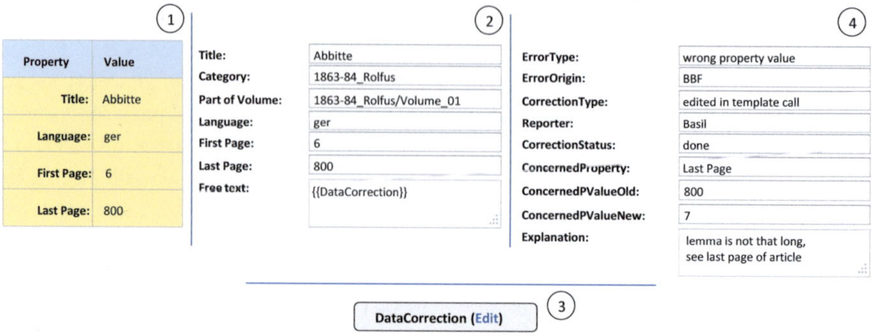

Figure 3.4: The data correction feature. The value 800 in (1) is wrong. The page can be edited with a form as shown in (2) and the value can be corrected. When saving the page the DataCorrection box is displayed on the page as shown in (3). The edit button within this box leads to an empty edit form where details about the correction can be provided as shown in (4).

Therefore, within the VRE the researchers can specify that they identified and corrected an error. They can describe in a *DataCorrection* element the value they replaced, the reason why it had to be changed and the source providing the evidence their decision is based on. Here, the corrective action can be the removal of a triple (such as *Josef Spieler*, *date of birth*, *1900*) or addition of a triple or both. These corrections are stored as objects carrying semantic properties which offers the possibility of tracing back the changes to structured data within the VRE and between the life-cycles. For example, a list of modifications can automatically be compiled with background information for a source such as a digital library, to inform the original provider of this data about the encountered errors and to publish these corrections so that other consumers can adapt their data as well. This list of modifications and justifications can be exported as RDF data. Once confirmed by a data provider, a correction performed within a VRE can be turned into, e.g., a SPARQL UPDATE or SQL INSERT command and executed by the provider of the remote data source.

The data correction workflow is depicted in Figure 3.4. In order to correct the data (which is either imported or created within the VRE), the researcher edits the respective wiki page where the imported data is stored, adds the code `{{DataCorrection}}` and saves the page. This leads to the display of a small box on the page which contains a link to a form where data about the correction can be entered. After editing the correction object, the box displays data entered via the form.

At present, no ontology exists that allows patches to ontologies to be represented. While a Graph Update Ontology[25] exists, this ontology is intended to describe which changes to apply to an ontology automatically. It does not allow for specifying the error and

[25] See http://webr3.org/specs/guo/

for providing evidence or arguments in natural language targeted at the data maintainer, who needs to decide whether to agree and apply each patch. However, this expressivity is a main need of the library to start their quality maintenance activities and requirement for interaction capacities between library and research life-cycles.

3.6.5 Exploring and Analyzing

For the purpose of exploring the VRE's content, researchers can create and embed queries written in ASK – the query language of SMW – and thus create dynamic views of the content. Examples for these queries are 1) a list of lexica that are relevant for a certain project and that contain a lemma that is annotated with certain terms from a taxonomy or 2) a depiction of dates of birth of lemma authors for a certain lexicon on a timeline. Figure 3.5 shows an example of a qualitative analysis: the visualization of reference types in annotated lemmata. A lemma can refer to another lemma within the same lexicon (internal reference), to an author (reference to author), and to another publication (reference to literature). For each type of reference each annotation is depicted with a square which is either grey-colored, if it does not represent a reference of this type, or colored, depending on the type of reference it represents.

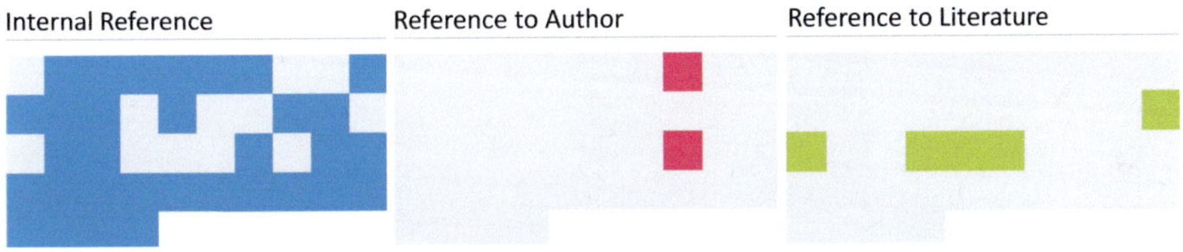

Figure 3.5: Qualitative analysis: visualization of reference types in annotated lemmata.

Figure 3.6[26] shows an example of what is known as a *snippet table*: it is queried for image annotations tagged with *classroom*. The selected sections of the images are displayed together with their tags and the name of the user that created the annotation.

We developed the *AnalysisTool*[27] that allows users of the VRE to create complex queries and explore content interactively. Researchers' query needs can be beyond the expressivity of ASK, the query language of SMW. While these queries can be realized using clever combinations of queries, templates, and parser functions, the implementation is time consuming and requires advanced programming skills. The AnalysisTool is a visual query builder where researchers can interact with menu elements, thereby creating a

[26]The original image the image sections are taken from is available online at http://commons.wikimedia.org/wiki/File:Bundesarchiv_Bild_183-S77144,_Schwerin,_bei_Naturkunde-Unterricht.jpg and is licensed under the Creative Commons Attribution-Share Alike 3.0 Germany license. Attribution: Bundesarchiv, Bild 183-S77144 / CC-BY-SA.

[27]The extension is available at: http://www.mediawiki.org/wiki/Extension:AnalysisTool.

Classroom

Snip	Tag	Created by
	Blackboard, Classroom	Basil
	Artefact, Classroom	Basil
	Teacher, Classroom	Basil

Figure 3.6: An example of a snippet table: image sections annotated with the tag *classroom* are listed. Sections of images have been annotated using the *SemanticImageAnnotator*.

complex query. Users can see the results of the current query and can use it to explore data by refining the query. Query results can be displayed in different formats such as a table, list, on a map, or as a graph. Users can save the query and export query results in various formats such as JSON and CSV.

Figure 3.7 shows a complex query created using the AnalysisTool. The query selects a lexicon if it has a volume that has a lemma that has a title that contains the string `rzieh`. Results of this query are lemmata such as *Erziehung* (German for education), *Erzieher* (German for educator), and *Auferziehung* (German for nurturing). The tool consists of three areas: the select area (shown in Figure 3.7), the display area, and the view area. The select area enables constraints to be built and constraints to be linked. In the example query, a category panel is used to specify a set of entities that belong to the category *lexicon*. Furthermore, the constraint is added that each member of this set (i.e., each lexicon) is related via the property *has volume* to an entity of a set *Cat 2*. *Cat 2* is defined with the second category panel. Here, a set of entities belonging to the category *volume* is specified where each member of this set (i.e., each volume) is related via the property *has lemma* to an entity of a set *Cat 3*. *Cat 3* defines a set of lemmata which have a lemma title that contains the string `rzieh`.

Besides the category panel, sets of entities can be specified via a property panel (e.g., entities that have a property *birthdate*) and an instance panel (for the purpose of using a concrete entity). Within the category and property panel, entities are either selected from a list, or constrained by defining filters over the entities' property values. In the areas not shown here, users can define for which properties to display values in the query result (display area), and how to format or export the results (view area).

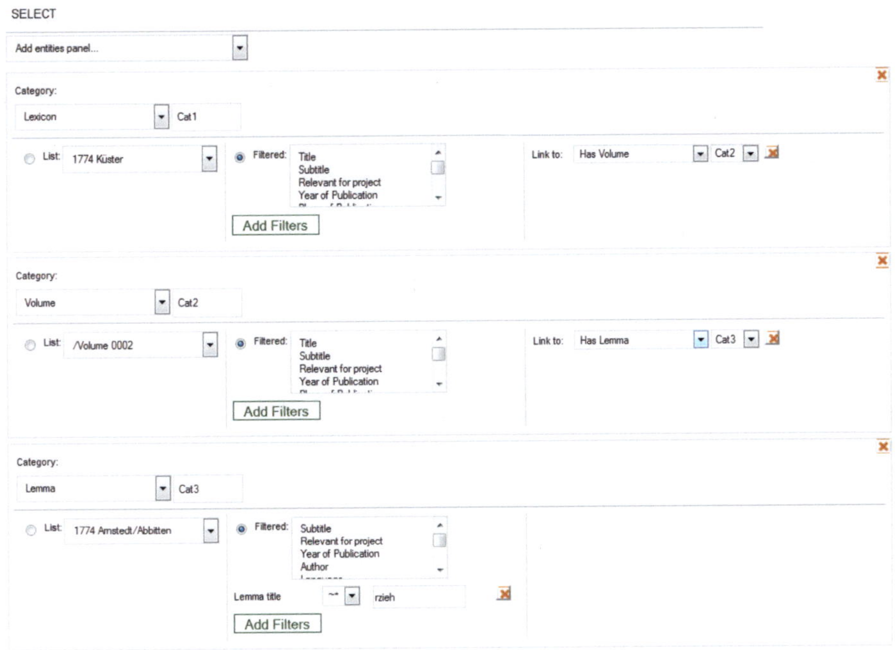

Figure 3.7: An example of a complex query created with the AnalysisTool: Lexica that have a volume that has a lemma title that contains the string `rzieh`.

3.6.6 Export and Sharing

SMW provides facilities to export query results in non-semantic formats such as CSV and JSON, but also to export content as RDF data. Besides sharing information and patches about incorrect data available in external sources as discussed in Section 3.6.4, results of the researchers' efforts (such as the efforts to enrich and interlink the research data and to create new entities) can be exported as well. Here, the identifiers from imported vocabularies, as described in Section 3.6.1 are used. For example, if the property *knows* is imported from the FOAF vocabulary, when exporting RDF data for an entity that uses this property, then instead of the wiki's own identifier for this property, *foaf:knows*, which is the identifier of the imported property is used. Using terms from well-known vocabularies increases the prospects of the exported data being readily reusable and integrable in other contexts.

3.7 Potential of Semantic Web Technologies

The realization of the VRE for the analysis of educational lexica offers several opportunities for interactions between researchers and research data and between life-cycles of digital libraries and research. On this basis we summarize the following potential:

- Import of research data from a digital library is preceded by importing existing vocabularies into the VRE. Research data can then be stored and represented using terms from standardized vocabularies. The benefits of using these vocabularies are the increased prospects for the data to be readily reusable and integrable in other contexts by third parties. Storing information about equivalent resources residing outside the VRE enables these entities to be referenced and externally available data to be displayed.
- The result of the enrichment activities – the semantic network – can be queried and serves as input to qualitative and quantitative analyses. Nevertheless, the layer of imported data and the layer of data created within the VRE remain separable and individually addressable. Results of analyses are dynamic since they depend on the query results as input thus reflecting the current state of the semantic network.
- Annotations created with the *SemanticImageAnnotator* allow for specifying which research project an annotation belongs to. This additional information allows the annotations of the distinct projects to be separated.
- The schema used to represent and link entities can be updated at any time by introducing and using new categories and properties. By using a so far unknown property or category the VRE's ontology is extended thus easily offering a semantic continuum for providing a free degree of formalization in articulation.
- Each object created using the *DataCorrection* feature stores information that enable users to compile lists of correction proposals for each source. Informing the data provider about errors can be beneficial for the provider as well as for other consumers of this data. Patches can be shared with other consumers as well.

- A missing value can be made explicit by using what is known as gardening properties. Regarding a missing value for a property *P* and entity *E*, for the property *missing value for property* the value *P* can be stored on the page *E*. A gardening page lists all pages where a certain property value is missing, thus listing that the entity *E* has no value for the property *P*. This can guide the enrichment process. For example, a template used on a page of a person may store a birthdate, where available, as value of the property *birthdate*. If this value is not available, the template stores the value *birthdate* for the property *missing value for property*.

3.8 Conclusion

In this chapter we described a semantically enhanced and wiki-based Virtual Research Environment that supports the tasks *importing research data*, *enriching research data*, *linking to external data*, *data cleansing*, *exploring and analyzing*, and *export and sharing* and which furthermore addresses socio-technical interactions between researchers and digital libraries offering new ways of collaboration throughout their different life-cycles. In detail, we showed how these interactions are supported and enhanced through Semantic Web technologies balancing thoroughly and fine-grained the intersections between library, research and the Semantic Web in general. While the benefits of the Semantic Web technologies utilized are manifold and enable heterogeneous data practices to be addressed and captured, the realization exemplifies the need to adjust the environment to these concrete practices. Different tasks and quality aspects of the life-cycles have thus been implemented. While the realization targets qualitative and quantitative analyses within a specific community rooted in the History of Education, the supported tasks, the technology and the method developed within the project can be transferred to and be reused in multiple research endeavors since the functionality they provide is not specific to the needs of this particular research. It remains to be evaluated whether in future expansion of our focus these tools are applicable. Concrete examples for transfer and reuse of technical developments are the extensions *OfflineImport*, *SemanticImageAnnotator*, *SemanticTextAnnotator*, *SemanticWebBrowser*, and *AnalysisTool*, as well as the established workflows for data corrections and the visualizations.

Furthermore, designing for concrete research practices and offering flexibility of the environment needs to take into account that ongoing support is required until the end of a research project in order to stabilize the endeavor and ensure a scientific output. Designing these interaction-aware Virtual Research Environments is one step towards future ecologies of small to large research projects and data providers where data flows between the participants lead to enriched and improved data thus providing benefits in a multitude of collaborations.

3.9 Contributions

The main contributions of this chapter are as follows:

- We addressed RQ1.1 *How can capabilities of researchers be enhanced by a semantically-enhanced Virtual Research Environment?* by identifying and supporting a set of research tasks: *importing research data, enriching research data, linking to external data, data cleansing, exploring and analyzing*, and *export and sharing*. These tasks are supported via a set of tools developed for this purpose as extensions to MediaWiki (*OfflineImport, SemanticImageAnnotator, SemanticTextAnnotator, SemanticWebBrowser* (co-developed), and *AnalysisTool*). The extensions are made publicly available. Furthermore, a data import tool, various visualizations such as the visualization of reference types in annotated lemmata and the snippet table and a data cleansing facility were developed.
- A lightweight collaborative and adaptive VRE was designed. Since the VRE is based on a flexible Open Source platform it can be tailored by the researchers towards their specific needs. Therefore, this lightweight environment may serve as a starting point for further re-uses and re-configurations in unforeseen research settings and required functionalities in the future.
- We closely engaged with a specific research community within the History of Education field and articulated requirements within the research community. A participatory design approach with agile development was carried out. Members working with a digital library as well as two researchers in the field of History of Education who are carrying out their research in the VRE were active participants in the requirement elicitation and realization process. Currently, collaborative qualitative and quantitative analyses of a large digital corpus of educational lexica are being carried out using this semantic and wiki-based research environment.
- We detailed in our discussion of the potential of Semantic Web technologies how previously unsupported interactions between life-cycles can now be enabled, thus addressing RQ1.2 *How can research interactions be enabled by a semantically-enhanced Virtual Research Environment?*

4 Labels in the Web of Data

4.1 Introduction

A growing number of applications are expected to use the Web of Data. They will discover descriptions of interesting entities on the Web, load these descriptions, and improve the user experience by being smarter, or enable completely new scenarios, by building on the knowledge found in the Semantic Web [BLHL+01]. These applications often need to expose the entities and the data they have gathered about these entities from the Web to the end user. In order to do so, labels are often used as human-readable names for the entities. Labels can be utilized for a number of different purposes:

- To display data (entities or a graph of entities) to end-users, instead of displaying the URIs, in tools that allow the navigation of RDF data such as Linked Data browsers.
- For searches over the Web of Data: in a query interface to RDF data for casual users, it cannot be expected that the user is capable of writing formal queries such as SPARQL queries. Instead, users would communicate their information needs via keywords or natural language questions. The interface may then try to map keywords or parts of the question to entities and relations in the knowledge base and generate a query. Mapping can be enabled by assigning human-readable labels to entities and relations in the knowledge base.
- For training and using annotation tools with a given knowledge base: labels allow human users to understand which content is available in a knowledge base.
- For generating natural language text from RDF and SPARQL: see Chapter 6 and Chapter 7 regarding Natural Language Generation from SPARQL and RDF, respectively.

Labels need to be made accessible to applications so that applications can utilize them. In the general case it is assumed that by dereferencing the URI of an entity using the hypertext transfer protocol (HTTP) – which means following Linked Data principles [BL06] –, the resulting RDF data contains labels and other information.

In reality, the situation is slightly more complicated. Issues such as internationalization, multiple labels for an entity, the computational costs associated with dereferencing, or the use of alternative labeling properties make the task of finding a label for a given entity much harder than expected. In this chapter, given a large subset of the Web of Data, we investigate how labeling on the Web of Data is actually carried out. The findings of our analysis allow us to derive a number of recommendations for data publishers. We define a number of metrics that provide a baseline for a quantitative analysis of the state of labeling on the Web of Data. Furthermore, we come up with suggestions on how to improve the current situation. The suggestions are aimed at simplifying the usage of data from the Semantic Web in applications.

In this chapter we answer the following three research questions:

RQ2.1 *Which properties are used for the purpose of labeling?*

RQ2.2 *Which metrics help study the properties of labeling within a dataset?*

RQ2.3 *What is the state of labeling in the Web of Data according to these metrics?*

The chapter is structured as follows. Section 4.2 describes related work, especially how current applications (mostly browsers for Linked Data) deal with the issue of labeling. Section 4.3 introduces the Billion Triples Challenge dataset that we use for our measurements. Section 4.4 draws the distinction between information resources and non-information resources, and how they are currently dealt with by data publishers with regard to labels. In Section 4.5 we investigate which properties are used to provide labels. Even though there is a labeling property defined in the RDFS standard, a number of vocabularies define alternative properties to provide labels. Based on those properties, we define metrics in Section 4.6 to assess the current state of labeling in the Web of Data, followed by the results of applying those metrics to a sample of the Web of Data in Section 4.7. We close with conclusions in Section 4.8, give a number of recommendations in Section 4.9, and highlight the main contributions of our research in Section 4.10.

4.2 Related Work

Applications enabling human users to exploit the Web of Data can be classified into three categories: Linked Data browsers, Linked Data search engines, and domain specific Linked Data applications [Hea08].

Linked data browsers, such as Disco [BG07], Tabulator [BL+06], VisiNav [Har10], FOAFNaut,[1] Fenfire [HCB08], Zitgist RDF Browser,[2] Humboldt [KD08], or Marbles [BB09], to name just a few, enable human users the to explore Linked Data similarly to how HTML browsers enable exploration of the traditional Web of Documents. Instead of navigating between HTML pages, they allow navigation between RDF documents

[1] See http://www.foafnaut.org (accessed in 2011, offline 2015-01-02)
[2] See http://dataviewer.zitgist.com/ (accessed in 2011, offline 2015-01-02)

following links in the data by following RDF links. Since applications consuming Linked Data, such as Linked Data browsers, are intended to be used by a broad audience, if the Web of Data becomes widely used, hiding technical details such as URIs when displaying facts to human users becomes crucial. For annotating entities with human-readable descriptions, the property `rdfs:label` from the RDF vocabulary is commonly used to provide a human-readable version of a resource's name besides its URI [BG04].

For example, when displaying data available in the Linked Data cloud for the artist Sidney Bechet using the Linked Data browser *Sig.ma*, the list of information items for his affiliation contains, amongst other items, the following three items:

- `http://rdf.freebase.com/ns/m.049jnng`
- `http://rdf.freebase.com/ns/m.043j22x`
- Sidney Bechet and His Orchestra

For the first two items no human-readable labels are available to Sig.ma, therefore the URI is displayed. The URI does not represent anything meaningful to the user besides the fact that Freebase contains information about Sidney Bechet.

If for a resource no label is known, an unexpected property is used for labeling, or the label is not retrieved by resolving the URI, developers of Linked Data browsers came up with a set of options when dealing with missing human-readable labels:

1. The URI itself is displayed to the user. The URI can be meaningful for some users that do not regard it as noise and that are capable of deriving the meaning from some readable strings in the URI. However, this requires URIs that have been created by following a convention to use meaningful names for URIs.[3] Displaying the URI also often leads to an overly technical feel of the interface.
2. The last part of the URI is used, i.e. the local name or the fragment identifier. For example for the URI `http://www.example.com/about#bob` the fragment identifier bob is used, and for the URI `http://www.example.com/people/alice` the last part of the path is used, i.e. `alice`.
3. A more complex mechanism, such as the one used in Protégé [Pro10], is used which allows the user to specify which properties to display values for.

Human-oriented search engines such as Falcons [CGQ08], Sindice [TDO07], MicroSearch [Mik08], Watson [d'A+07b], SWSE [Hog+11], and Swoogle [Din+04] provide keyword-based search services. Keyword search on graphs relies on the existence of nodes that are labeled, thus allowing keywords to be matched to nodes via their labels [He+07; Tra+09], or on meaningful URIs.

[3] However, http://www.w3.org/Provider/Style/URI (last accessed 2015-01-02) recommends not using topic names in a URI since thereby URI creators binds themselves to some classification that can be subject to change, and would therefore require a renaming of the URI, which is considered undesired.

Although human-readable labels are, as we argue, relevant for certain applications, and although measurements of the Web of Data have been performed before [DF06; WPH06; d'A+07a], an analysis of labels in the Web of Data has not been performed. However, Azlinayati et al. [MBS10] analyzed identifiers and labels in 219 OWL ontologies. Given that the Web of Data mainly consists of instance data, their analysis regarding schema data can be seen as complementing our approach which analyses instance data.

4.3 Billion Triples Challenge Dataset

The Billion Triples Challenge (BTC) 2010 corpus[4] is a dataset consisting of Linked Data crawled from the web. This snapshot of the Web of Data is input to our experiments. The data is stored as *ntriples*. Each of the 3,167,799,445 ntriples[5] is a quad constituted by a subject, a predicate, an object, and a context, where the context is the URI of the resource the triple has been crawled from. When ignoring the context, thus reducing the quads to triples, the dataset contains 1,441,499,718[6] distinct triples.

4.4 Information Resources and Non-Information Resources

URIs are used to identify resources, where a resource might be anything from a person to an abstract idea to a simple document on the Web [JW14]. *Information resources* (IR) are resources that consist of information and therefore all of their essential characteristics can be conveyed in a message and be transported over protocols such as HTTP. IRs can be copied from and downloaded via the Internet given their URLs. Disjoint from this set of resources is the set of *non-information resources* (NIR) – resources that cannot be accessed and downloaded via the Internet – such as a person or a country. Nevertheless, a non-information resource can be identified with a URI. Resolving the URI should result in metadata that describes the non-information resource. This idea is part of the Linked Data principles [BL06].

The distinction between information and non-information resources is relevant for the further investigation of labeling on the Web of Data: whereas NIRs are not directly accessible to the machine (i.e., the machine can talk *about* a resource, but not access or transform it), IRs can be downloaded, displayed, and further processed. IRs do not

[4] Available at http://km.aifb.kit.edu/projects/btc-2010/ (last accessed 2015-01-02)

[5] Thus representing 12,57% of the estimated size of the Web of Data, which consists of 25,200,042,407 triples according to http://www4.wiwiss.fu-berlin.de/lodcloud/ (accessed May 2011).

[6] See http://gromgull.net/blog/2010/09/redundancy-in-the-btc2010-data-its-only-1-1b-triples/ (last accessed 2015-01-02)

necessarily require labels in order to be useful to the end-user, whereas for NIRs there is not much else besides the URI and related entities that can be used to represent them in the user interface. IRs can be represented by themselves (in case of a picture), or by a hyperlink to the document, or by the document title (in case of an HTML page or Office document). Applications such as Linked Data browsers should thus be aware of the difference, and treat NIRs and IRs differently. Indeed, some browsers do so. Tabulator [BL+06], Explorator [ASB09], and Graphite[7] display, for instance, images inline with the other data in the browser.

Whether a URI refers to an information resource or to a non-information resource should be determined as follows according to [BCH07]: Non-information resources should have a hash URI or, if they have a slash URI, resolving the URI should lead to an HTTP `303 See Other` response. Hash URIs include a fragment, with a special part that is separated from the rest of the URI by a hash symbol # [SC08].[8] URIs of information resources on the other hand should ultimately resolve with the given information resource, which means with an HTTP response code `200 OK` (after following redirects). When we receive an error when resolving a URI (i.e., a response in the `4xx` or `5xx` range), we cannot infer whether this URI refers or has referred to an information resource or a non-information resource.

Even though URIs are supposed to be opaque [BLFM05], an analysis performed on URIs with extensions from the BTC 2010 corpus[9] revealed that URIs with file name extensions such as `.html` or `.jpg` often refer to information resources. In order to test this hypothesis, we collected all URIs ending in extensions from the BTC 2010 corpus. The Billion Triples Challenge (BTC) 2010 corpus[10] is a dataset consisting of Linked Data crawled from the Web which is stored as *ntriples*. Looking through the corpus, we found 75,6 million distinct URIs that appeared either in the subject or the object position.[11] Of these, 10,3 million URIs ended in an extension (13,6%). For each extension, we selected a random sample of 50 URIs, and issued HTTP `HEAD` requests. The aim of the request was not to retrieve the whole resource, but only the HTTP header information. If the response to the request was a `303 See Other`, the URI would have identified a non-information resource even though the URI ended in a file extension. Extensions that appear more than 100,000 times in the BTC 2010 corpus are `.jpg`, `.html`, `.rdf`, `.bml`, `.do`, `.json`, `.ttl`, `.jsp`, `.xml`, `.php`, `.htm`, `.png`, and `.gif`. The percentage of NIRs among those resources is 0% – indeed not a single URI returned a `303 See Other` among these extensions. A complete list of all extensions and results can be found online.[12] The results show that almost all URIs ending with an

[7] See http://graphite.ecs.soton.ac.uk/ (last accessed 2015-01-02)

[8] E.g., `http://www.example.com/about#alice`

[9] See Section 4.3 for more information about this dataset.

[10] Available at http://km.aifb.kit.edu/projects/btc-2010/, (last accessed 2015-01-02)

[11] We also looked at the URIs in the property positions, but within a sample of ca. 40 million triples we only found a single URI with an extension, and subsequently ignored this case.

[12] See http://km.aifb.kit.edu/sites/label/btc/

extension are indeed information resources, as expected. The only surprising number we encountered was among `.svg` files, which were encountered 3,287 times. Of these SVG URIs, 31% gave a `303 See Other` response. We further investigated the matter, and found that all those URIs came from DBpedia [Aue+07], and can be traced back to DBpedia's extraction mechanism, which transforms infobox links to local SVG files on Wikipedia articles as properties of a given entity.

The BTC 2010 corpus also provides a file that contains for each URI for which a server responded with a `303 See Other` response the URI the server redirected to.[13] This list contains about 6 million URIs. Some of them point to HTML documents and not to RDF files, but in general we assume that this list contains a subset of the NIRs that are within the BTC 2010 corpus.

4.5 Labeling Properties

The RDFS standard defines the property `label`, which can be used to connect an entity to a human-readable name [BG04]. But `rdfs:label` is only one of the many means that are actually used to assign a human-readable name to an entity. There are several different reasons for using alternative labeling properties. Some vocabularies prefer to use more specific properties to assign names. For example, the FOAF vocabulary [BM05] defines `foaf:name` to assign a name to a person, as it sounds much more acceptable to give a person a name than a label. The SWRC ontology [Sur+05] provides `swrc:name` as well. SKOS even provides a set of properties for preferred and alternative labels [MB09], as the simple label property from RDFS is not sufficient for the needs of SKOS.[14] Other vocabularies might provide an alternative labeling property due to legacy reasons. FOAF introduces a `foaf:LabelProperty` class for labeling such properties, but this is not used even within FOAF itself.[15]

To find out which properties are used for labeling, we examined the BTC 2010 corpus. We extract the property of each quad with a literal with datatype `xsd:string` or with a literal without a given datatype. We counted the number of occurrences for each such property. From the set of 178 properties that occurred at least 100,000 times[16] we manually assessed whether the property is used for the purpose of labeling. To do so we performed a URI lookup on the property itself, checking the label and the description of the property, and then looked at instance data. This resulted in a list of 36 properties

[13] The name of the file is `redirects.nx` in the BTC 2010 corpus.

[14] The idea here is that no two concepts should be given the same preferred label for any given language tag for information retrieval and information organization purposes. Alternate labels allows multiple same-language descriptors for a concept. See http://www.unc.edu/~prjsmith/skos_guide.html (accessed in 2011, offline 2015-01-02).

[15] In the latest *FOAF Vocabulary Specification 0.99* from 14 January 2014 (avaiable at http://xmlns.com/foaf/spec/20140114.rdf, last accessed 2015-01-02), this class is commented as a candidate for replacement.

[16] The whole set consisting of 179 properties is available at http://km.aifb.kit.edu/sites/label/btc/.

Table 4.1: Most often used properties for labeling purposes.

Property: Short Name and URI	**#quads**
rdfs:label, http://www.w3.org/2000/01/rdf-schema#label	184,763,752
foaf:nick, http://xmlns.com/foaf/0.1/nick	71,290,327
dc:title, http://purl.org/dc/elements/1.1/title	16,940,134
rss:title, http://purl.org/rss/1.0/title	7,081,008
foaf:namehttp://xmlns.com/foaf/0.1/name	6,007,766
dcterms:title, http://purl.org/dc/terms/title	2,895,504
geo:name,http://www.geonames.org/ontology#name	2,789,894
foaf:nickname, http://xmlns.com/foaf/0.1/nickname	2,398,760
swrc:name, http://swrc.ontoware.org/ontology#name	1,638,784
cyc:label, http://sw.cyc.com/CycAnnotations_v1#label	1,497,882
lastfm:title, http://rdf.opiumfield.com/lastfm/spec#title	1,125,943
po:ResidueName, http://www.proteinontology.info/po.owl#ResidueName	1,012,286
po:Atom, http://www.proteinontology.info/po.owl#Atom	706,700
po:Element, http://www.proteinontology.info/po.owl#Element	706,700
po:AtomName, http://www.proteinontology.info/po.owl#AtomName	706,700
po:ChainName, http://www.proteinontology.info/po.owl#ChainName	657,371
uniprot:fullName, http://purl.uniprot.org/core/fullName	537,734
uniprot:title, http://purl.uniprot.org/core/title	485,432
ao:has-title, http://www.aktors.org/ontology/portal#has-title	451,727
skos:prefLabel, http://www.w3.org/2004/02/skos/core#prefLabel	429,330
ao:name, http://www.aktors.org/ontology/portal#name	403,119
foaf:givenName, http://xmlns.com/foaf/0.1/givenName	389,219
pim:fullName, http://www.w3.org/2000/10/swap/pim/contact#fullName	357,282
foaf:surName, http://xmlns.com/foaf/0.1/surName	335,516
swrc:title, http://swrc.ontoware.org/ontology#title	333,804
swrc:booktitle, http://swrc.ontoware.org/ontology#booktitle	314,946
ao:hp-name, http://www.aktors.org/ontology/portal#has-pretty-name	290,178
uniprot:orfName, http://purl.uniprot.org/core/orfName	282,049
uniprot:name, http://purl.uniprot.org/core/name	251,480
daml:name, http://www.daml.org/2003/02/fips55/fips-55-ont#name	206,148
geo:alternateName, http://www.geonames.org/ontology#alternateName	185,630
uniprot:locusName, http://purl.uniprot.org/core/locusName	156,062
skos:altLabel, http://www.w3.org/2004/02/skos/core#altLabel	131,566
cc:attributionName, http://creativecommons.org/ns#attributionName	125,425
ao:family-name, http://www.aktors.org/ontology/portal#family-name	124,256
ao:full-name, http://www.aktors.org/ontology/portal#full-name	124,216

shown in Table 4.1 that are used for the purpose of labeling. Note that the numbers in Table 4.1 should not be read as the number of labeled entities since an entity can have multiple labels or an entity can be labeled several times in multiple contexts.

Most of these properties are not connected to `rdfs:label` in a way that would allow machines to automatically discover the alternative labeling property.[17] From the given list, only FOAF [BM05], SKOS [MB09], and Geonames[18] explicitly connect their labeling properties to `rdfs:label` via the `rdfs:subPropertyOf` property. Under both RDFS [BG04] and OWL 2 semantics [Gra+08], this would allow for automatically inferring that any literal connected with the alternative labeling property is also a valid value for `rdfs:label`.[19] Also, the pattern occurs so frequently that it might be worthwhile to hard-code it into an application, to avoid the overhead implied by the usage of a reasoner. Note that the protein ontology[20] contains multiple properties used for labeling due to the fact that these properties are annotated as functional properties[21] with a given domain. For example the domain of the property `po:Atom` is the class `po:Atoms`. It means that when using such a property, besides labeling an entity, the entity can be uniquely referred to via that label and it can be inferred that this entity belongs to class `po:Atoms`.

4.6 Metrics

In this section we define a number of metrics that help the study the properties of labeling within a dataset. In the following section we will discuss the results of measuring a large subset of the Web of Data along these metrics.

4.6.1 Completeness

All non-information resources should have labels. The labeling completeness metric LC tells us if this is indeed the case. The metric is defined as the ratio of all URIs with at least one value for a labeling property to all URIs in a given knowledge base. The metric is extended with three parameters: the actual properties used to assign the label, the entities to be regarded by the metric, and the dataset.

[17] As of October 10, 2014, only the properties http://xmlns.com/foaf/0.1/name, http://www.w3.org/2004/02/skos/core#prefLabel, http://www.geonames.org/ontology#alternateName, and http://www.w3.org/2004/02/skos/core#altLabel are subproperties of `rdfs:label`.

[18] See http://www.geonames.org (last accessed 2015-01-02)

[19] Note that this was not true for the OWL 1 Lite and DL semantics since `rdfs:label` is an `owl:AnnotationProperty` [SWM04], but OWL 2 was extended to enable this pattern.

[20] This ontology is not available anymore at http://proteinontology.info. However, a publication is available: [Sid+05].

[21] For example using the following statement: `po:Atom rdf:type owl:FunctionalProperty`.

Labeling properties are indicated by the subscript of the metric. They may be defined strictly as only `rdfs:label` (LC_{rdfs}), or including any formally defined subproperty of `rdfs:label` (LC_{rdfs+}), or as any other set of labeling properties lp (LC_{lp}) (such as the set presented in Section 4.5, which we call BTC).

The considered entities are defined by the superscript. Most often, we will only want to consider the non-information resources (LC^{NIR}). For an automatic assessment of this metric we must also devise a method to decide whether a given URI is an information resource, or a non-information resource, as discussed in Section 4.4. One might also argue that some non-information resources actually do not require labels, as some resources are basically artifacts of the knowledge representation (LC^{-}). In RDFS and OWL this would most prominently include nodes that model n-ary relations [Noy+06].

The third parameter is given as the argument of the metric. Thus $LC(D)$ is the labeling completeness of the dataset D. We expect $LC(D)$ to always be 1 for a knowledge base D.

Note that a dataset may include data from several RDF files, and indeed most of the time LC is defined over the merged data from a whole site. In this chapter we regard the BTC dataset, the merged data from several million lookups, as a whole.

4.6.2 Efficient Accessibility

A wide-spread method of working with data from the Semantic Web is called *follow your nose*, which works due to the Linked Data principles (see Section 2.1.2 and [BL06]): whenever an application encounters an unknown URI, it can simply dereference the URI in order to access information about the entity identified by the URI. The retrieved information will usually include a label for the entity of interest, and it will also include links to other entities to which the given entity is connected, so that the application can further dereference these as well.

Assume that for the URI `ex:Berlin` the result of this exercise looks as follows:

```
ex:Berlin ex:location ex:Germany .
ex:Berlin rdfs:label "Berlin"@en .
```

A Linked Data browser can display the string *Berlin* to represent the resource of interest, but it has to look up both `ex:location` and `ex:Germany` before it can represent the single fact that is included in the response. If an RDF graph contains 50 triples, with about 60-80 different URIs, the application actually needs to make several dozen of HTTP requests in order to display the facts within that single resource. This turns out to be the main reason for the slow performance of Linked Data browsers [Vra+11]: a single browsing step can fire dozens, if not hundreds, of requests. Imagine instead that the response were:

```
ex:Berlin ex:location ex:Germany .
ex:Berlin rdfs:label "Berlin"@en .
ex:location rdfs:label "Location"@en .
ex:Germany rdfs:label "Germany"@en .
```

Now the application can display the fact without any additional lookup. This approach has nevertheless several disadvantages: it implies redundancy, and leads to larger data files. In general it is expected to nevertheless *reduce* the load and bandwidth of serving Linked Data as the amount of requests would be significantly reduced.

We define the metric *LE* as the ratio of all mentioned URIs with at least one value for a labeling property to all mentioned URIs in a given RDF graph. The subscript and superscript are defined as for *LC*, the superscript can further define a background set of known labels (e.g., for a widely deployed vocabulary such as FOAF or GoodRelations [Hep08]). For example, the following graph would have a LE^{foaf-}_{rdfs} of 1, but a LE^{-}_{rdfs} of 0.5 (since the `foaf:img` property has no label). Note that for brevity RDF and RDFS are always assumed to be known.

```
ex:Basil foaf:img ex:basil.jpg .
ex:Basil rdfs:label "Basil"@en .
```

Whereas for the *LC* metric we can always look up a given URI, this is not allowed for *LE*. Nevertheless, *LE* with sensible parameters should always be 1 in order to increase the utility of any given response for inquiring applications.

4.6.3 Unambiguity

Each entity can have a whole set of different labels attached to it. This will likely yield meaningful results if the application can distinguish between these labels: SKOS includes different properties for denominating preferred and alternative labels [MB09], and given a multi-lingual knowledge base we expect to have several labels for a given entity, one in each language (see the following section).

But an entity can also have several labels that are not at all differentiated. In this case an application has to select one of the labels. And unless it does not have a deterministic selection procedure, the application might end up being inconsistent, displaying a different label every time the entity is displayed – which might easily lead to confusion for the user of the application. Even if the application provides a deterministic selection procedure, as long as this procedure is not common among all applications the user uses to interact with a given knowledge base, the user will be exposed to confusing inconsistencies across interfaces.

We introduce the metric LU_f which is the ratio of all URIs that have exactly one preferred label according to a selection procedure f to all URIs with any label in a given knowledge base. The superscript is the same as for LC, but the subscript is replaced by the selection procedure f, which might be, in the simplest case, just selecting any value of `rdfs:label` (LC_{rdfs}), but could also include a more sophisticated preference function (e.g., if there is a `skos:prefLabel` take that, otherwise any `rdfs:label`).

As with all the previous metrics presented in this chapter, a knowledge base should have a LU of 1.

4.6.4 Multilinguality

Language tags can be used on plain literals to state the natural language used by the literal. This enables applications to select the most appropriate literals based on their user's language preferences. An example for a literal with a language tag is `"university"@en` or `"Universität"@de`.

In order to measure multilinguality we define LLN, the number of languages used with a labeling property. The same subscripts and superscripts apply as for LC.

4.7 Results

We used the metrics defined in the previous section on the BTC 2011 corpus. We did not consider entailments as defined by the formal semantics of RDFS or OWL. In particular we did not regard the equivalency of entities that could be derived via `owl:sameAs` statements or inverse functional properties, but regarded them URI by URI.

The BTC2011 corpus consists of 219 chunks. From each chunk we extracted the URIs from the first 100 nquads which resulted in 7195 URIs. For each URI we performed a lookup and identified 1376 NIRs by `303 See Other` redirect. By following the redirect and analyzing the RDF data we found that for 526 NIRs at least one label exists given the properties in Table 4.1. This means that only 38.2% of the analyzed NIRs have a label. Table 4.2 shows which properties are used to assign labels.

$$LC_{BTC}^{NIR}(BTC2011) = 38.2\%$$

In order to measure the efficient accessibility, we looked through a sample of up to five random graphs from each second level domain in the BTC 2011 corpus. This resulted in a set of 741 graphs. The results are given in Figure 4.1. The histogram shows that for 109 graphs no entity is labeled within a graph. However, there are 26 graphs for which each entity is labeled within the graph. In order to define a set of known vocabularies `voc`, we

Table 4.2: Completeness of NIR labels.

Number of NIRs	Labeling property
451	http://www.w3.org/2000/01/rdf-schema#label
73	http://xmlns.com/foaf/0.1/name
53	http://purl.org/dc/elements/1.1/title
20	http://xmlns.com/foaf/0.1/givenName
13	http://purl.org/dc/terms/title
5	http://xmlns.com/foaf/0.1/nick
4	http://www.w3.org/2004/02/skos/core#prefLabel

took the ten most widely used vocabularies in the BTC 2010 corpus (see Table 4.3). The average completeness per dataset regarding voc is 33.82%. 25% of the datasets have up to 11% completeness, 50% of datasets have up to 27% completeness, and 75% of datasets have up to 56% completeness.

$$LE_{voc}^{NIR}(BTC2011) = 33.82\%$$

Table 4.3: Top ten most frequently occurring vocabulary namespaces in the BTC 2010 corpus (according to http://gromgull.net/2010/10/btc/explore.html).

Vocabulary namespace	Number of occurences
http://www.w3.org/2000/01/rdf-schema#	845,952,387
http://data-gov.tw.rpi.edu/vocab/p/90/	651,432,324
http://www.w3.org/1999/02/22-rdf-syntax-ns#	567,247,265
http://purl.org/goodrelations/v1#	527,323,224
http://xmlns.com/foaf/0.1/	209,249,423
http://purl.uniprot.org/core/	41,961,030
http://purl.org/dc/elements/1.1/	29,596,285
http://www.proteinontology.info/po.owl#	13,661,605
http://purl.org/dc/terms/	12,579,646
http://www.w3.org/2002/07/owl#	12,362,503

We measured the unambiguity of labels in the corpus. From the set of 57,532 NIRs that have at least one label in the corpus, 903 NIRs have multiple labels – either multiple labels for at least one of the labeling properties shown in Table 4.1, or multiple labels for at least one property and language. This results in an unambiguity ratio of 0.98.

$$LU_{f}^{NIR}(BTC2011) = 98.0\%$$

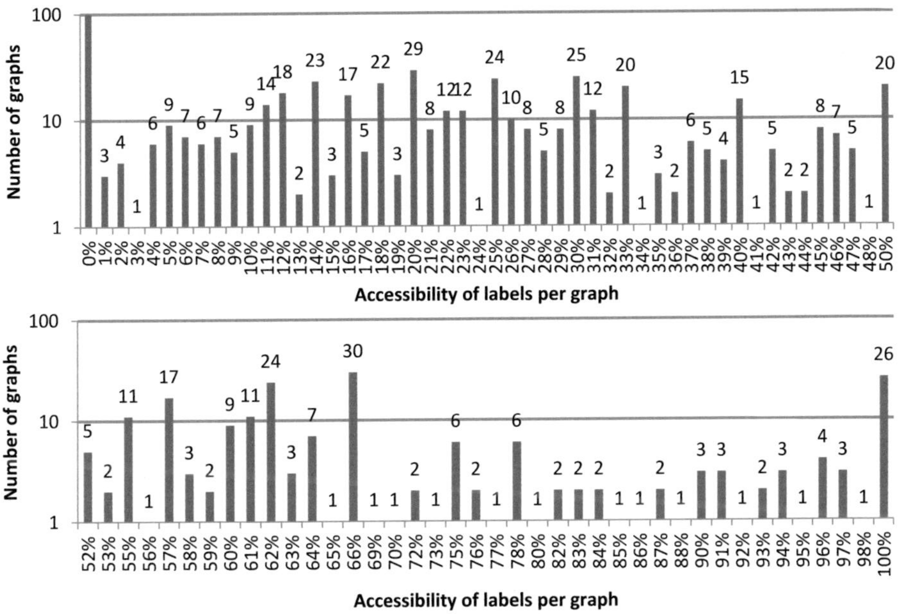

Figure 4.1: Histogram of LE_{BTC}^{top} of up to five random graphs from each of the domains in the BTC 2011 corpus, for a total of 741 graphs (logarithmic scale).

Here, the selection function f selects a label for any of the labeling properties in Table 4.1.

Finally, we measured the multilinguality of the Web of Data. Figure 4.4 (placed at the end of this chapter due to its size) is a Sankey diagram that shows i) how often each labeling property occurred (e.g., the property `ao:full-name` occurred 124, 216 times), ii) how often a language tag occurred (e.g., 371, 140 times a Japanese (ja) label was assigned to an entity; 112, 060, 382 times no language tag (nolang) was assigned), and iii) it shows which language tags are used for which labeling property (e.g., most literal values assigned to an entity via the property `rdfs:label` have an English language tag; most literals assigned to an entity via the property `foaf:nick` are not language-tagged). Language tags used less than 5000 times for a property are aggregated as `etc`.

In Figure 4.2 we visualize the number of language tags for each property – these are the LLN values for each property. Note that for those of the 36 properties that are not listed in this figure no language tag was used. We selected the most prominent labeling property, `rdfs:label`, and display in Figure 4.3 how often each language tag is used with this property. We cut off language tags used less than 1000 times.

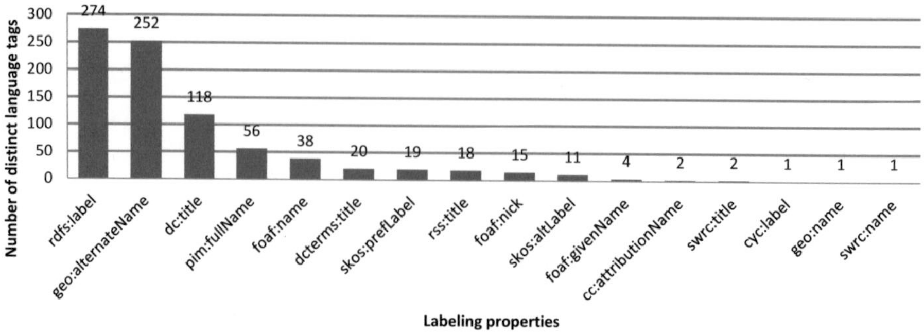

Figure 4.2: LLN: Number of distinct languages used with labeling properties.

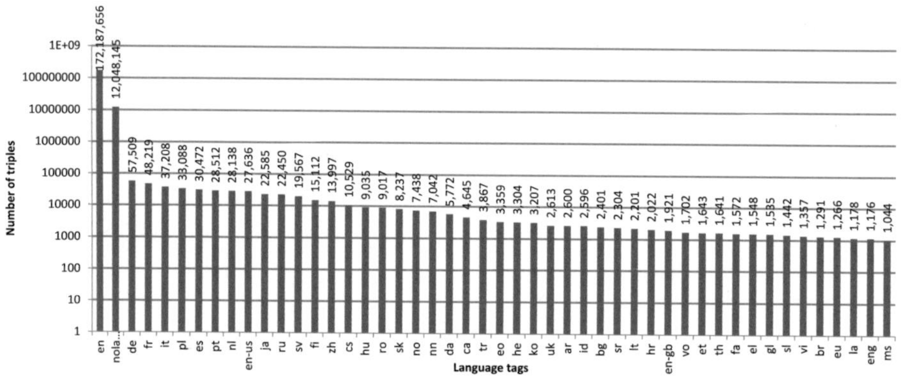

Figure 4.3: Language tags used with the labeling property `rdfs:label` (logarithmic scale).

Labels are used to provide human-readable names for entities. Labels should be provided in multiple languages which is rarely the case. Thus, a potential benefit of the Semantic Web, i.e., the language-independence of the Web of Data, is underexploited.

4.8 Conclusion

Our work has investigated the current state of labeling the Web of Data given a large subset. We have defined metrics to assess the completeness, efficient accessibility, unambiguity, and multilinguality. These metrics address issues that are problematic during the development of applications. The list is not complete but sound, given that they are all based in previous experience. While defining the metrics, we noticed that we had to include a number of parameters that depend on the application that will use the knowledge. This is not surprising: data on the Web of Data is hardly ever evaluable by itself – it greatly benefits from knowing the context of an application that will use the data. The parameters in the metrics allow the customization of the metrics based on the given application, on the labeling properties the application expects, and on the set of entities that are expected to play a role.

4.9 Suggestions

Based on our findings as well as the argumentation leading to the definition of our metrics, we can make a number of suggestions on how to improve the quality and usefulness of labels:

- For all URIs *mentioned* in a given RDF graph labels should be provided and not only for the *main entities*, as this will considerably speed displaying the data with human-readable names and reduce the number of requests significantly.
- A complete set of labels should be provided in all supported languages. One of the biggest advantages of the Web of Data is its inherent multilinguality, but currently this is a tremendously underused feature of the architecture.
- If a proprietary labeling property is used, then the property should be connected to `rdfs:label` explicitly with the `rdfs:subPropertyOf` property. `rdfs:label` should be used redundantly as well since many tools will not provide the inferencing needed to understand the proprietary labeling property. If possible, proprietary labeling properties should be avoided.
- No more than one obvious preferred label for each entity should be provided to decrease the possible confusion for the end-user using an application accessing the data.

The suggestions given above lead to an obvious problem: even a moderately small RDF graph with about 100 triples will include about 150 entities. Labeling all these entities in, e.g., ten languages will lead to an extra 1500 triples – a huge overhead (and not even considering the costs for creating those labels). While one could devise new protocols to deal with these problems, there is an under-utilized existing solution: HTTP allows the `Accept-Language` header, that defines a set of natural languages the response should cover [Fie+99], to be set. By using the HTTP headers a data provider could both provide all labels necessary for an efficient exposure of the data, without unnecessarily inflating the size of the response by only providing labels for the requested languages.

Labels should follow a style guide and be used consistently. A style guide should define if classes are labeled with plural or singular nouns, if properties are labeled with nouns or verbs, etc. Labels should never use camel case or similar escape mechanisms for multi-word terms, but instead simply use space characters (or whatever is most suitable for the given language). I.e., an URI `http://example.org/LargeCity` should have a label `"large city"@en`. External dictionaries such as WordNet [Fel98] can be used to check consistency with regards to a style guide.

In an environment where datasets are assembled on the fly from multiple datasets [Ala06], the assembled parts may follow different style guides. The assembled dataset will then not adhere to a single style guide and thus offer an inconsistent user interface. It is not expected that a single style guide will become ubiquitous on the whole Web. Instead, a dataset may specify explicitly what style guide it follows, and even provide labels following different style guides. This would allow a subproperty of `rdfs:label` to be introduced that is style guide specific, which would in return allow assembled datasets to be displayed consistently.

Even when subproperties of `rdfs:label` are defined, there should always be one label (per supported language) given explicitly by using `rdfs:label` itself. Even though this is semantically redundant, many tools (especially visualization tools) do not apply reasoning for fetching the labels of an entity but simply look for the explicit triple stating the entity's label.

Many of the problems described in this chapter are a consequence of publishing data using the Linked Data principles. It is not clear if following these principles is the best way to publish data on the Web of Data. Serving data through a SPARQL endpoint provides a viable alternative, with the advantage that the application can, in a very fine-grained way, describe exactly what kind of information, labels, and languages it needs. The SPARQL endpoint can then try to understand the query and do its best to provide a viable response.

Labeling may be just a small piece, but at the same time it is an absolutely essential piece of the puzzle that is needed for the Web of Data to finally become widely used.

4.10 Contributions

The main contributions of this chapter are as follows:

- For the purpose of addressing RQ2.1 *Which properties are used for the purpose of labeling?* we identified the 36 properties shown in Table 4.1.
- We introduced four label-related metrics thus addressing RQ2.2 *Which metrics help study the properties of labeling within a dataset?*: completeness, efficient accessibility, unambiguity, and multilinguality.
- For the purpose of addressing RQ2.3 *What is the state of labeling in the Web of Data according to these metrics?* we analyzed the Billion Triples Challenge dataset and found that: regarding completeness, only 38.2% of all non-information resources have a label; regarding efficient accessibility, labels of non-vocabulary URIs are only provided within a dataset in 33.82% cases; regarding unambiguity, most labels (98.0%) are unambiguous; and multilinguality is a strongly underexploited feature. Either no language tag is used, or few languages such as English, German, and French are dominating.
- The findings of our analysis allow us to derive a number of recommendations for data publishers. Furthermore, we came up with suggestions on how to improve the current situation. The suggestions are aimed at simplifying the usage of data from the Semantic Web in applications.

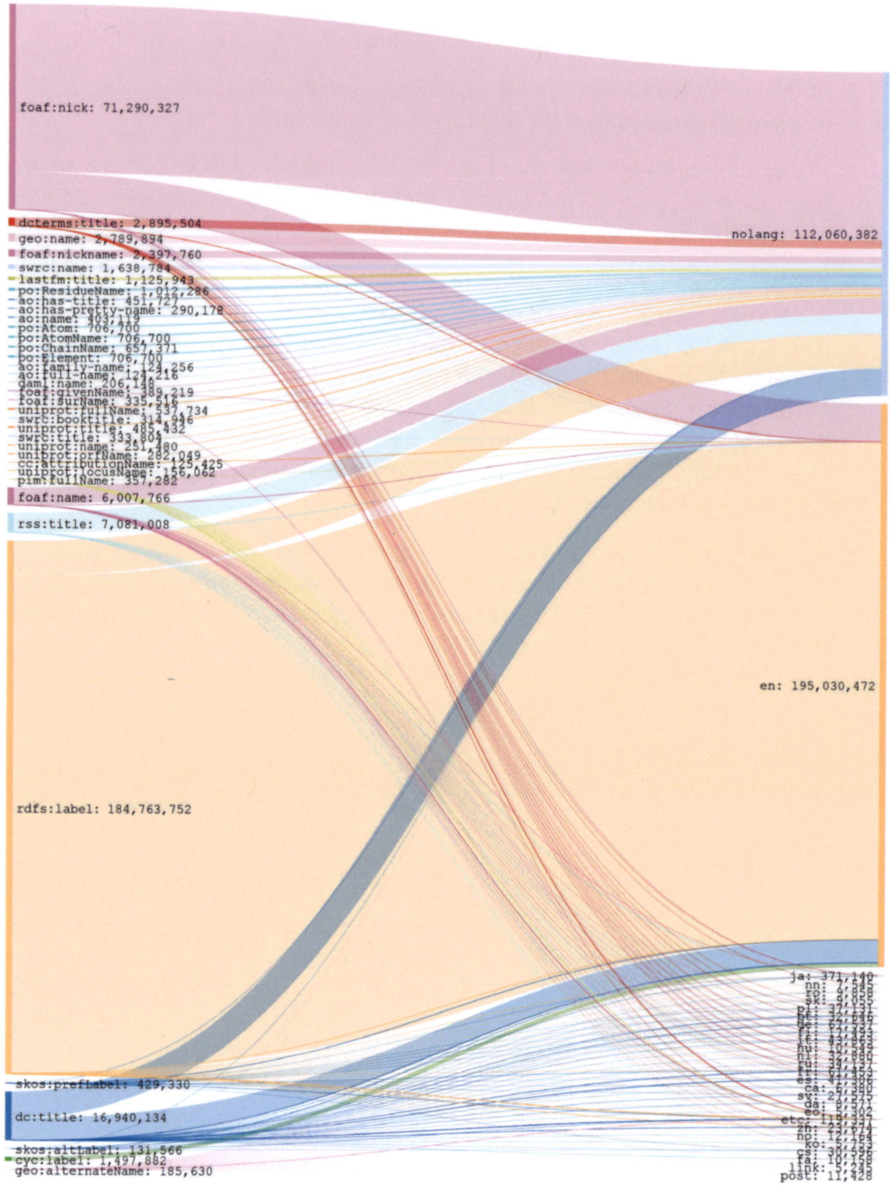

Figure 4.4: Sankey diagram depicting how often within the BTC 2010 dataset language-tagged literals appear with each property and how often each language tag occurs.

5 Deriving Human-Readable Labels from SPARQL Queries

5.1 Introduction

The Semantic Web is built on the concept of unique identifiers for entities and relations. Entities are identified by Uniform Resource Identifiers (URIs) that enable the identification of both web documents and real-world objects [SC08]. Whenever a user interacts with an application performing queries on Linked Data, such as Linked Data browsers [Hea08] (e.g., Sig.ma [Tum+10], VisiNav [Har10], or Tabulator [BL+06]), the retrieved data needs to be presented in a user-friendly way thus allowing the application to be usable also by people not proficient in Semantic Web technologies. The properties `rdfs:label`[1] and `rdfs:comment` from the RDF vocabulary may be used to provide a human-readable version of a resource's name besides its URI [BG04].

As seen in the previous chapter, a large percentage of entities on the Semantic Web lack a human-readable label. A lack of labels hampers the ability of any tool that uses Linked Data to offer a meaningful interface to human users. We argue that methods for deriving human-readable labels are essential in order to allow the usage of the Web of Data. In this chapter we provide and evaluate a method for deriving human-readable labels from variable names used in a large corpus of SPARQL queries that we extract from a set of log files. We analyze the structure of SPARQL graph patterns and offer a classification scheme for graph patterns. Based on this classification, we identify graph patterns that allow us to derive useful labels. We also provide an overview of the current usage of SPARQL in the corpus.

Identifiers in programming languages and software systems can be arbitrarily chosen by developers (besides the lexical constraints given by the respective programming language). However, using meaningful identifiers and following naming conventions increases the productivity and quality of the software during software maintenance [DP06; Pig96], evolution [Leh03], and program comprehension [DP06]. To compensate for missing labels of URIs we derive labels that are meaningful to users by analyzing how

[1] Throughout this chapter we omit prefix definitions for the sake of readability and brevity but use common prefixes where their expansion is known by the service provided at http://prefix.cc (last accessed 2015-01-02).

Linked Data is interacted with. SPARQL (introduced in Section 2.1.3) is a query language for RDF data. Issuers of these queries may chose meaningful identifiers for the same reasons as in programming languages. Therefore, a SPARQL query may contain meaningful identifiers of variables in the context of URIs. By analyzing SPARQL query logs we can observe how users, be it human or non-human agents, interact with Linked Data. We extract SPARQL queries from the web server log files of two prominent data sources in the LOD cloud, namely *DBpedia* [Aue+07] and *Semantic Web Dog Food (SWDF)* [Möl+07], and show to which extent meaningful identifiers are used and how labels for URIs can be derived to compensate for missing labels. To the best of our knowledge, no approach exists to systematically derive labels for resources.

In this chapter we answer the following two research questions:

RQ3.1 *How can human-readable labels be derived from variable names in SPARQL queries?*

RQ3.2 *Which SPARQL graph patterns are common?*

The remainder of this chapter is structured as follows. We describe our analysis and findings in Section 5.2, carry out an evaluation in Section 5.3, present related work in Section 5.4, draw conclusions in Section 5.5, and highlight the main contributions in Section 5.6.

5.2 Analysis

5.2.1 USEWOD2011 Dataset

The USEWOD2011 corpus[2] contains server log files from *DBpedia* [Aue+07] and *Semantic Web Dog Food* (SWDF) [Möl+07]. In total the dataset contains 19,770,157 log items for DBpedia and 7,992,850 log items for SWDF. The number of SPARQL queries is 5,159,387 (26.10%) for DBpedia and 2,033,021 (25.44%) for SWDF.

Semantic Web Dog Food (SWDF) is a dataset of publications, people and organizations in the Web and Semantic Web area, covering several of the major conferences and workshops, including the International World Wide Web Conference (WWW), the International Semantic Web Conference (ISWC), and the Extended Semantic Web Conference (ESWC). The dataset consist of SWDF log files from 2008 November 01 to 2010 December 14.

[2] See http://data.semanticweb.org/usewod/2011/

```
0.0.0.0 - - [01/Jul/2009:10:15:44 +0100]
↳ "GET␣/sparql?query=SELECT...␣HTTP/1.1"
↳ 200 1183 "-" "Java/1.6.0_13" "FR"
↳ "5ee07b08fad8d44d388c6aff91651f1db70e2c23"
```

Figure 5.1: An example entry in Apache Combined Log format.

The DBpedia 3.5 knowledge base has been created by extracting information from Wikipedia, thus covering many domains, and contains 672 million RDF triples. The USEWOD2011 corpus contains the log files from 27 days between 2009 and 2010.

The log files conform to the Apache Combined Log Format[3] with small modifications: for the purpose of anonymization the IP in the IP address field is replaced with 0.0.0.0. To allow location-based analyses, a field with the country code of the original IP is appended to the log entry. Moreover, a hash of the original IP is appended to allow users to be distinguished. The log entry shown in Figure 5.1 consists of the blank IP address (`0.0.0.0`), empty userid, request date (`01/Jul/2009:10:15:44 +0100`), abbreviated request string (`GET ...`), response code (`200`), response size (`1183`), empty referrer (`-`), user agent (`Java/1.6.0_13`), country code (`FR`), and the hash of the original IP (`5ee07b08fad8...`). Note that the example log entry is actually a single line that was broken into 4 lines for the purpose of readability, denoted by ↳.

Some log entries represent SPARQL SELECT queries [PS08], such as the query in Listing 5.1, taken from the DBpedia logs:

```
PREFIX rdfs: <http://www.w3.org/2000/01/rdf-schema#>
PREFIX dbpprop: <http://dbpedia.org/property/>
SELECT DISTINCT ?x ?abstract
WHERE {
  ?x rdfs:label "Fanfare_Ciocarlia".
  OPTIONAL {
    ?x dbpprop:abstract ?abstract .
  }
}
```

Listing 5.1: A SPARQL query extracted from the DBpedia query logs.

The query requests entities that have an `rdfs:label` `Fanfare_Ciocarlia` and, if available, `dbpprop:abstract`'s value for this entity. The query contains two triple patterns. In the example, the first triple pattern

[3]See http://httpd.apache.org/docs/current/logs.html (last accessed 2015-01-02)

?x rdfs:label "Fanfare_Ciocarlia" .

consists of a variable, a URI, and a literal. The second triple pattern

?x dbpprop:abstract ?abstract .

consists of a variable, a URI, and a variable.

5.2.2 Preprocessing

From the 19,770,157 (DBpedia) and 7,988,587 (SWDF) lines in the log files, where each log event, such as a SPARQL SELECT event or other HTTP requests, is represented by one line, we extracted 5,147,626 (DBpedia) and 2,037,238 (SWDF) SPARQL SELECT queries. Furthermore, for each set of identical queries only one instance is selected and the other instances are ignored. The remaining sets contain 1,212,932 (DBpedia) and 195,641 (SWDF) SPARQL SELECT queries. The queries were parsed using the Perl module RDF::Query::Parser::SPARQL which is available at CPAN.[4] When querying the SPARQL endpoint of DBpedia, providing namespace definitions for common prefixes is unnecessary. However, the parser could not successfully process a query in the absence of namespace definitions for prefixes used in the query. For each of the prefixes[5] we added the usual prefix definition where necessary to parse these queries successfully.

The result of the preprocessing phase is a list of 1,212,932 SPARQL SELECT queries for DBpedia and 195,641 SPARQL SELECT queries for SWDF consisting of 2,242,800 and 213,029 triple patterns respectively. In the case of DBpedia 3,933,989 queries (76.44%) were ignored and 705 queries could not be parsed, whereas in the case of SWDF 1,841,472 queries (90.39%) were ignored and from those that were not ignored 125 queries could not be parsed.

5.2.3 Query Patterns

Figure 5.2 (note the logarithmic scale) presents the number of triple patterns per query – both for DBpedia and SWDF. Most queries are rather simple with only one to three triple patterns.

[4] Version 2.903 was used but is not available anymore. Instead, version 2.912 is available, http://search.cpan.org/dist/RDF-Query/lib/RDF/Query/Parser/SPARQL.pm (last accessed 2015-01-02)

[5] Supported prefixes: annotation, cc, cohere, conf, dbo, dbpedia, dbpedia-owl, dbpprop, dc, dcterms, foaf, geo, georss, gr, ical, kuaba, lsdis, mo, nao, nco, nfo, nid3, nie, nmo, opo, owl, rdf, rdfs, rss, scot, sioc, sioct, skos, and vs.

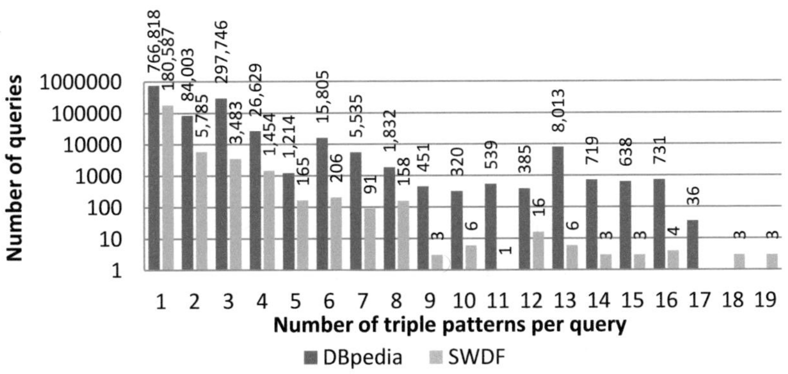

Figure 5.2: Number of triple patterns per query in DBpedia and SWDF (logarithmic scale).

We classify triple patterns into the set of triple pattern classes P where $P := \{R, V, B\} \times \{R, V, B\} \times \{R, V, B, L\}$, where R denotes that a triple pattern's element (subject, predicate, or object) is a resource, V denotes that a triple pattern's element is a variable, B denotes that a triple pattern's element is a blank node, and L denotes that a triple pattern's element is a literal. For example, the triple pattern

dbpedia:Karlsruhe dbo:populationTotal ?population .

belongs to class RRV since the triple pattern's subject and predicate are resources and the triple pattern's object is a variable. Given this classification, triple pattern classes exist that do not contain a variable, such as RRR. These are ignored since within the scope of this work we focus on variables.

Knowing about frequent common structures of SPARQL queries and their number of occurrences in a real dataset is valuable information for RDF database engine (known as triple stores) developers. The information can be helpful for designing indexing and caching strategies for the purpose of increasing the performance of query engines. We analyzed which triple pattern classes constitute SPARQL queries. Figure 5.3 and Figure 5.4 present basic graph structures as hypergraphs. For example, in the DBpedia dataset we found 11,282 SPARQL SELECT queries that consist of three triple patterns of class RRV and three triple patterns of class VRV. Circular nodes represent hyperedges and rectangular nodes represent triple pattern classes. Each hyperedge is a group of triple pattern classes and contains all triple pattern classes that it connects to via multi-edges. The number of occurrences of each graph structure is denoted by the number in the circular node. To focus on the most common patterns in the figures, we pruned the graph to show only those patterns that occur more than 5000 times in case of DBpedia and 1000 times in case of SWDF. Before pruning, the graphs depicted 329 (112) graph

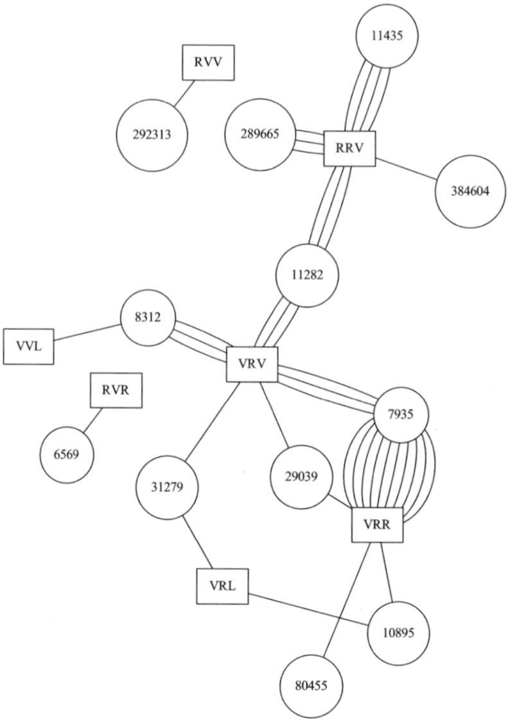

Figure 5.3: Hypergraph of most frequent query patterns in DBpedia (with more than 5000 occurrences).

patterns for DBpedia (SWDF). Most queries (766,662; 63.29%) in DBpedia consist of only one single triple pattern of class RVV, whereas in the SWDF dataset most queries (180,670; 94.11%) consist of one single triple pattern of class RRV. From the visualization of the pruned graphs it can be derived how often a certain triple pattern occurs at least in the respective dataset. For example, the triple pattern RRV occurs at least $4 * 11,435 + 384,604 + 3 * 289,665 + 3 * 11,282$ times in the DBpedia dataset. Due to the pruning this number can be smaller than the actual number.

The hypergraphs can also be used to predict how likely an instance from another class will co-occur in a SPARQL query for a given triple pattern class. For example, in the case of SWDF, a triple pattern of class VRR is more likely to occur with a VRV triple than with a VVV triple since 3130 (=1205 + 1925) queries contain at least a VRR and a VVV triple pattern and 4758 (=1628+1925+1205) queries contain at least a VRR and a VRV triple pattern. This information can be interesting for developers of SPARQL query builders when supporting users in extending queries.

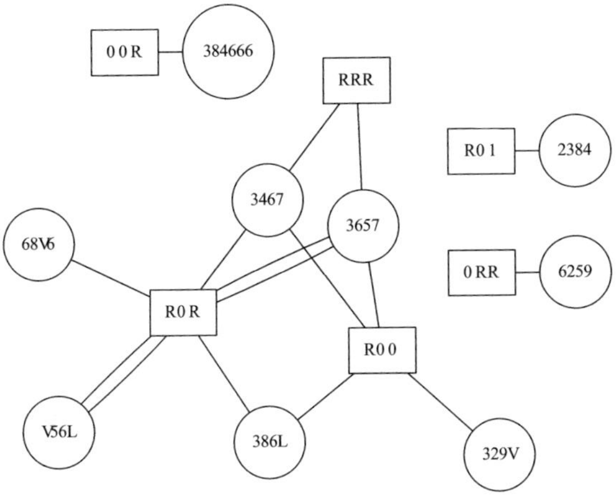

Figure 5.4: Hypergraph of most frequent query patterns in SWDF (with more than 1000 occurrences).

5.2.4 Analyzing Variable Names

We classify variable names as follows:

short A variable name is considered *short* if it has a string length up to 2 characters. Variable names of that type that frequently occur are `s`, `p`, `o`, and `x`.

stop A variable name is considered as a *stop* word if it is not *short* and does not add information that could be used to describe a URI, such as a variable named `subject` in subject position. For each position (subject, predicate, object) we created the lists of stop words manually while exploring the data resulting in three lists containing 31, 25, and 28 words respectively. Table 5.1 shows the top stop words for each of the three possible positions in a triple pattern and how often they occurred in the data. The complete list of stop words is available online.[6]

lang If a variable name is neither *short* nor a *stop* word and if it belongs to a natural language, such as the word `artist`, which belongs (non-exclusively) to the English language, then it is classified as *lang*. Strings that contain the separator character "_" or that are in camelCase are split into its constituent parts. Each constituent of length $\geqslant 4$ needs to be classified as *lang* in order for the string to be classified as *lang*. For checking which language a word most likely belongs

[6]See http://people.aifb.kit.edu/bel/label/sparql_logs/

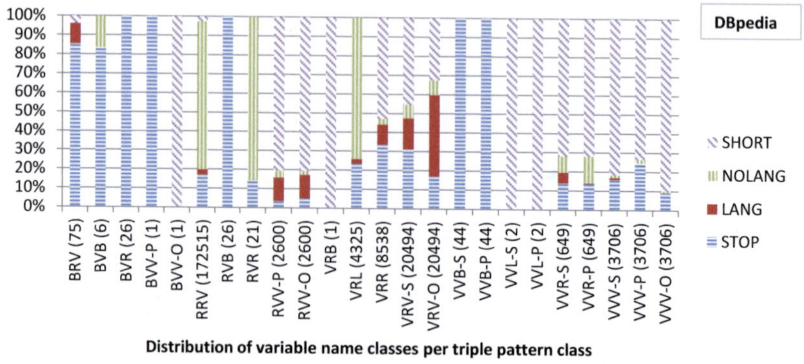

Figure 5.5: Distribution of classes of variable names for each triple pattern class for DBpedia.

Table 5.1: Most frequent variable names that are stop words in DBpedia queries.

Subject position		Predicate position		Object position	
variable:	frequency:	variable:	frequency:	variable:	frequency:
resource	158244	property	7592	category	12358
res	61803	pred	134	uri	11775
category	12639	left	56	url	8375
subject	8224	predicate	39	value	6452
instance	3013	prop	27	hasValue	457

to we use the Corpex[7] webservice. The Corpex dataset consists of all words and their frequencies as extracted and counted from instances of Wikipedia in multiple languages [VSS11]. For each language $l \in \{de, en, es, fr, it\}$ we request the number of exact occurrences in the dataset derived from the respective Wikipedia corpus and normalize this value by dividing it by the total number of words in this corpus for language l. We ignore words for which this results in a value less than $5 * 10^{-7}$, which corresponds to words that occur less than 1000 times in the English Wikipedia. The language for which this score is highest is assumed as the language to which this word belongs to.

nolang Variable names that are not *short*, not *stop*, and not *lang*, are classified as *nolang*.

Figure 5.5 and Figure 5.6 show the distribution of classes of variable names for each triple pattern class for the DBpedia and the SWDF datasets.

[7] See http://km.aifb.kit.edu/sites/corpex/ (accessed in 2011, offline 2015-01-02).

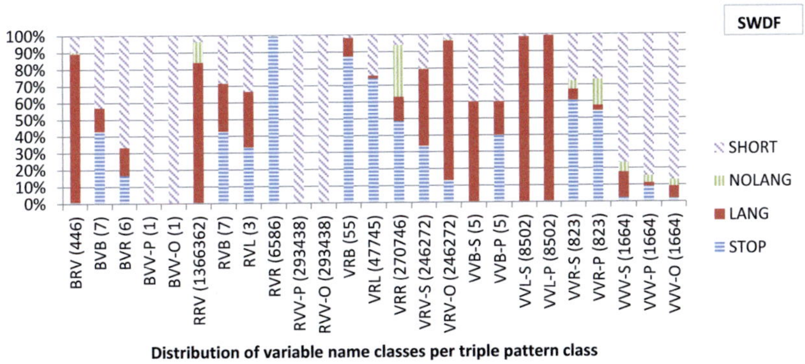

Figure 5.6: Distribution of classes of variable names for each triple pattern class for SWDF.

5.2.5 Query Pattern Classes

We distinguish between query patterns and triple patterns, where a query pattern is a set of triple patterns. We ignore anything but triple patterns inside the SPARQL query, e.g., `UNION`, `OPTIONAL`, etc. For each pattern that we describe we provide an example from the actual data and formulate an assumption about how this triple pattern class can be used to derive labels. An evaluation of these assumptions is presented in Section 5.3. In the following, we discuss six of the query pattern classes.

5.2.5.1 1 × RVV

A query pattern of class 1 × RVV consists of one triple pattern of class RVV which consists of a resource as the subject, a variable as the predicate, and a variable as the object. 292,313 queries (24.13 % of all DBpedia queries) of this class were extracted from the DBpedia dataset and 2,407 queries (1.25 % of all SWDF queries) from the SWDF dataset. For example:

dbpedia:Claude_Debussy ?p ?place .

Most variable names are either short (99.47% in predicate position, 99.41% in object position) or stop words (0.25% in predicate and object position). Therefore, this query pattern is not a fruitful source for deriving labels. However, we found queries containing RVV patterns where additional information about the property is encoded in a filter expression as in the query shown in Listing 5.2:

```
SELECT ?label WHERE {
  <http://data.semanticweb.org/person/daniel-herzig>
    ?label_prop ?label .
  FILTER(REGEX(str(?label_prop),
    "(label|summary|name)$", "i"))
} LIMIT 1
```

Listing 5.2: A SPARQL query where additional information about the property is encoded in a filter expression.

A user issuing this query seems to be striving to find something that is expected to be human-readable. The query returns a list of all values for properties that end with `label`, `summary`, or `name`, such as the properties `rdfs:label` or `foaf:name`. In the current approach we ignore this additional information.

5.2.5.2 1 × RRV

A query pattern of class 1 × RRV consists of one triple pattern of class RRV which consists of a resource as the subject, a resource as the predicate, and a variable as the object. 384,604 queries (31.75% of all DBpedia queries) of this class were extracted from the DBpedia dataset, 169,222 (88.15% of all SWDF queries) from the SWDF dataset. For example:

dbo:NASA <http://www.w3.org/2003/01/geo/wgs84_pos#lat> ?lat .

In this example the name of the variable ("lat") in the triple $R_1 R_2 V$ is equal to the local name or fragment identifier of R_2, as in the following example where the local name is the part behind the last slash:

dbo:NASA <http://dbpedia.org/property/agencyName> ?agencyName .

Our assumption is that V' is a meaningful label for R_2 in $R_1 R_2 V$ iff $eq_{ln}(R_2, V) \wedge lang(V)$ where $eq_{ln}(R_2, V)$ stands for the string equality of the local name or fragment identifier of the URI R_2 and the name of the variable V, and $lang(V)$ evaluates to true if the name of the variable V is considered as *lang*, thus being a word from a natural language as checked using the Corpex webservice. V' can be derived from V by substitution of separators "_", "+", and "-" to spaces and splitting camel-cased words into its constituents.

5.2.5.3 3 × RRV

A query pattern of class 3 × RRV consists of three triple patterns where each triple pattern is of class RRV and consists of a resource as the subject, a resource as the predicate, and a variable as the object. 289,665 queries (23.91 %) of this class were extracted from the DBpedia dataset. The homogeneity of this set of graph patterns is high: when ignoring the subjects, which are the same in every triple pattern of a query, then the number of distinct queries is 3. While the structure of each query is the same, the 3 queries differ in the variable's names and properties used. For example:

```
SELECT ?image ?abstract ?redirect WHERE  {
  {
    dbpedia:Tiger_Rag dbo:thumbnail ?image
  } UNION {
    dbpedia:Tiger_Rag rdfs:comment ?abstract
    FILTER ( lang(?abstract) = "en" )
  } UNION {
    dbpedia:Tiger_Rag dbpedia2:redirect ?redirect
  }
}
```

Due to the small number of distinct query types, these queries are expected to be application-specific and not repeatedly issued by a human agent. Due to the small number of unique queries, queries from this class are not promising to be analyzed to harvest labels.

5.2.5.4 1 × VRR, 1 × VRV

A query pattern of class 1 × VRR, 1 × VRV consists of one triple pattern of class VRR and one triple pattern of class VRV. 29,039 queries (2.40 %) of this class were extracted from the DBpedia dataset. For example:

```
?artist
  skos:subject
    dbpedia:Category:People_from_Karagandy_Province .
?artist rdfs:label ?label .
FILTER (lang(?label)='en') .
FILTER (?artist != dbpedia:Aslan_Maskhadov) .
```

87.85% of all queries of class *1 × VRR, 1 × VRV* have a similar structure: the variables in the subject position are equal in both triple patterns, the two variables in the VRV triple pattern are different, the properties in both triple patterns are different, the property in the VRR triple pattern is not `rdfs:type`, the property in the VRV triple pattern is `rdfs:label`, and the variables are `artist` and `label`. An agent seems to be iterating over a set of entities and creating a query for each entity. Thereby, the names of the variables are the same for each such query. Due to the homogeneity of queries from this class, and due to the small number of distinct variable names used, this class is not promising to be analyzed in order to harvest labels.

5.2.5.5 2 × VRV

A query pattern of class 2 × VRV consists of two triple patterns of class VRV. 3,028 queries (1.58 %) of this class were extracted from the SWDF dataset. For example:

```
?person foaf:name ?name .
OPTIONAL { ?person foaf:mbox ?email }
```

This pattern seems promising at first glance: it seems that we can derive labels for the properties from the variables in the object position. But in 98.22% of such queries, the variable names are either short or stop words. Therefore, queries from this class are not promising to be analyzed in order to harvest labels.

5.2.5.6 Any Graph with VRR

Finally, we discuss graph patterns that contain at least one VRR triple pattern. For example:

?Player dbo:Athlete dbo:SoccerPlayer .

This pattern occurs 270,746 times (22.32%) in the DBpedia dataset. The assumption is, that V' is a human-readable label for R_2 in VR_1R_2 iff $lang(V) \wedge R_1 =$ rdf:type, as in the following example:

?person rdf:type foaf:Person .

If the property is not `rdf:type`, then the name of the variable in the subject position can not be used to derive a label. That means that in this example `Person` can be derived as a label for the class `foaf:Person`. The following examples demonstrate that in each case the variable's name could be used for a different purpose:

Case 1: ?ground skos:subject dbpedia:Category:Parks_in_Indiana .

Case 2: ?singer foaf:page <http://en.wikipedia.org/wiki/Bob_Dylan> .

Case 3: ?airline dbo:headquarter dbpedia:Germany .

Case 4: ?maceo owl:sameAs dbpedia:Maceo_Parker .

The variable names could be used as follows: The variable name in Case 1 could be used as a label for the resource in object position, the variable name in Case 2 could be used as a label for class of the resource in object position, the variable in Case 3 could be used as a label for a class in the domain of the property, and the variable in Case 4 could be used as a name of the instance in object position.

5.3 Evaluation

For the assumptions presented in the previous section we performed the following evaluation: For every tuple consisting of a URI and a label that we derived from analyzing the query log of a data source (the *guessed label*), we query the data source in order to see if a label already exists (via either the `rdfs:label`, `rdfs:comment`, `dc:title`, or `foaf:name` properties).[8] If no given label exists in the data sources, we analyze whether the BTC2010 corpus provides a label. If this also fails, we dereference the URI to access their RDF description and see if this RDF description provides a label. We regard this as the *given label*. We then compare given labels with guessed labels.

We consider a guessed label as being correct if it is equal to the given label or if the given label is a substring of length $\geqslant 4$ of the guessed label or if the guessed label is a substring of length $\geqslant 4$ of the given label or if the Levenshtein edit distance between given and guessed label is $\leqslant 4$. If a guessed label did not meet these criteria we manually evaluated for a random subset of all those cases whether this label was meaningful and appropriate for the resource. Two patterns have been selected for evaluation that were the most interesting and most frequently occurring classes.

5.3.1 1 × RRV

In the DBpedia dataset for all 1,366,362 triples of class RRV we found 549,093 triples where the condition $eq_{ln}(R_2, V)$ holds, and 916,673 triples where the condition $\neg eq_{ln}(R_2, V)$ holds. From these triples we extracted 226 pairs of URIs and guessed labels. We started with an automatic evaluation by comparing the guessed labels with the given labels. This resulted in 54.5% guessed labels being correct. Then we evaluated the remaining guessed labels manually. The overall evaluation resulted in 68.5% being correct, 9.1% being correct within a given context, and 22.4% as being wrong. Examples for guessed labels that are considered as being correct in a certain context only are `actor` for the property `dbo:starring` or `location` for the property `dbo:residence`.

[8] Other labeling properties presented in Chapter 4 are not used in the datasets and are therefore excluded.

An example of a guessed label that was considered wrong is the label `contained in` for the property `dbpprop:creator` for which the `rdfs:label creator` is known.

5.3.2 Any Graph with VRR

80,455 queries in the DBpedia dataset contain a triple pattern of class VRR. For 60 distinct URIs we derived 36 labels for classes – some labels were derived for multiple URIs, such as `river` for both `dbo:River` and `dbpedia:Category:Rivers_of_Spain`. We began by checking the labels automatically. 25% of the guessed labels where automatically confirmed as being correct. The remaining guessed labels were checked manually. Of the labels derived from this class, 53.3% were correct, 46.7% were considered as being wrong. An example for a guessed label considered as being correct is `station` for the class `dbo:RadioStation`. An example for a guessed label considered as being wrong is the label `scientist` for the class `dbo:SoccerPlayer`.

5.4 Related Work

Query logs have already been analyzed with different intentions in the context of the Semantic Web:

- Gallego et al. [Gal+11] aim to find the most frequently used language elements focusing on the most expensive SPARQL operations. These results may assist designers of indices, stores, optimizers, and benchmarks in making reasonable assumptions and make sound decisions. They also perform their analysis on the USEWOD2011 corpus.
- While Mika, Meij, and Zaragoza [MMZ09] also analyze query logs, the authors are focusing on the *semantic gap* – the gap between the content provided in the Semantic Web, and the information needs as expressed by web users submitting keyword queries to search engines.
- Möller et al. [Möl+10] analyze a similar dataset consisting of access logs and find out whether a human user or a machine agent is consuming Linked Data. They perform an analysis of the SPARQL queries found in the log files and expect these results to be beneficial when choosing which indexes to pre-compute and store for serving LOD data.

To the best of our knowledge SPARQL queries have not yet been analyzed with a focus on exploiting variable names. Moreover, no approach exists to systematically derive labels for resources in the Web of Data.

5.5 Conclusion

We presented an approach for automatically deriving labels for entities based on the extensive analysis of a big corpus of SPARQL queries. The methods that we have developed have achieved an acceptable precision as evaluated on the DBpedia and SWDF datasets. That means, most of the labels that we guessed based on the SPARQL queries matched the already given labels.

Regarding the quality of variable names used in SPARQL queries for labels we found out that guessed labels can be less specific than it is useful since in the context of a query a variable name may be only as specific as necessary for the purpose of disambiguation. For example in the following query it is sufficient to name the variable `artist` instead of e.g. `MusicalArtist`:

```
SELECT ?artist ?x WHERE {
  ?artist rdf:type dbpedia-owl:MusicalArtist .
  ?x dbprop:influencedBy ?artist .
}
```

We noticed that in most cases the labels were useful for terminological entities, i.e., classes and properties. We have, for now, only regarded the queries by themselves. In future work, queries could be analyzed in parallel with the data, especially with the given answers.

We have published the derived labels on the Web, so that the results can be inspected and also used by Web of Data applications.[9]

The regarded datasets (DBpedia and SWDF) provide through the process they are created an almost full coverage with labels for all their entities, which makes them highly atypical as we have seen in our analysis of labels in the Web of Data in Chapter 4. At the same time, this enables us to thoroughly evaluate our approach since we can use the already given labels, allowing us to automatically evaluate our approach. We expect that the same methods can be applied to other datasets where labels are missing and SPARQL query logs are available With the methods presented here we can automatically derive labels for properties and classes in these datasets, thus taking an important step towards a higher reusability of the knowledge published on the Web of Data.

[9] See http://people.aifb.kit.edu/bel/label/sparql_logs/

5.6 Contributions

The main contributions of this chapter are as follows:

- We address RQ3.1 *How can human-readable labels be derived from variable names in SPARQL queries?* by presenting and executing an approach to derive human-readable labels from variable names in SPARQL queries. The evaluation shows that the approach is applicable for deriving human-readable labels.
- For the purpose of addressing RQ3.2 *Which SPARQL graph patterns are common?* we analyzed a large set of SPARQL queries extracted from the DBpedia and SWDF query logs. We developed a hypergraph-based visualization of the most frequently occurring graph patterns and applied it to visualize our measurement results in Figure 5.3 and Figure 5.4.

6 Verbalization of SPARQL Queries

6.1 Introduction

SPARQL (introduced in Section 2.1.3) is the W3C Recommendation for querying and accessing RDF data [HS10]. While SPARQL has found broad acceptance among semantic application developers, the usage of SPARQL among those who possess limited to no expertise in Semantic Web technologies remains understandably limited.

A wide variety of systems propose different means for users to express what they are looking for: (i) keywords, as supported by systems such as SemSearch [LUM06] and SWIP [PHH12]; (ii) free-text questions, sometimes using a controlled language, such as ORAKEL [Cim+08], FREyA [DAC12], and the approach introduced in [Ung+12]; and (iii) pre-defined forms [Men+08; HO11]. Independently of how the input is given, SPARQL queries are generated and evaluated.

The system we introduce in this chapter, Spartiqulation, is complementary in functionality and purpose to these approaches. More concretely, we address the question of query verbalization, by which the meaning of a query encoded in SPARQL is conveyed to the user via English text. The verbalization allows a potential discrepancy between an intended question and the system-generated query to be observed by a user. In addition, Spartiqulation offers an easy-to-use means to gain better insight into the operation of a search system.

We illustrate a potential discrepancy via an example. Assume the information need of the user is: *The second highest mountain on Earth.* If the system does not know the meaning of the term *second*, it will very likely simply ignore the qualifier and display the highest mountain. Using Spartiqulation, the meaning of the generated SPARQL query can be communicated to the users in a comprehensible way and eventually inform them that the system understood a different question.

Further scenarios, in which SPARQL verbalization could play a key role, are learning environments and (iterative) query editors. Creating natural-language representations of SPARQL queries while learners are writing these queries is expected to help them gain a better command of the semantics of the language, and understand the reasons why in some cases the results returned by a query engine differ from the original intention of the learner. For example, regard the query in Listing 6.1 in which the variable *?pop* is defined as optional in the OPTIONAL block and where the optionality of the variable is countermanded by the filter expression that explicitly requests the variable to be bound. This query can be verbalized as *Cities and their population values* in which the eventually intended optionality is missing.

```
SELECT * WHERE {
  ?x rdf:type :city .
  OPTIONAL {
    ?city :populationTotal ?pop .
  }
  FILTER ( BOUND(?pop) )
}
```

Listing 6.1: Example query with a countermanded optionality.

Spartiqulation uses template-based natural language generation (NLG) techniques, as well as linguistic cues in labels and URIs of resources mentioned in a SPARQL query to generate English text. The approach is schema-agnostic (besides being tied to the RDF vocabulary itself), and is thus applicable to various domains and application scenarios.

In this chapter we answer the following research question:

RQ4 *How can SPARQL queries be verbalized in a mostly schema-agnostic manner?*

The chapter is structured as follows. The approach is described in Section 6.2, followed by a description of the template engineering process in Section 6.3. We present an evaluation in Section 6.4, followed by a discussion of related work in Section 6.5. We draw conclusions in Section 6.6 and highlight the main contributions in Section 6.7.

All verbalizations presented as captions of query listings are generated using Spartiqulation.[1] Additional material, such as the evaluation sheets, is available online.[2]

[1] We would like to thank Jia-Yan Gu for her help in improving the verbalizations in terms of correct use of the English language as well as the 20 participants that participated in an online evaluation and gave valuable feedback for a previous version of our verbalizer.

[2] See http://km.aifb.kit.edu/projects/spartiqulator/ESWC2014SPARQL

6.2 The Spartiqulation Approach

6.2.1 Coverage

According to the SPARQL W3C Recommendation [HS10], SPARQL knows the query forms `SELECT`, `CONSTRUCT`, `ASK`, and `DESCRIBE`. Tools such as SemSearch [LUM06], ORAKEL [Cim+08], FREyA [DAC12], and TcruziKB [Men+08] that translate user input into SPARQL queries generate `SELECT` queries (e.g., Listing 6.2) and `ASK` queries (e.g., Listing 6.3), which are also the query forms that our approach supports. In the current form our approach verbalizes SPARQL 1.1 `SELECT` and `ASK` queries where the `WHERE` clause is a connected basic graph pattern that may contain certain filter expressions. The aggregation function `COUNT` and the solution modifiers `DISTINCT`, `HAVING`, `LIMIT`, `OFFSET`, and `ORDER BY` may be used. Currently not supported are unconnected basic graph patterns, variables in predicate positions, negations via the language features `EXISTS` and `MINUS`, subqueries, the language features `BIND` and `VALUES`, the solution modifier `REDUCED`, aggregation functions besides `COUNT`, graph names, and path matching.

6.2.2 Anatomy of a Verbalization

Our approach is template-based and inspired by the pipeline architecture for NLG systems and the tasks these systems commonly perform, as introduced by Reiter and Dale [RD00], see Section 2.3.3. In particular, inspired by [Hew+05] and [SM07], we have manually collected a series of schema-independent templates, which are used in the verbalization process to generate coherent natural-language text from the different parts of a SPARQL query. These templates could be extended to capture user-, domain- or application-specific information to further improve the verbalization results. Our approach supports such extensions, but already delivers meaningful results in its current generic form.

The anatomy of a verbalization consists of up to four parts:

Main entity (ME): `SELECT` and `ASK` queries contain a `WHERE` clause containing a basic graph pattern. Verbalization of a graph or graph pattern requires a starting point. We refer to the node that we chose to begin with as the *main entity*. The main entity is rendered as the subject of the verbalization in singular or plural, with a definite or an indefinite article, and may be counted. Examples are: *Persons* for the `SELECT` query in Listing 6.2 and *a record* for the `ASK` query in Listing 6.3. Further examples are *The country* in Listing 6.4, *Not more than 10 distinct african*

$$
\begin{aligned}
Verbalization &::= ME\ [\text{"that has"} \mid \text{"that have"}] \\
&\qquad ConsList?\ \text{"Show also"}?\ ReqList?\ MOD? \\
ConsList &::= CONS\ (\text{"and"}\ ConsList) \\
ReqList &::= REQ\ (\text{"and"}\ ReqList)
\end{aligned}
$$

Figure 6.1: Anatomy of the verbalization of a SELECT query.

countries[3] in Listing 6.5, *Number of distinct european countries* in Listing 6.6, and *Books* in Listing 6.7.

Constraints (CONS): `CONS` covers restrictions regarding the main entity, such as the relations with other resources and literals. Constraints are rendered in singular or plural, depending on the number of the main entity, and may contain information from the `ORDER BY` and `LIMIT` parts of the query, as well as from `FILTER` expressions. Examples are: *that have a birth place*, *that have the surname "Elcar"*, *that have "Dana" as an English given name*, and *that have an alias that matches "Dana"* in Listing 6.2, *has a maker that has the name "Pink Floyd"* in Listing 6.3, *has the highest number of languages* in Listing 6.4, *do not have borders with oceans* in Listing 6.5, *have government types that match "monarchy"* in Listing 6.6, and *are labeled "The Pillars of the Earth" in English* in Listing 6.7.

Requests (REQ): `REQ`, which is only created for `SELECT` queries, includes the projection variables (those that appear in the `SELECT` clause) besides the main entity of a query. Examples of requests are *these birth places* and *if available, these person's English labels* in Listing 6.2, *if available, its English labels* in Listing 6.4, and *these book's authors* in Listing 6.7. Renderings of requests may include information from `FILTER`s and from domain/range information of properties and whether the variable is optional.

Modifiers (MOD): `MOD` expresses the features `LIMIT`, `OFFSET`, and `ORDER BY` and applies to `SELECT` queries. `MOD` can be partially included within other parts of the verbalization, for example, in the ME part (*Not more than 10 persons*), within constraints (*that has the highest number of languages*, as in Listing 6.4), or as an own sentence (*Omit the first 10 results; show not more than 10 results.*) for the features `LIMIT 10 OFFSET 10`.

The four parts are then joined to create the complete verbalization as described in Section 6.2.8 and as shown in Figure 6.1.

[3]The approach does not consider that national and regional adjectives are capitalized in English and therefore generates *european* instead of *European*, *african* instead of *African* and so forth.

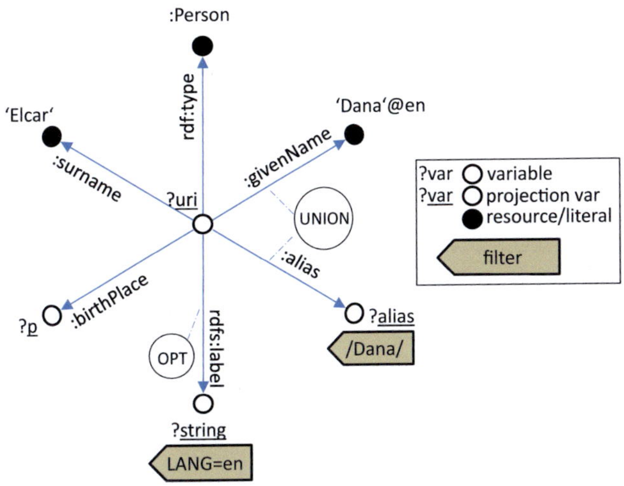

Figure 6.2: Visual representation of the query shown in Listing 6.2.

```
SELECT ?uri ?string ?p WHERE {
  ?uri :birthPlace ?p . ?uri :surname 'Elcar' .
  ?uri rdf:type foaf:Person.
  { ?uri foaf:givenName 'Dana'@en. } UNION {
    ?uri prop:alias ?alias . FILTER(regex(?alias,'Dana')) .
  }
  OPTIONAL {
    ?uri rdfs:label ?string . FILTER(lang(?string) = 'en')
  }
}
```

Listing 6.2: *Persons that have a birth place and that have the surname "Elcar" and that have "Dana" as an English given name or that have an alias that matches "Dana". Show also these birth places and, if available, these person's English labels.* See Figure 6.2 for a visualization of the query graph.

```
ASK WHERE {
  ?album rdf:type mo:Record.
  ?album mo:release_status mo:bootleg.
  ?album foaf:maker ?artist.
  ?artist foaf:name 'Pink␣Floyd'.
}
```

Listing 6.3: *Is it true that there is a record that has a maker that has the name "Pink Floyd" and that has the release status bootleg?*

```
SELECT ?uri ?string WHERE {
  ?uri rdf:type onto:Country .
  ?uri onto:language ?language.
  OPTIONAL {
    ?uri rdfs:label ?string.
    FILTER (lang(?string) = 'en')
  }
} ORDER BY DESC(COUNT(?language)) LIMIT 1
```

Listing 6.4: *The country that has the highest number of languages. Show also, if available, its English labels.*

```
SELECT DISTINCT ?state WHERE {
  ?state rdf:type ex:AfricanCountry .
  OPTIONAL {
    ?state ex:bordersWithOceans ?ocean .
  }
  FILTER(!BOUND(?ocean))
} LIMIT 10
```

Listing 6.5: *Not more than 10 distinct african countries that do not have borders with oceans.*

```
SELECT COUNT(DISTINCT ?uri) WHERE {
  ?uri rdf:type yago:EuropeanCountries .
  ?uri dbo:governmentType ?govern .
  FILTER(regex(?govern,'monarchy'))
}
```

Listing 6.6: *Number of distinct european countries that have a government type that matches 'monarchy'.*

6.2.3 Content Determination

In natural language generation the system decides which parts of the input are communicated to the user as human-readable text. In our case, this decision is rather trivial, as the complete SPARQL query is verbalized. An exception in this approach are PREFIX definitions such as PREFIX foaf: <http://xmlns.com/foaf/0.1/>; we leave these out for reasons of conciseness of the output.

6.2.4 Document Structuring

The system constructs independently verbalizable messages from the input query and determines an appropriate ordering and structure. We first identify the subject of the verbalization, transform the graph, and then create and classify the messages which will be processed by the subsequent tasks.

6.2.4.1 Main Entity Selection

SELECT queries are a means to retrieve bindings for variables. We assume that a user is more interested in variable values than in entities used in the query. *Projection variables* are those variables that appear in the SELECT clause and in the WHERE clause, such as the variable ?title in Listing 6.8. Only bindings retrieved for projection variables are returned as result of a query execution. Therefore, only projection variables are candidates for the main entity selection. Furthermore, only non-optional projection variables come into consideration. A variable is a non-optional variable if within the WHERE clause it does not only appear within OPTIONAL blocks. For example, in Listing 6.4 the variable ?uri is non-optional and the variable ?string is optional. Due to their nature of being optional and thus less relevant than non-optional variables, only non-optional projection variables come into consideration. The variables for which a NOTBOUND filter (e.g. !bound(?var)) is specified are treated as optional variables during main entity selection.

```
SELECT ?uri ?book WHERE {
  ?book rdf:type onto:Book .
  ?book onto:author ?uri .
  ?book rdfs:label 'The␣Pillars␣of␣the␣Earth'@en .
}
```

Listing 6.7: *Books that have the label "The Pillars of the Earth" in English and that have an author. Show also these books' authors.*

```
SELECT DISTINCT ?track ?title
WHERE {
  ?track rdf:type mm:Track.
  ?track dc:title ?title.
  ?track dc:creator ?artist.
  ?artist dc:title 'Petula␣Clark'.
}
```

Listing 6.8: A SELECT query with two non-optional projection variables: *?track* and *?title*.

Table 6.1: Different CONS part verbalizations for different main entity selections for the query shown in Listing 6.8.

ME	Verbalization
`track`	*Distinct tracks that have a creator that has the title "Petula Clark".*
`title`	*Distinct things that are titles of tracks that have a creator that has the title "Petula Clark".*

ASK queries are a means to assess whether a query pattern has a solution. If ASK queries contain variables then the selection procedure is the same as for projection variables in SELECT queries. Otherwise, we select the triple's subject.

In order to identify the main entity we define Algorithm 6.1 which applies the ordered list of rules R shown in Figure 6.3. The rules propose the exclusion of members from a candidate set. We derived the rules by looking at queries within the training set[4] having multiple candidates. The candidate set C is initialized as the set of projection variables and the algorithm eliminates candidates step by step. Q denotes the set of triples within the WHERE clause of a query, R_t is the property `rdf:type` and R_l is a labeling property from the set of 36 labeling properties identified in previous experiments and presented in Chapter 4, Table 4.1. The application of an exclusion rule R_i to a candidate set C given a query Q, denoted by $R_i(C, Q)$, results in the removal of the set E proposed by the reduction rule.

[4]See Section 6.4.3 for more information about our training set.

Rule 1 removes candidates that appear in an `OPTIONAL` block of the `WHERE` clause. For example, in a query `SELECT ?a WHERE { ex:R1 ex:R2 ?a . OPTIONAL { ?a ex:R3 ?b . } }` the variable `?b` is removed from the candidate set `{?a, ?b}`.

Rule 2 excludes variables that are not constrained via `rdf:type` in queries that contain variables that are constrained via `rdf:type`. For example, in a query `SELECT ?a ?b WHERE { ?a rdf:type ex:R1 . ?b ex:R2 ex:R3 . }` with `ex:R2` $\neq$ `rdf:type`, the variable `?b` is removed from the candidate set `{?a, ?b}`.

Rule 3 eliminates those variables, for which the existence of a label is not constrained or requested. This applies to queries, which use variables for which the existence of a label is constrained, or in which a label is requested. For example, in a query `SELECT ?a ?b WHERE { ?a` <R_l> `?l . ?b ex:R2 ex:R3 . }` where R_l is a labeling property such as `rdfs:label`, the variable `?b` is removed from the candidate set `{?a, ?b}`.

Figure 6.3: Exclusion rules used by Spartiqulation.

The rules can be described as follows where the numbers show how often a rule was successful in reducing the candidate set for the 209 queries within our training set:

- *Rule 1* (85, 40.67%) proposes removing candidates that appear within the WHERE clause only within OPTIONAL blocks.
- *Rule 2* (12, 5.74%) proposes removing candidates that represent subjects that are not constrained via `rdf:type` in the case that there are candidates that are constrained via `rdf:type`.
- *Rule 3* (48, 22.97%) proposes removing candidates for which no label is constrained or requested in the case that there are candidates for which this is the case.

In some cases (64, 30.62%) no rule was applied since the candidate set contained only a single variable. For all queries given these rules the main entity has been identified. While our actual list of exclusion rules contained more rules these were never applied for the given training data and are thus omitted here.

Algorithm 6.1 Applying reduction rules to candidate set.

```
procedure ReduceCandidateSet(C, R, Q)
    if |C| = 1 then
        return C
    while |C| > 1 do
        for each R_i ∈ R do
            if |R_i(C, Q)| > 0 then
                C ← R_i(C, Q)
                if |C| = 1 then
                    return C
    return ∅
```

Table 6.2: Message types used by Spartiqulation.

nr	name	nr	name	nr	name
(1)	*PATH*	(2)	*VAR*	(3)	*ORDERBY*
(4)	*LIMIT*	(5)	*OFFSET*	(6)	*HAVING*

If a SELECT query has multiple non-optional projection variables, a choice is made among these candidates. For example, given the query shown in Listing 6.8, selecting `?track` would result in *Things that have a creator that has the title "Petula Clark"*; selecting `?title` would result in *Distinct things that are titles of tracks that have a creator that have the title "Petula Clark"*. A choice may have an influence on the verbalization's total length and understandability. In the current approach among the remaining candidate variables the first variable in lexicographic order is selected. However, future extensions of this approach may decide based on the estimated total length and understandability.

6.2.4.2 Graph Transformation

We perform a transformation of the query graph since it simplifies the Linguistic Realization task as discussed in Section 6.2.7. If the query does not come in that shape already, we transform queries in a way that the query graph is converted into a graph where the main entity is the root node and all edges point away from the root, as shown in Algorithm 6.2. Therefore, the algorithm maintains three sets of edges P, F, and T: edges that are already processed (P), edges that need to be followed (F), and edges that need to be transformed (T), which means reversed. An edge is reversed by exchanging subject and object and by marking the property (p) as being reversed with a prepended '`-`' (as in $-p$).

Algorithm 6.2 Graph Transformation

```
P←∅, F←{(s,p,o) ∈ Q | s=m}, T←{(s,p,o)∈Q | o=m}                (init)
while F ≠ ∅ or T ≠ ∅ do
    for each (s_i, p_i, o_i) ∈ F do
        for each (s_j, p_j, o_j) ∈ Q\(P ∪ F ∪ T) do
            if o_i = s_j then
                F ← F ∪ {(s_j, p_j, o_j)}
            else if o_i = o_j then
                T ← T ∪ {(s_j, p_j, o_j)}
        Move (s_i, p_i, o_i) from F to P
    for each (s_i, p_i, o_i) ∈ T do
        for each (s_j, p_j, o_j) ∈ Q\(P ∪ F ∪ T) do
            if s_i = s_j then
                F ← F ∪ {(s_j, p_j, o_j)}
            else if s_i = o_j then
                T ← T ∪ {(s_j, p_j, o_j)}
        T ← T\{(s_i, p_i, o_i)}
        P ← P ∪ {(o_i, −p_i, s_i)}
return P
```

6.2.4.3 Message Creation and Classification

SPARQL queries are represented as sets of messages. Table 6.2 shows the different types of messages that are necessary for representing the subset of SPARQL processable by our approach (see Section 6.2.1). The query graph is split into independently verbalizable messages which represent paths that start at the main entity and consist of sets of triple patterns. For the query in Listing 6.7, where the variable `?uri` is selected as the main entity, two path messages are created. The first message represents the path `(?uri -onto:author ?book. ?book rdf:type onto:Book.)`.[5] The second message represents the path `(?uri -onto:author ?book. ?book rdfs: label 'The Pillars of the Earth'@en.)`. Further messages are created for variables and contain information about filters, as well as information related to the SPARQL features `HAVING`, `LIMIT`, `OFFSET`, `OPTIONAL`, `ORDER BY`, and `UNION`.

A message that represents a variable consists of a list of key value pairs. It uses boolean values to express whether the variable is the main entity (*main*), whether the count aggregation function is used for this variable in the `SELECT` clause (*count*), whether the `DISTINCT` modifier is used for this variable in the `SELECT` clause (*distinct*), whether the variable is a projection variable (*project*), and whether the variable appears only within an `OPTIONAL` part (*optional*). Integer values are used to store the value of the `LIMIT` and

[5]Note that the minus symbol in `-onto:author` indicates that the property is reversed.

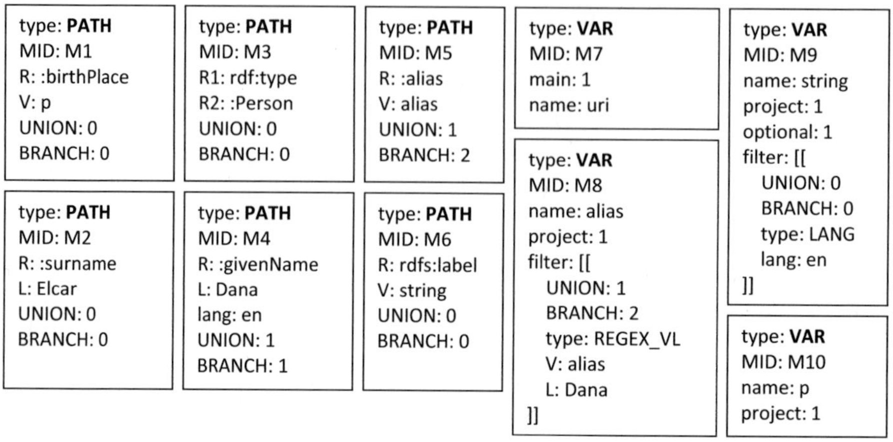

Figure 6.4: A set of messages that represents the SPARQL query in Listing 6.2.

`OFFSET` modifiers (*limit* and *offset*). The name of the variable, e.g. *artist*, is stored as a string (*name*). Moreover, an array of filters is stored (*filters*). Common filters are *LANG* as in `FILTER(lang(?str)='en')`, `BOUND` as in `FILTER(bound(?v))`, `NOTBOUND` as in `FILTER(!bound(?v))`, `RELATIONAL_VL` as in `FILTER(?v > 10)`, and `REGEX_VL` as in `FILTER(REGEX(?v, '^A', 'i'))`. Since a variable can occur in multiple different branches of a UNION where in each branch another FILTER regarding this variable is defined, each member in the array of filters stores in which union and which branch it is defined.

The messages that represent the `SELECT` query from Listing 6.2 are depicted in Figure 6.4. The query is represented using 6 path-representing messages (M1-M6) and 4 variable-representing messages (M7-M10). The main entity is represented with message ID (MID) M7. The query contains one `UNION` with 2 branches. Note that the `REGEX_VL` filter related to the variable `alias` in M8 is specific to branch #2 in `UNION` #1.

Each message that consists of triple patterns is classified according to the role the underlying information will play in the verbalization, as introduced in the anatomy of a verbalization in Section 6.2.2. The classification distinguishes among (i) CONS messages, in which the main entity is constrained; (ii) REQ messages, which contain a projection variable other than the main entity; and (iii) MOD messages, which includes features such as `OFFSET`, `ORDER BY` and `LIMIT`. Information about filters is stored within messages that represent variables.

Messages that represent a path are classified as `CONS`. In case of a `SELECT` query if the path contains a projection variable besides the main entity, then the path-representing message is also classified as `REQ`. In Figure 6.4, the path-representing messages M1, M5, and M6 are classified as `REQ` messages.

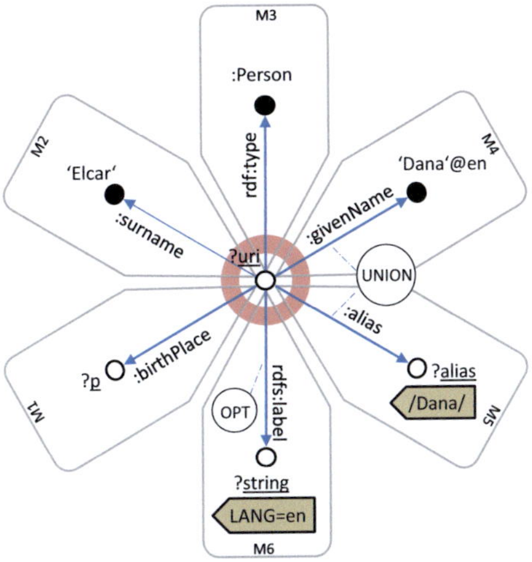

Figure 6.5: Visual representation of the query shown in Listing 6.2. How the query graph is split into messages shown in Figure 6.4 is depicted. The main entity is highlighted (center).

6.2.5 Lexicalization

During lexicalization the system determines the actual wording to denominate an entity; in our case, such entities are RDF resources represented by URIs or variables. Further details about the wording (e.g., the usage of singular or plural, the capitalization) are considered in the referring expression generation task (Section 6.2.6) and the linguistic realization task (Section 6.2.7).

For each entity the URI representing the entity is dereferenced; to do so the `Accept` field of the HTTP request header is set to `application/rdf+xml` in order to explicitly request RDF data. If RDF data is available, the system checks if an English label is available using one of the 36 labeling properties presented in Chapter 4, Table 4.1. If the entity appears within a triple pattern in predicate position in the SPARQL query, then further information about the property is collected from the RDF data obtained by dereference; namely, the system checks whether its inverse property is specified and labeled, and whether the property is symmetric. This information is used when rendering reversed properties. In OWL, the inverse property can be specified using `owl:inverseOf`, as it is the case, for instance, in `ex:hasChild owl:inverseOf ex:hasParent`. A property is known to be symmetric if it is an instance of the class *owl:SymmetricProperty*. Both directions of a symmetric property are lexicalized in the same way.

Should no label be available for a given entity with any known labeling property, a label is derived from the URI's local name or fragment identifier. For instance, the label *music group* can be derived by de-camelcasing and lowercasing `MusicGroup`, which is the local name of the URI `http://purl.org/ontology/mo/MusicGroup`.

Variables are expressed in natural language either using their type constraints or, if absent, using the term *thing*. A variable can be explicitly constrained by its type such as the variable `?v` in `?v rdf:type ex:Actor`. In this case, we lexicalize the variable using the label of the typing class, that is *actor*. Such typing information can also be determined taking into account the domain and range of a property. For example, in the triple pattern `?var1 dbo:capital ?var2` with domain of `dbo:capital` defined as *PopulatedPlace*, we can derive `?var1` as *populated place*.

If multiple types exist, then the conjunction of types can be verbalized, e.g. as *things that are A as well as B*. Moreover, by analyzing the part of speech of the label or the local name of the property, in the case that this label or local name or fragment identifier is identified as a noun, then this noun can be used as a type for a variable. For example, the local name *capital* of the property in the triple pattern `?var1 dbo:capital ?var2` is a noun and the variable *?var2* can be referred to as *capital*.

6.2.6 Referring Expression Generation

Referring expression generation is the task of deciding how to refer to a previously introduced entity. For example, the query in Listing 6.7 asks for books that have a certain label and known authors. The variable `?uri` is introduced and rendered as *authors* within the `CONS` part *have authors*. Since the `SELECT` clause contains a second variable `?uri` besides the main entity `?book`, the verbalization needs to communicate that entities that can be bound to `?uri` need to be part of the query result. This is achieved by adding the phrase *Show also these books' authors* to the verbalization, where *these books' authors* is the referring expression corresponding to the variable `?uri`.

On the one hand, a referring expressions needs to unambiguously refer to an entity. On the other hand, a referring expression should be concise to aid the understandability of a verbalization. For example, for the `SELECT` query in Listing 6.2, the projection variable can be verbalized as *these birth places* or as *these persons' birth places*. Since within the query *birth place* does not occur multiple times, it is sufficient to generate *these birth places*, which means that from the `REQ` message only the projection variable itself needs to be verbalized. If this leads to an ambiguity, which means that the referring expressions generated for two distinct variables are identical or substring of each other, then the part of the `REQ` message that is actually verbalized needs to be extended step by step until the full path between that variable and the main entity is verbalized. We perform this extension until the set of all referring expressions is free of ambiguities (no two variables are verbalized identically and no variable's verbalization is substring of another variable's verbalization) or if the full paths have already been verbalized which means that in this case we cannot generate unambiguous referring expressions.

$A \triangleq$ The DISTINCT modifier is used
$B \triangleq$ Main entity is counted as in `SELECT(COUNT ?main)`
$C \triangleq$ Result set is limited with LIMIT as in `LIMIT 10`
$D \triangleq$ ME needs to be verbalized in singular (LIMIT = 1)
$E \triangleq$ Main entity is ordered as in `ORDER BY DESC(?main)`
$F \triangleq$ Main entity has multiple types as in
`?main rdf:type ex:A. ?main rdf:type ex:B.`

Figure 6.6: The set of variables that control how the main entity is verbalized within the verbalization template, as shown in Figure 6.7 (left side).

6.2.7 Linguistic Realization

Abstract representations of sentences are translated into actual text. Verbalization of the `MOD` part of a query is straightforward; the verbalization of `REQ` messages is similar to the verbalization of `CONS` messages. Therefore, the remainder of this section will focus on the realization of the messages corresponding to the main entity and the `CONS` part.

A template contains a set of slotted strings where a slotted string is a string containing variables that are filled in later steps. Which slotted string is selected for the linguistic realization is controlled by a set of variables, which depend on the context of the part to be realized. For example, variables enable to specify whether the singular or plural form needs to be created. Furthermore, the template is provided with data that is used to fill the slots. For example, this could be the type of an entity.

A set of 6 boolean variables, shown in Figure 6.6, is necessary to fully capture the variations for the main entity template. In Figure 6.7 an excerpt of the main entity template is shown on the left

The string *Distinct scientists* is one possible result which is created using this template. Besides these boolean variables the template is provided with a hash map `$D` that contains strings that are either literals appearing in the query or labels of resources. For example, `$D{TPL}` is the variable's type in plural,[6] `$D{TSI}` is the variable's type in singular, `$D{MULTPL}` is a list of multiple types in plural such as *scientists as well as astronauts*, and `$D{L}` is a limit value as specified using the SPARQL `LIMIT` feature. The strings, such as `Abcdef`, indicate which of the boolean variables is true. Capital characters indicate a true value, lowercase characters indicate a false value.

[6] We use the Perl module Lingua::EN::Inflect in order to convert a word to plural.

`Abcdef`	'Distinct ' . $D{TPL} → Distinct scientists
`aBcdef`	'Number of ' . $D{TPL} → Number of scientists
`AbcdEf`	'The distinct ' . $D{TPL} → The distinct scientists
`abCdef`	'Not more than ' . $D{L} . ' ' . $D{TPL} → Not more than 10 scientists
`abcDEf`	'The ' . $D{TSI} → The scientist
`abcdeF`	'Things that are ' . $D{MULTPL} → Things that are scientists as well as astronauts

`abcdefghIJ`	'that has no ' . $D{PSI} → that has no email
`abcdEFGHij`	'that have the highest number of ' . $D{PPL} → that have the highest number of languages
`abcDefghIj`	'that is not ' . $D{A} . ' ' . $D{PSI} . ' of a thing' → that is not a holder of a thing

Figure 6.7: On the left: Excerpt of the main entity template. On the right: Excerpt of the CONS-RV-C1 template (for properties such as *email* or *hasColor*).

`CONS` messages are verbalized in smaller parts, each with the help of a template, which are then joined together. Consider, for example, a `CONS` message that represents a path consisting of two triples `?main :prop1 ?v1.  ?v1 rdfs:label "x"`. This path is split into the parts (i) `:prop1 ?v1` (a part of type RV – consisting of a resource R and a variable V), and (ii) `rdfs:label "x"` (a part of type RL – consisting of a resource R and a literal L). For the first part, a specific `RV` template is selected based on the linguistic properties of that resource. Classes of properties and example verbalizations are shown in Table 6.3.[7] For example, if the property label is a noun, then the template `CONS-RV-C1` is selected. Similar to the main entity verbalization, the specific verbalization procedure is controlled by a set of variables as shown in Figure 6.8. Given these variables the template produces verbalizations as shown in Figure 6.7 (on the right).

For each of the seven property classes shown in Table 6.3, and for each of the possible types of parts $T = \{RR, RL, RV, R_lR, R_lV, R_lL, R_tR, R_tV, R_tL\}$ (where R_l is a labeling property and R_t is the property `rdf:type`), we developed CONS and REQ templates.

Due to the graph transformation shown in Algorithm 6.2, every path message consists of a (potentially empty) list of RV parts and ends with a part of type $t \in T$. Without the graph transformation, additional part types such as *VR* need to be handled and further templates would be necessary.

[7] We use the Stanford parser [KM03] to identify the part of speech (POS) of a property's label, local name or fragment identifier to choose the most appropriate lexicalization. These property patterns are based on the work by Hewlett et al. [Hew+05].

Table 6.3: Classes of properties, examples with POS tag patterns, expansions, and expansions of the reversed properties.

№	Examples	Expansions
1	email (NN)	X has/have an email Y
		Y is/are (an) emails of X (reversed)
	hasColor (*has* + NN)	X has/have a color Y
		Y is/are (a) color/colors of X (reversed)
2	knows (VBZ)	X knows/know Y
		Y is/are known by X (reversed)
3	brotherOf (NN + *of*)	X is/are brother/brothers of Y
	isBrotherOf (*is* + NN + *of*)	Y has/have a brother X (reversed)
4	producedBy (VBN + IN)	X is/are produced by Y
		Y produces/produce X (reversed)
	isMadeFrom (*is* + VBN + IN)	X is/are made from Y
		Y is/are used to make X (reversed)
5	collaboratesWith (NNS + *with*)	X collaborates/collaborate with Y
		Y collaborates/collaborate with X (reversed)
6	visiting (VBG)	X is/are visiting Y
		Y is/are visited by X (reversed)
7	marriedTo (VBN + TO)	X is/are married to Y
		Y is/are married to X (reversed)

$$
\begin{aligned}
A &\triangleq \text{the variable is the first optional variable} \\
&\ \text{and this variable is not NOTBOUND} \\
B &\triangleq \text{the variable has exactly one type} \\
C &\triangleq \text{the variable has more than one type} \\
D &\triangleq \text{the property is reversed} \\
E &\triangleq \text{the variable is counted} \\
F &\triangleq \text{plural form is required} \\
G &\triangleq \text{ordered by variable} \\
H &\triangleq \text{descending order} \\
I &\triangleq \text{the variable is OPTIONAL and NOTBOUND} \\
J &\triangleq \text{the property is numeric}
\end{aligned}
$$

Figure 6.8: The set of variables that control within the verbalization template how a CONS part is verbalized as shown in Figure 6.7 (on the right).

6.2.8 Aggregation

Aggregation maps the structures created so far onto linguistic structures such as sentences and paragraphs. Verbalization consists of at least one and no more than three sentences in case of `SELECT` queries and of one sentence in case of `ASK` queries. The first sentence begins with the verbalization of the main entity (ME) followed by *that is* or *that are* followed by the verbalized and joined `CONS` messages. The second sentence begins with *Show also* followed by the verbalized and joined `REQ` messages. If there are no `REQ` messages then we omit the sentence. The third sentence verbalizes all `MOD` messages if they have not yet been verbalized as part of the main entity verbalization. If there are no further `MOD` messages then this sentence is not created. Verbalizations of `ASK` queries consist of exactly one sentence which verbalizes the main entity and the `CONS` messages. They begin with *Is it true that* followed by *there is* or *there are* followed by the verbalized and joined `CONS` messages. REQ and MOD messages are not created for ASK queries since the SPARQL features they express exist for SELECT queries only.

`UNION`s are dealt with in the aggregation step as follows. For the set of `CONS` messages that do not belong to any `UNION`, their verbalizations are joined with and. For the query in Listing 6.2, verbalization of the `CONS` messages M1 and M2 results in the string *that have a birth place and that have the surname "Elcar"*. For a set of `CONS` messages that belong to the same branch of a `UNION`, the `CONS` verbalizations are joined by *and* to create the branch verbalization. Each `UNION` is verbalized by joining the branch verbalizations by *or* to create the `UNION` verbalization, for example, resulting in *that have "Dana" as an English given name or that have an alias that matches "Dana"*.

Another aspect of the aggregation is the inclusion of the `LIMIT`, `OFFSET` and `ORDER BY` modifiers into the main entity verbalization, as shown in Section 6.2.5. This form of aggregation allows verbalizations to be more concise compared to the more wordy alternative where a dedicated sentence is created.

6.3 Template Engineering

The quality of verbalization results strongly depends on the quality of the verbalization templates. In this section we describe our approach to developing and testing templates – demonstrated using the example of the main entity template.

The upper bound to the size of a template in terms of the number of slotted strings it holds is constrained by the number of boolean variables. A template with n variables contains up to 2^n slotted strings. However, in cases where variables are dependent, this number can be reduced. For the main entity template we identified the set of dependencies shown in Figure 6.9. The variables A–E are explained in Figure 6.6. These dependencies can be explained as follows:

$$B = 1 \rightarrow C = 0 \quad (D1)$$
$$B = 1 \rightarrow D = 0 \quad (D2)$$
$$B = 1 \rightarrow E = 0 \quad (D3)$$
$$C = 0 \rightarrow E = 0 \quad (D4)$$
$$D = 1 \rightarrow E = 0 \quad (D5)$$
$$D = 1 \rightarrow A = 0 \quad (D6)$$

Figure 6.9: Dependencies between ME template variables.

(D1–D3) If the main entity is counted ($B = 1$), then the limit parameter can be ignored (set C to 0), the main entity needs to be verbalized in plural (set D to 0), and the result ordering can be ignored (set E to 0).

(D4) If the result set is not limited ($C = 0$), then the ordering can be ignored (set E to 0) since ordering is, in this case, not verbalized as part of the main entity. For example, as in *Books published by Urs Widmer. Show also these book's publication dates. Order by publication date.*

(D5–D6) If the main entity needs to be verbalized in singular form ($D = 1$), then the ordering can be ignored (set E to 0) and the `DISTINCT` modifier can be ignored (set A to 0).

For example, given two sets of variable assignments with $B = 1$ that differ only in the values assigned to C, the verbalization results for both assignments are identical, thus reducing the number of distinct slotted strings the template contains from $2^6 = 64$ to 17.

Relevant quality criteria are the correctness and completeness of the template. For the purpose of assessing a template according to these criteria, it is beneficial that we can pass a set of boolean variables and data to the template. This allows us, given a hash map `$D` of values used to fill the slots, to iterate over all possible assignments of boolean values to variables.

Given the hash map `$D`, shown in Figure 6.10, iterating over all possible variable assignments leads to the list of distinct realizations shown in in Table 6.4. Note that for the purpose of increasing readability we denote the assignment of boolean values to variables as a string. For example, the string `Abcdef` indicates that only the variable A is true, which for the main entity means that the `DISTINCT` modifier is used. We expect that this fact can be derived from `Abcdef` more easily than from `100000`.

$$LIMIT \leftarrow \text{"10"}$$
$$MULTPL \leftarrow \text{"scientists as well as astronauts"}$$
$$MULTSI \leftarrow \text{"a scientist as well as an astronaut"}$$
$$TPL \leftarrow \text{"scientists"}$$
$$TSI \leftarrow \text{"scientist"}$$

Figure 6.10: Example hash map `$D`.

Table 6.4: Example realizations created with the main entity template and the data shown in Figure 6.10.

Realization result	**Example case**
Number of things that are scientists as well as astronauts	aBcdeF
A scientist	abcDef
The distinct scientists	AbcdEf
Distinct scientists	Abcdef
Not more than 10 distinct things that are scientists as well as astr.	AbCdeF
Things that are scientists as well as astronauts	abcdeF
A thing that is a scientist as well as an astronaut	abcDeF
Not more than 10 distinct scientists	AbCdef
The scientists	abcDEf
Number of scientists	aBcdef
The scientist	abcDEf
Number of distinct things that are scientists as well as astronauts	ABcdeF
Number of distinct scientists	ABcdef
Not more than 10 scientists	abCdef
Not more than 10 things that are scientists as well as astronauts	abCdeF
Scientists	abcdef
Distinct things that are scientists as well as astronauts	AbcedF

```
SELECT DISTINCT ?uri ?string
WHERE {
        res:Bill_Clinton dbo:child ?child .
        ?child dbp:spouse ?string .
        ?uri rdfs:label ?string .
}
```

Listing 6.9: Example SPARQL query for DBpedia

6.4 Evaluation

6.4.1 Overview

According to Mellish and Dale [MD98], evaluation in the context of an NLG system can be carried out for the purpose of assessing: (i) the properties of a theory; (ii) the properties of a system; and (iii) the application potential. We focused on the second aspect: on the quality of our system in terms of a set of specific dimensions. We (i) performed a comparative evaluation where we compared Spartiqulation against the (to the best of our knowledge) only other alternative, SPARQL2NL [NN+13]; and (ii) assessed the performance of our system according to these dimensions.

A user-driven evaluation was necessary because no gold standard is available for the type of task addressed by our system. Even though our data set contains questions and their SPARQL equivalents, these questions are underspecified, and therefore do not qualify for a gold standard. For example, the question associated with the query in Listing 6.9 is *"Who is the daughter of Bill Clinton married to?"* From this question it cannot be derived that the query asks for the URIs of the requested entities, and optionally also for their English labels. Moreover, if Bill Clinton has a son, this query would also return that son's spouse.

6.4.2 Dimensions

The evaluation dimensions, inspired by [LP97; MD98; RB09], are defined as follows:

Coverage: the ratio of SPARQL queries the system accepts – a dimension that can be measured automatically.

Accuracy: the degree to which the verbalization conveys the meaning of the SPARQL query. This quality is measured through human judgment using a 4-point scale adapted from [NTN85]:

(1) The meaning of the verbalization neither leaves out any aspect of the SPARQL query, nor adds anything to it.

(2) The meaning of the SPARQL query is not adequately conveyed to the verbalization. Some aspects are missing.

(3) The meaning of the SPARQL query is not adequately conveyed to the verbalization. Most aspects are missing.

(4) The meaning of the SPARQL query is not conveyed to the verbalization.

Syntactic correctness: the degree to which the verbalization is syntactically correct, in particular whether it adheres to English grammar. This criterion is measured using a 4-point scale:

(1) The verbalization is completely syntactically correct.

(2) The verbalization is almost syntactically correct.

(3) The verbalization presents some syntactical errors.

(4) The verbalization is highly syntactically incorrect.

Understandability: The level of understandability of the verbalization, which is adapted from [NTN85]. This quality is assessed manually by external judges in terms of a 5-point scale:

(1) The meaning of the verbalization is clear.

(2) The meaning of the verbalization is clear, but there are some problems in word usage, and/or style.

(3) The basic thrust of the verbalization is clear, but the evaluator is not sure of some detailed parts because of word usage problems.

(4) The verbalization contains many word usage problems, and the evaluator can only guess at the meaning.

(5) The verbalization cannot be understood at all.

Adequacy and Efficiency According to Dale [Dal89], criteria relevant for referring expressions are *adequacy* and *efficiency*. A referring expression is adequate if it allows the referent to be identified unambiguously. It can be measured as the ratio of expressions for variables within the REQ part that unambiguously identify a variable. In addition, a referring expression is said to be efficient if it is perceived to not contain more information than necessary. Since these criteria are clearly defined and objective, they are manually evaluated by the authors.

6.4.3 Dataset

We created a corpus of SPARQL queries using data from the QALD-1[8] and the ILD2012 challenges.[9] The aim of these challenges was to answer natural language questions against data from DBpedia[10] and MusicBrainz.[11] The organizers provide a training set

[8] See http://www.sc.cit-ec.uni-bielefeld.de/qald-1
[9] See http://greententacle.techfak.uni-bielefeld.de/~cunger/qald/
[10] See http://www.dbpedia.org/
[11] See http://musicbrainz.org/

encompassing questions and the corresponding SPARQL queries. Our corpus refers to 291 of a total of 300 queries, more precisely `SELECT` and `ASK` queries. Nine of the questions in the original data set were eliminated since no SPARQL equivalent was specified as they were out of scope of the data sets used in the challenges.[12] We randomly split the data into a training set (251 queries) which we used while developing our approach and an evaluation set (40 queries) as follows:

Training data set: 44 queries from *2011-dbpedia-train*, 44 queries from *2011-music brainz-train*, 79 queries from *2012-dbpedia-train*, and 84 queries from *2012-musicbrainz-train*. The set contained 251 queries (228 SELECT queries, 23 ASK queries) which is about 86% of the full corpus.

Evaluation data set: 6 queries from *2011-dbpedia-train*, 6 queries from *2011-music brainz-train*, 14 queries from *2012-dbpedia-train*, and 14 queries from *2012-musicbrainz-train*. The set contained 40 queries (35 SELECT queries and 5 ASK queries) which is about 14% of the full corpus.

6.4.4 Comparative Evaluation

We compared our work with SPARQL2NL[13] in a blind setting with the help of six evaluators who had experience with writing SPARQL queries. The evaluators were not aware of the fact that the verbalizations were generated by different systems that were developed by two disjunct groups of researchers. In cases where both systems successfully verbalized a query (38/40 queries), their task was, given a query and two verbalizations, to compare the first verbalization with the second regarding accuracy, syntactic correctness, and understandability. For example, we asked *Compare the two verbalizations regarding accuracy* where we provided the options (i) *The first one is more accurate*, (ii) *They are equally accurate*, (iii) *The first one is less accurate*, and (iv) *Not applicable (Please explain)*.

6.4.5 Non-Comparative Evaluation

After the comparative evaluation we asked the same group to evaluate the *accuracy*, *syntactical correctness*, and *intelligibility* of verbalizations generated by Spartiqulation. Given the set of 40 successfully verbalized queries, we asked the evaluators to assess the verbalizations along these three criteria. For each SPARQL query we showed the verbalization and for each criteria we presented the respective scale as introduced in Section 6.4.2.

[12] These are the queries #94, #95, #96, #97, #98, #99, and #100 in 2012-dbpedia-train and the queries #49 and #72 in 2012-musicbrainz-train.

[13] We would like to thank Christina Unger from the SPARQL2NL team for sharing her verbalization results with us.

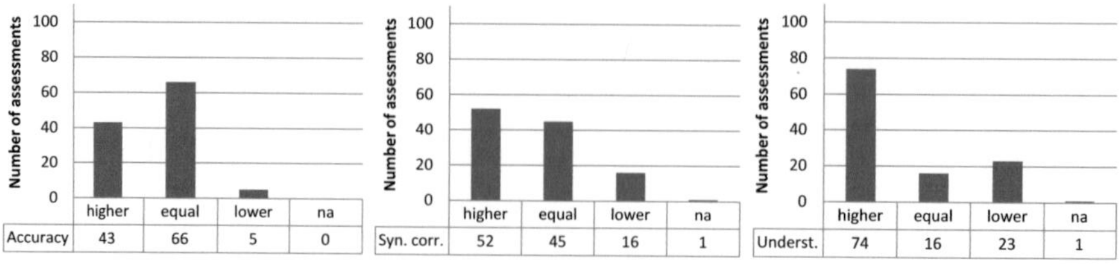

Figure 6.11: Results regarding accuracy, syntactical correctness, and understandability from the comparative evaluation.

Coverage, adequacy, and efficiency of referring expressions were assessed as follows. Coverage was measured as – per definition – the ratio of queries accepted by our system both in the training and the evaluation data set. Adequacy and efficiency of referring expressions were evaluated manually by the authors. Since these criteria, unlike accuracy, syntactic correctness, and understandability, are unambiguously defined in the literature, we evaluated them ourselves without diminishing the objectivity of the remaining findings.

6.4.6 Results

6.4.6.1 Comparative Evaluation

Figure 6.11 shows the results of the comparative evaluation. 38 verbalizations were assessed by the 6 evaluators, leading to a total number of 114 assessments.[14] *"na"* means not answered by the participant. Higher accuracy was reported in 43 cases (37.72%), equal accuracy was reported in 66 cases (57.89%), higher syntactical correctness was reported in 52 cases (45.61%), equal syntactical correctness was reported in 45 cases (39.47%), higher understandability was reported in 74 cases (64.91%), and equal understandability was reported in 16 cases (14.04%). We used Krippendorff's alpha [HK07] to measure inter-rater agreement regarding whether our results are comparable or better. The results are $\alpha = 0.56$ for accuracy, $\alpha = 0.726$ for syntactical correctness and $\alpha = 0.676$ for understandability.[15]

[14] Each of the 38 query verbalizations was evaluated by 3 evaluators, thus resulting in 114 assessments.

[15] According to [Kri04] "*to assure that the data under consideration are at least similarly interpretable by two or more scholars (as represented by different coders), it is customary to require* $\alpha \geqslant .800$. *Where tentative conclusions are still acceptable,* $\alpha \geqslant .667$ *is the lowest conceivable limit.*"

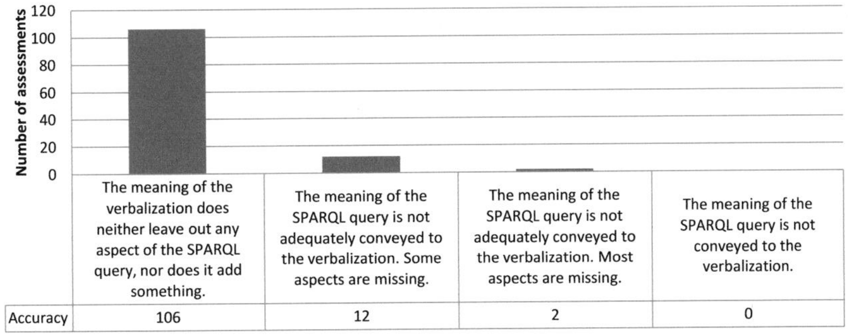

Figure 6.12: Results regarding accuracy from the non-comparative evaluation.

6.4.6.2 Non-Comparative Evaluation

Coverage:
We counted how many queries contain features that our system does not support using the data set described in Section 6.4.3. Within the evaluation set of 40 queries, every query was verbalizable. Within the training set of 251 queries, four queries did not meet the limitations described in Section 6.2.1. Each of these queries[16] contained two disconnected basic graph patterns in the `WHERE` clause that were only connected via FILTER expressions, such as `FILTER(?allelevation > ?elevation)`, `FILTER(REGEX(?design, ?mdesign))`, and `FILTER(?large = ?capital)`. This means that the system obtained a total coverage of 287/291 (98.6%).

Accuracy, syntactical correctness, and understandability:
Figure 6.12, Figure 6.13, and Figure 6.14 show the results for the dimensions of accuracy, syntactical correctness, and understandability, respectively, with respect to the 40 evaluation queries that were were assessed by the 6 evaluators, leading to a total number of 120 assessments.[17] Verbalizations show a high accuracy, high syntactical correctness, and good understandability. 106 out of 120 times the evaluators awarded the best accuracy score (88.33%). Regarding syntactical correctness and understandability there is room for improvement, 70 out of 120 times the evaluators awarded the best score for syntactical correctness (58.33%), 47 out of 120 times the evaluators awarded the best understandability score (39.16%).

Adequacy and minimality of referring expressions:
Among the 40 queries in the evaluation set, for 25 queries referring expressions had to

[16]These were the queries #40 in 2011-dbpedia-train.xml, #26 in 2012-dbpedia-train.xml, #61 in 2012-dbpedia-train.xml which is the same as #40 in 2011-dbpedia-train.xml, and #19 in 2012-dbpedia-train.xml.

[17]Each of the 40 query verbalizations was evaluated by 3 evaluators, thus resulting in 120 assessments.

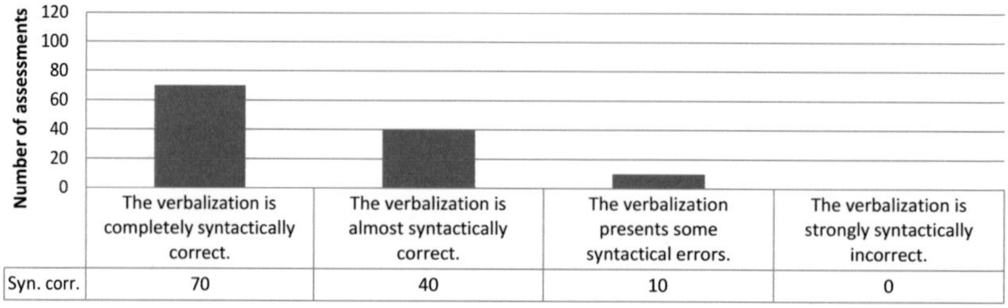

Figure 6.13: Results regarding syntactical correctness from the non-comparative evaluation.

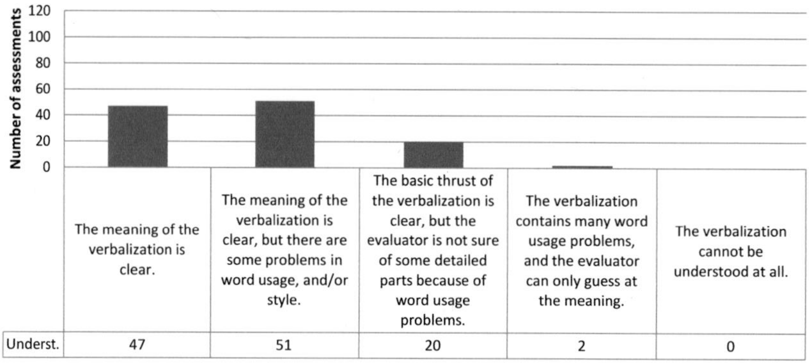

Figure 6.14: Results regarding understandability from the non-comparative evaluation.

be generated. In 24 cases the referring expressions were unambiguous which means an adequacy of 96%. In 3 out of 25 cases the referring expression was not efficient. For example, a query was verbalized as *Distinct things that are presidents of the united states or that are presidents that have President of the United States as a title. Show also, if available, these things' (that are presidents of the united states or presidents) English labels.* Here, the referring expression *these things' (that are presidents of the united states or presidents) English labels* could by reduced to *these things' English labels.*

6.4.7 Discussion

What makes the verbalization generated by the SPARQL2NL system less understandable for complex queries is the fact that variable names are included in the verbalization, such as in *"This query retrieves distinct countries ?uri and distinct values ?string such that ?string is in English. Moreover, it returns exclusively results that the number of ?uri's official languages is greater than 2."* In comparison, our system verbalizes the same query as *"Distinct countries that have more than 2 official languages. Show also, if available, these countries' English labels."* In some cases experts tended to prefer the variant with variable names since this seems to be more natural to them, as they told us after the evaluation. However, the experts pointed out their belief that verbalizations containing variables will be hard to understand by non-experts. We claim that as long as experts are not the only intended users of semantic search engines this verbalization style is inappropriate. Especially, variable names in automatically generated queries may carry little information.

An interesting feature of SPARQL2NL is that datatypes are utilized as in the verbalization of the literal `?date <= '2010-12-31'^^xsd:date` to *?date is greater than or equal to January 31, 2010.* Finally, SPARQL2NL was capable of verbalizing the 4 queries that were rejected by our system.

Both systems faced problems arising from four sources:

1. Missing labels for entities. Relying on local names or fragment identifiers leads to results such as *that have the release type type soundtrack* for the triple pattern `?album mm:releaseType mm:TypeSoundtrack`.
2. The way the data is modeled complicates the verbalization as in *Things that are begin dates of things that have to artists that have the title "Slayer".* Here, the verbalization of the property in `?bandinstance ar:toArtist ?band` as *to artist* is currently the best guess the system can make.
3. Missing linguistic information about properties. The property `dbo:crosses` in the triple pattern `res:Brooklyn_Bridge dbo:crosses ?uri` can be interpreted as the plural of the noun *cross* or an inflected form of the verb *to cross.*

Here, verbalization could be improved if linguistic information was attached to the vocabulary, for example, using the *lemon model* [MSC12].

4. Problems with pluralization and capitalization exist and could also be fixed given a lexicon. For example, in the verbalization of the query in Listing 6.5, *african countries* needs to be capitalized as *African countries* and *european countries* in Listing 6.6 needs to be capitalized as *European countries.*

6.5 Related Work

To the best of our knowledge SPARQL2NL [NN+13] is the only approach which is similar to ours in scope and functionality. One part of our evaluation was dedicated to the comparison along a number of quality dimensions established in the field of Natural Language Generation, to which both solutions belong. The evaluation revealed that both approaches have advantages and disadvantages, whereas Spartiqulation seems to perform better for cases dealing with complex queries with multiple variables.

Both approaches are geared towards a similar subset of SPARQL. How a triple is verbalized depends on linguistic cues found in property labels and type information extracted from the queries. The main differences are two-fold:

1. SPARQL2NL maps each atom (property, resource, literal) to its realization, stores these realizations as dependency trees and aggregates these trees in a later step. In our approach, we fragment the query graph into independently verbalizable parts (messages). This higher level of granularity has positive influences on conciseness of the resulting verbalization.

2. SPARQL2NL does not map variables to realizations, which means that names of variables appear in verbalizations as they are in the query. Even in a scenario where variable names are meaningful, this is expected to have a negative impact on the understandability of the verbalization for non-experts. Moreover, meaningful variable names cannot be guaranteed if queries are generated by a natural language query interface. In cases where variables have been introduced due to filters, SPARQL2NL is capable of removing those variable names from the verbalizations using aggregation.

Further related work comes from three areas: verbalization of RDF data [Dav+08; SM07; SM07; MS06; SM06], verbalization of OWL ontologies [TWP11; Wil03; BW04; Ste+10; Agu+98; Hew+05; KF07; GA07; GTS09; LSR11; Sch09; FKV10; CSM07], and verbalization of SQL queries [Min05; Min10; KSI10]. The first two fields provide techniques that we can apply to improve the lexicalization and aggregation tasks, such as the template-based approach presented in [Dav+08].

The main difference between Spartiqulation and the work by Minock [Min10; Min05], which focuses on relational queries over tuples, is that our approach is schema-agnostic. Besides some dependencies to RDF(S) and OWL, our system does not require any information about the domain of the application, and about the vocabularies used to encode knowledge about this domain. By contrast, the verbalizer by Minock foresees manually created patterns covering all possible combinations of relations in the schema.

Koutrika et al. [KSI10] annotate query graphs with template labels and explore multiple graph traversal strategies. Moreover, they identify a main entity (the query subject), perform graph traversal starting from that entity, and distinguish between *CONS* (*subject qualifications*) and *REQ* (*information*). Templates need to be defined for each property, whereas in our approach templates are automatically selected based on the class the property's label (or the URI's local name or fragment identifier) belongs to. In this way our approach is schema-agnostic and can thus verbalize queries that use vocabularies that were unknown during the construction of the verbalization system and its templates.

6.6 Conclusion

In this chapter we presented our approach to SPARQL query verbalization. Our aim was to create natural-language descriptions of queries to communicate the meaning of these queries to users who are not familiar with the intricacies of the query language. To do so, we realized an approach which is based on an established natural language generation pipeline complemented by templates which we manually derived through the analysis of a representative set of SPARQL queries which is used by the community in related research challenges.

The results of our work could be beneficial for a variety of Linked-Data-related scenarios in which SPARQL cannot be assumed to be the most appropriate form of interaction between an application and its users. In particular, verbalization could complement the functionality of information retrieval systems, which transform unstructured or semi-structured user queries into SPARQL, as the availability of human-readable renderings of SPARQL queries allows users to gain a better understanding of the way the information retrieval system matches their information needs to resources, and of the reasons why certain resources are included in the result set. One can distinguish between three categories of systems, depending on the specific types of input they are able to handle: keywords (e.g., SemSearch [LUM06], ONTOSEARCH2 [TPS07], SPARK [Zho+07], SearchWebDB [Wan+08b], Q2semantic [Wan+08a], Hermes [TWH09], and SWIP [PHH12] as well as the approaches in [Tra+09; She+11]), questions in free-text or using a controlled version of the language (e.g., Querix [KBZ06], GINO [BK06], OntoNL [KZC07], Panto [Wan+07], NLP-Reduce [KBF07], ORAKEL [Cim+08], NLION [RK09], SemanticQA [TAN10], Alexandria [WGD12], DEQA [Leh+12], DEANNA

[Yah+12], FREyA [DAC12], and the approach introduced in [Ung+12]), and forms (e.g., [HO11; Men+08]).

Furthermore, verbalization would be a welcome add-on to learning environments and query editors for SPARQL, as it provides novices with means to become familiar with the capabilities of the language through human-readable representations of the queries they create.

Spartiqulation does not make any domain- or application-specific assumptions. The templates that guide its operation could be extended to capture additional information, presumably leading to improved results on queries complying to the corresponding assumptions. Independently of these considerations, our evaluation shows some interesting directions for future research. While our system seems to perform better for complex queries with multiple variables, experts did not perceive the verbalization style of SPARQL2NL, which keeps variables in the output text, to be hampering the understandability of the queries; additional experiments involving laymen or people with considerably less knowledge of the query language are needed in order to lead to conclusive results about this matter.

Further improvements to our system could be achieved foremost by considering punctuation and shortening the length of sentences.

The comparative evaluation revealed a number of problems both approaches are confronted with, which can be mostly traced back to the quality of Linked Data datasets, in particular when it comes to the availability of human-readable labels for classes and properties, and unconventional modeling decisions which require special treatment at the level of the templates that are used during the verbalization. As Linked Data is getting increasingly used in real-world applications, we expect such quality issues to be gradually resolved.

6.7 Contributions

Our main contributions are:

- We argue that SPARQL query verbalizations are beneficial to users of a keyword-based or natural language question-based semantic search interface since the verbalization allows a potential discrepancy between an intended question and the system-generated SPARQL query to be observed.
- We introduced a domain-independent SPARQL query verbalization approach based on domain-independent templates thus addressing RQ4 *How can SPARQL queries be verbalized in a mostly schema-agnostic manner?* Being schema-agnostic renders the verbalization system potentially applicable in many domains.
- We verbalize a query in a top-down manner by breaking a query into independently verbalizable parts. This allows verbalizations to be more concise compared to a bottom-up manner where the smallest parts of a query are mapped to their realization and then combined.
- In a comparative evaluation our approach outperformed SPARQL2NL by obtaining higher (43 cases, 37.72%) or equal (66 cases, 57.89%) accuracy, higher (52 cases, 45.61%) or equal (45 cases, 39.47%) syntactical correctness, and higher (74 cases, 64.91%) or equal (16 cases, 14.04%) understandability.
- In a non-comparative evaluation our system successfully verbalized 98.6% (287/291) of our query dataset built from queries from the QALD (Question Answering over Linked Data) challenges. In 70 out of 120 cases the evaluators awarded the best score for syntactical correctness (58.33%), in 47 out of 120 cases the evaluators awarded the best understandability score (39.16%).

7 Induction of RDF Verbalization Patterns

7.1 Introduction

With the rise of the Semantic Web, more and more data encoded using the Semantic Web standard RDF have become available. RDF is oriented towards use by machines: designed to be easily processable by machines it is difficult to understand for casual users. Transforming RDF data into human-comprehensible text by an NLG system would facilitate the assessment of this information by non-experts.

Natural Language Generation (NLG) systems require resources such as templates or rules. Template-based systems are natural language generating systems that map their non-linguistic input directly (i.e., without intermediate representations) to the linguistic surface structure [RD00].[1] These resources limit the variability and the domain-specificity of the generated natural language output and manual creation of these resources is tedious work. Therefore, *trainable NLG* strives to automatically induce these resources from example data, thus removing this knowledge acquisition bottleneck.

In this chapter we present a language-independent method for extracting RDF verbalization templates from a parallel corpus of text and data. Our method is based on distant-supervised simultaneous multi-relation learning and frequent maximal subgraph pattern mining. We demonstrate the feasibility of our method on a parallel corpus of Wikipedia articles and DBpedia data for English and German. Whereas related works in trainable NLG required a semantically annotated corpus, which again represents a bottleneck since this annotation needs to be carried out manually, our approach does not require the corpus to be semantically annotated.

The approach is language-independent since it does not rely on pre-existing language resources such as parsers, grammars or dictionaries. **Input** is a corpus of parallel text and data consisting of a set of documents D and an RDF graph G, where D and G are related via a set of entities E where an entity can be described by a document in D and

[1] According to [DKT05], NLG approaches were perceived to be inferior regarding their maintainability, linguistic well-foundedness, and quality of output. However, template-based systems may profit from corpus-based approaches and may perform all NLG tasks in a linguistically well-founded way. A complex set of templates may be as powerful as a set of rules.

described by data in G. **Output** is a set of templates. Templates consist of a graph pattern that can be applied to query the graph and of a sentence pattern that is a sentence containing variables into which parts of the query result are inserted. A template enables a subgraph of G to be verbalized as a complete sentence.

An example is shown in Figure 7.1.[2] The graph pattern gp can be transformed into a SPARQL query q_{gp}. Given the results of querying the RDF dataset G, the graph G_{gp} can be created. G_{gp} can be verbalized as an English (German) sentence s_{en} (s_{de}) using the sentence pattern sp_{en} (sp_{de}).

The approach employs the distant supervision principle [CK99; BM07; Car+09; Min+09; Wel+10; Hof+11; Sur+12] from relation extraction: training data is generated automatically by aligning a database of facts with text; therefore, no hand-labeled training data is required. We apply simultaneous multi-relation learning [Car+09] for text-data alignment and frequent maximal subgraph pattern mining to observe commonalities among RDF graph patterns.

Besides the general idea of allowing non-experts to assess information encoded in RDF, we envision the application of these verbalization templates in three scenarios:

(1) In query interfaces to RDF databases, casual users – usually are not capable of writing formal queries – specify their information needs using keywords [LUM06; TPS07; Wan+08b], questions in free-text or using a controlled language [KBZ06; Cim+08; WGD12; DAC12], or forms [HO11; Men+08]. The system then queries an RDF database according to its interpretation(s) of the input. Query results could be verbalized using templates.

(2) Since the introduction of the Google Knowledge Graph,[3] when searching for an entity such as the city of Karlsruhe via Google, besides the search results shown on the left a table is displayed on the right which provides a short description of the entity taken from Wikipedia. While these descriptions are decoupled from data in the knowledge graph – the short description from Wikipedia may contain facts not contained in the knowledge graph and vice versa – the descriptions could be generated automatically thus reflecting the actual data.

(3) The collaboratively-edited knowledge base Wikidata provides machine-readable data which can be used, e.g., by Wikipedia. The Wikidata browsing interface *reasonator* currently explores the use of template-based NLG in order to provide human-readable descriptions of its entities.[4] Since the templates are created manually, currently verbalizations can only be provided for a few types of entities.

[2] Further examples and the evaluation material can be found on our website at http://km.aifb.kit.edu/sites/bridge-patterns/INLG2014.

[3] See http://googleblog.blogspot.com/2012/05/introducing-knowledge-graph-things-not.html (accessed 2014-03-20)

[4] See, for example, the page about Johann Sebastian Bach: http://tools.wmflabs.org/reasonator/?q=Q1339 (accessed 2014-03-20).

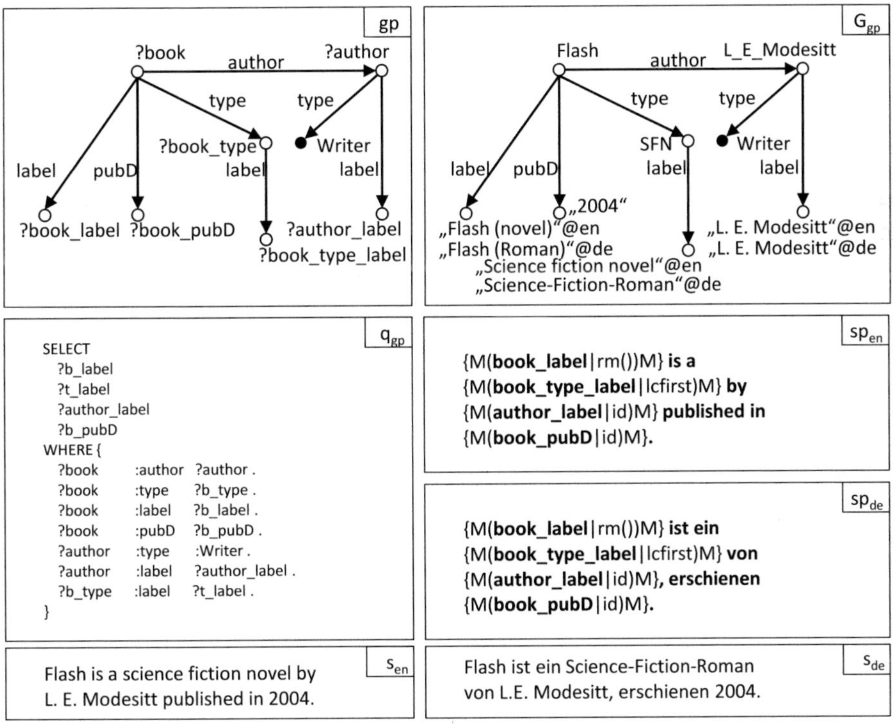

Figure 7.1: A template consists of a graph pattern gp and a sentence pattern sp. The graph pattern gp can be transformed into a SPARQL query q_{gp}. Given the results of querying the RDF dataset G, the graph G_{gp} can be created. This graph can be verbalized as an English sentence s_{en} using the English sentence pattern sp_{en} or as a German sentence s_{de} using the German sentence pattern sp_{de}. The modifiers, e.g. `rm()` and `lcfirst`, are explained in Table 7.1. The figure presents two templates, one being (gp, sp_{en}) and the other being (gp, sp_{de}).

In this chapter we answer the following research questions:

RQ5.1 *How can RDF graphs be verbalized as a single sentence using a template?*

RQ5.2 *How can RDF verbalization templates be learned from a parallel text-data corpus?*

The remainder of this chapter is structured as follows. We continue the introduction with basic definitions and give an overview of how a NLG system generating text from RDF could use RDF verbalization templates. The definition of and requirements for a parallel corpus are given in Section 7.2, the approach is explained in Section 7.3 followed by experiments (Section 7.4), an evaluation (Section 7.5), and related work (Section 7.6). We draw conclusions in Section 7.7, and highlight our main contributions in Section 7.8.

7.1.1 Definitions

- A **template** is a tuple (sp, gp) where sp is a sentence pattern and gp is a graph pattern. We denote the set of variables within a sentence pattern sp as $Vars_{SP}(sp)$ and the set of variables within a graph pattern gp as $Var_{GP}(gp)$. A template (sp, gp) is *safe* if the set of variables within the sentence pattern is a subset of the set of variables within the graph pattern: $Vars_{SP}(sp) \subseteq Var_{GP}(gp)$.
- A **sentence pattern** (sp) is a string that consists of terminals and non-terminals where non-terminals consist of variables and modifiers. Within a sentence pattern a (variable, modifier) tuple (v, m) is denoted as `{M(v|m)M}`. `{M(` and `)M}` serve as delimiters of a (variable, modifier) tuple.
- A **graph pattern** is a set of triple patterns (s, p, o) where $s \in \mathcal{U} \cup \mathcal{V}$, $p \in \mathcal{U} \cup \mathcal{V}$, and $o \in \mathcal{U} \cup \mathcal{L} \cup \mathcal{V}$. $\mathcal{U}$ is a set of identifiers, $\mathcal{L}$ is a set of literals, and $\mathcal{V}$ is a set of variables. Note that, in contrast to the definition of graph patterns in Section 2.1.3, here we omit blank nodes.
- A **modifier** $m \in M$ is a function applicable to the value of a variable v – denoted by $m(v)$. A list of example modifiers that we use in our experiment is shown in Table 7.1. For example, the modifier `enD_M_Y` transforms the value `"2014-03-22"^^xsd:date` into `22 March, 2014`.

7.1.2 Template-Based Natural Language Generation

In order to support the NLG tasks, a template can be applied for Natural Language Generation (see Section 2.3) as follows: Given an RDF data graph G and a template (sp, gp), a SPARQL SELECT query can be created: `SELECT PV WHERE {` gp' `}`. The list of projection variables `PV` is the list of variables $v \in Vars_{SP}(sp)$. gp' is constructed by adding each triple pattern of gp to gp'. An example of a query (q_{gp}) created from a graph pattern (gp) is shown in Figure 7.1.

Executing a query results in a solution sequence[5] which is a list of solution mappings $\mu : V \rightarrow \mathcal{T}$ from a set of variables V to a set of RDF terms $\mathcal{T} = \mathcal{U} \cup \mathcal{L}$.

For each non-terminal in sp representing a variable-modifier tuple (v, m), the modifier m is applied on $\mu(v)$ resulting in $m(\mu(v))$. Finally, the tuple (v, m), expressed as `{M(v|m)M}`, is replaced in sp with $m(\mu(v))$. After replacing each such tuple the sentence creation is complete.

According to Reiter and Dale [RD00], the NLG process consists of several tasks – see Chapter 2. In a system that generates text from RDF using RDF verbalization templates as presented here, templates can be applied in several tasks. For a subset of these tasks where templates are relevant we discuss how they can be applied.

Content determination is the task of deciding which information to communicate in the text. Which content to select may depend on a communicative goal, a user model and a discourse history. However, content determination is constrained by the templates available that enable the verbalization. The set of templates available to an NLG system can thus be applied to reduce the available data to the potentially verbalizable data.

Lexicalization is the task of deciding what specific words to use for expressing the content. A template may specify that an entity has to be expressed in a sentence using the value of the property `foaf:name` and not using the value of the property `rdfs:label`. Thereby, a template reduces the number of possible choices. However, there may still be multiple values for that entity and the property `foaf:name` so that alternatives remain.

A template may also contain terminals that represent decided lexical alternatives. For example: in the sentence pattern *V1 is a book by V2*[6] (where `V1` is the label of an entity e_1, `V2` is the label of an entity e_2, e_2 is the author of e_1, and e_1 is a book), choices are already materialized regarding how to verbalize the facts that: i) the entity e_1 is a book; and ii) the label of the author property does not need to be inserted into the sentence.

Referring expression generation is the task of deciding how to refer to an entity. Similar to lexicalization where terminals may represent decided lexical alternatives, this is partially the case for referring expressions. Consider, for example, the sentence pattern *V1 is a novel by V2 which he wrote while living in V3.* Here, the pronoun *he* refers to the entity expressed with *V2*. The pronoun takes into

[5] We adopt the terminology from the SPARQL 1.1 Query Language documentation available at http://www.w3.org/TR/2013/REC-sparql11-query-20130321/ but ignore blank nodes.

[6] For the purpose of readability we simplify our notation by omitting the modifier and the (variable, modifier) tuple delimiters `{M(` and `)M}`. Thus, `V1` stands for `{M(V1|id)M}`.

account the gender of the entity referred to and the fact that this entity is a person. However, each template creates a single sentence and referring expressions can be necessary to link two sentences and linking between sentences is not covered by templates.

Aggregation is the task of deciding how to map abstract representations onto linguistic structures such as sentences and paragraphs. Since templates define how to map content to single sentences, which sentences to arrange as a paragraph is not covered.

Linguistic realization is the task of converting abstract representations of sentences into real text. Sentence patterns contain terminals that represent linguistic realizations. Applying modifiers to the values of variables is another aspect of the process of linguistic realization. The terminals and the modified variable names may take inflections into account. Consider the following two German sentence patterns that are part of two templates:

(1) *V1 ist ein Roman des deutschen Autors V2.*

(2) *V1 ist ein Roman der deutschen Autorin V2.*

Here, the graph patterns of both templates share that an entity is a German author and that a novel was written by this author. The first template applies to male authors and the second template applies to female authors. The difference in gender is taken into account in the sentence patterns. The author's gender has an influence on the article (*der* vs. *die*) and on the noun (*Autors* vs. *Autorin*). Note that *Autor/Autorin* is not inserted by a variable and that the genitive case is correctly expressed.

Structure realization is the task of adding markup such as HTML code to the generated text in order for it to be interpreted by the presentation system, such as a web browser. If the documents in the parallel corpus contain not only pure text but also markup, then this markup is contained in the extracted templates. For example, a sentence pattern such as *V1 can be reached via email (<a href="mailto:V4">V2</a>) or phone (V3)* could be extracted. As for the aggregation task, markup for paragraphs cannot be captured by templates unless sentence patterns are extended to larger units such as paragraphs.

7.2 Parallel Corpus

Our approach requires a parallel corpus of text and data where texts describe entities in natural language and a data graph semantically describes entities.

Formally, the parallel corpus consists of a set of entities E, a set of documents D, and an RDF data graph G. An entity can be described by a document in a certain language. The relation $document \subseteq E \times L \times D$ relates an (entity, language) tuple to a set of documents. $document(e, l)$ denotes the (potentially empty) set of documents that describe an entity $e \in E$ in language $l \in L$.

G is a set of triples (s, p, o) where $s, p \in \mathcal{U}$, and $o \in \mathcal{U} \cup \mathcal{L}$. Each literal has a datatype, returned by the function $datatype : \mathcal{L} \rightarrow T$. Literals of type *string* can be language-tagged. The function $l_l : \mathcal{L} \rightarrow L$ returns the language $l_l(r) \in L$ for a literal $r \in \mathcal{L}$ if it exists. An entity can have a human-readable form which is a language-tagged literal. The relation $\lambda \subseteq E \times L \times \mathcal{L}$ relates an entity $e \in E$ to a (possibly empty) set of literals $\lambda(e, l) \subseteq \mathcal{L}$ in language $l \in L$. $\lambda(e, l)$ are the human-readable forms of entity e in language l. The property p_λ relates an entity with its label. For example, p_λ can be one of the labeling properties from Table 4.1 in Chapter 4. Each entity $e \in E$ occurs in the data graph. This means that G contains a triple (s, p, o) where $s = e$ or $o = e$.

7.3 Approach

Our approach consists of six steps:

1. For each entity $e \in E$ we collect sentences from documents about the entity that mention the entity. The intention is to reduce the probability of introducing word sense disambiguation-related problems. For example, if a text about jaguar (the animal) mentions jaguar, then most likely in the text it is referred to the animal and not to jaguar, the aircraft or jaguar, the brand (Section 7.3.1).
2. For each sentence we align the sentence and the data graph by iteratively exploring the vicinity of the entity within the graph. This leads to a set of identified entities: entities that are believed to be mentioned within the sentence; and a set of observations. The subgraph of G that consists of all triples that contain an identified entity serves as an hypothesis graph: the assumption is that no fact that is not expressed in the subgraph is expressed in the sentence. Thereby, entities that were not identified can also be contained in the hypothesis graph. For example, this non-identified entity can be a class related to an identified entity via `rdf:type` and may later constrain applicability of the template to entities of a certain type (Section 7.3.2).

3. Each (sentence, identified entities, graph) tuple is abstracted by replacing identified literals in the sentence and in the graph with variables and by replacing identified entities in the graph with variables. This step can lead to multiple distinct (sentence pattern, graph pattern) tuples for each sentence. This abstraction enables different sentences that share the same sentence pattern after abstraction to be compared (Section 7.3.3).
4. A set of (sentence pattern, graph patterns) tuples is built for each sentence pattern (Section 7.3.4).
5. For each (sentence pattern, graph patterns) tuple the set of graph patterns is analyzed regarding their commonalities. This is realized via the frequent and maximal subgraph pattern extraction (fmSpan) algorithm which results in a set of graph patterns that are subgraph patterns to the input graph patterns. Thereby, this step realizes multi-relation learning: multiple relations are learned together and not in isolation (Section 7.3.5).
6. Given the output of the fmSpan algorithm and the abstracted sentences the templates are created (Section 7.3.6).

7.3.1 Sentence Collection

Given a language name l, a set of entities E, a set of documents D, and an ordered list of modifiers M, for each entity $e \in E$ for each document $d \in document(e,l)$ (which describes e in language l) the document is split into a set of sentences. For each sentence that has an acceptable length (measured as the number of characters), for each label $x \in \lambda(e,l)$ and for each string modifier $m \in M_{string}$, we store the (sentence, entity, left, right, λ, matched) tuple if the modified label $m(x)$ matches the sentence. See Algorithm 7.3.

Algorithm 7.3 Collect example sentences

```
procedure COLLECT EXAMPLE SENTENCES(l, E, D, M)
 for each e ∈ E do
  for each d ∈ document(e, l) ∈ D do
   for each s ∈ sentences(d, l_min, l_max) do
    for each x ∈ λ(e, l) do
     for each m ∈ M_string do
      if applicable(m, x) then
       (left, right, x') ← MatchesLiteral(s, x, m)
       if (left, right, x') ≠ ∅ then
        Output (s, e, left, right, x, x', m)
        Continue with next sentence
```

Algorithm 7.4 MatchesLiteral

```
procedure MatchesLiteral(s, x, m)
 if datatype(x) = "xsd:string" ∨ datatype(x) ≠ "xsd:integer" then
  if length(x) ⩾ 4 then
   if s matches (\W|^)\w{l_0,l_1}m(x)\w{r_0,r_1}(\W|$) then
    return (left, right, matched)
 else if type(x) = "xsd:integer" then
  if s matches (\D|^)m(x)(\D|$) then
   return (left, right, matched)
  return ∅
```

Details to the Algorithm 7.4:

- $\backslash W$ denotes a non-word character (such as a blank).
- $\backslash D$ denotes a non-digit.
- $\backslash w$ denotes a word character[7] (such as "x"), $\backslash w\{a, b\}$ denotes a sequence of at least a word-characters and not more than b word characters,
- l_0 and l_1 are the minimum and maximum number of word characters that may appear on the left side of the modified string $m(x)$ between this string and a non-word character or the beginning of the sentence (^).
- r_0 and r_1 are the corresponding numbers regarding the right side of the modified string.
- $ denotes the end of the sentence.
- In case of a match, the string that is matched by $\backslash w\{l_0, l_1\}$ is stored as *left*, the string that is matched by $\backslash w\{r_0, r_1\}$ is stored as *right* and the part that matches $m(x)$ is stored as *matched*. Note that *matched* can be different from $m(x)$ since the application of the modifier m to the string x can result in a regular expression that contains information for the matcher specifying that a part of the string needs to be matched case-insensitively.

Allowing a certain number of characters to be added to the left and to the right of a string has the intention of matching strings even though prefixes and postfixes are added. For example, `German` can be matched within its plural form `Germans` and `magic` can be matched within `magician`.

[7] Note that word and non-word characters are language-specific and may be defined for each language individually.

7.3.2 Sentence and Data Alignment

The sentence and the data graph are aligned by iteratively exploring the vicinity of an entity within the graph. The exploration is described by Algorithm 7.5 which builds a set of observations *obs*. A member of *obs* is a 7-tuple where the first three members form a triple (entity, property, literal value), followed by the strings matched to the left and the right, the matched string and the modifier. Moreover, the algorithm creates a graph $graph \subseteq G$ consisting of all triples that contain an identified entity. An entity e is identified if a modifier $m \in M$ exists such that an $x \in \lambda(e, l)$ exists such that the sentence matches $m(x)$. Output is the original sentence, the set of identified entities, the set of observations, and the subgraph.

The graph consisting of all triples that contain entities identified for a sentence constitutes a hypothesis graph for a sentence – it represents what the sentence may express. For example, given the sentence *Paris is the capital of France*, where the entities `:Paris` and `:France` were identified, the hypothesis graph contains all triples with `:Paris` in subject or object position as well as all triples with `:France` in subject or object position. Moreover, the hypothesis graph contains all information available about these two entities, such as the postal code of Paris, the population value of Paris and France and so forth.

Ideally, the sentence is completely explained by a subset of the hypotheses. In this step the hypothesis graph contains hypotheses that are not expressed in the sentence, such as the population value of France. Later steps in our approach try to remove hypotheses from the hypothesis graph. If relevant hypotheses are missing in the hypothesis graph, then unless this information is missing for most of similar sentences, then this sentence cannot be used to induce an RDF verbalization template.

7.3.3 Sentence and Graph Abstraction

In the previous step, ambiguities may exist. For example, given two triples (e_1, p_1, v) and (e_2, p_2, v) where v is a literal value, $e_1 \neq e_2$, and the entities e_1 and e_2 are identified; if the value v is found in the sentence, then it cannot be resolved whether the sentence expresses the fact (e_1, p_1, v) or (e_2, p_2, v). Therefore, for each situation where a value appears in two distinct contexts or where values overlap (two values overlap if the intervals of their character positions overlap), the sentence and graph pattern is copied and on each copy another abstraction is performed thus leading to multiple abstractions per sentence. Algorithm 7.6 iteratively creates all sentence abstractions given a language name l, a sentence s, and a set of observations *obs*. The function `poss` evaluates the set of observations that are still valid. The function `apply` replaces a string in a sentence with variable and modifier. Thereby, the *left* and *right* parts are added to the modifier. For an observation (e, p, o, l, r, o', m), the string concatenation $l + o' + r$ is replaced with `{M(`v_i`|m')M}`. For each observation a new variable v_i is introduced. m' is a modifier to

Algorithm 7.5 Data Collection

```
procedure CollectData(s, e, lang, left, right, x, x', m0)
  identified = ∅; todo = (e); done = ∅;
  graph = ∅; obs = {(e, p_l, x, left, right, x', m0)}
  while todo ≠ ∅ do
    e ← todo.first
    todo ← todo \ {e}; done ← done ∪ {e}
    for each (e, p, o) ∈ G do
      graph ← graph ∪ {(e, p, o)}
      if o is a URI then
        if o ∉ done ∧ o ∉ todo then
          todo.add(e)
      else if o is a literal then
        for each m ∈ M do
          (l, r, m') ← MatchesLiteral(s, o, m)
          if (l, r, m') ≠ ∅ then
            obs ← obs ∪ {(e, p, o, l, r, m', m)}
            if p = p_λ ∧ l_l(o) = l then
              identified ← identified ∪ {e}
    for each (e2, p, e) ∈ G do
      graph ← graph ∪ {(e2, p, e)}
      if e2 ∉ done ∧ o ∉ todo then
        todo.add(e2)
    Output (sentence, identified, obs, graph)
```

which the modifiers `+l(l)` and `+r(r)` are appended which denote that certain strings are added to the left and the right of the literal. The graph is abstracted by replacing the triple (e, p, o) with the triple pattern (e, p, v_1). After completely abstracting a sentence pattern, each identified entity is replaced by a variable; triples that do not contain any variable are removed.

Algorithm 7.6 Sentence Abstraction

```
procedure AbstractSentence(l, s, obs)
P ← poss(l, s, obs)
if P = ∅ then
  Output(s)
else
  O ← overlap(s, P)
  for each p ∈ P do
    if p ∉ O then
      s ← apply(s, p)
  if O = ∅ then
    Output(s)
  else
    for each p ∈ O do
      s′ ← apply(s, p)
      AbstractSentence(l, s', P)
```

As an example, consider the sentence s = "Michael Jordan is professor of Computer Science." and an entity e exists that has an `rdfs:label` "Michael Jordan", a `foaf:givenName` "Michael", and a `foaf:surName` "Jordan". Sentence and data alignment results in three observations o_1, o_2, and o_3:

$o_1 = (e,$	`rdfs:label`,	"Michael Jordan",	ϵ,	ϵ,	"Michael Jordan",	"id")
$o_2 = (e,$	`foaf:givenName`,	"Michael",	ϵ,	ϵ,	"Michael",	"id")
$o_3 = (e,$	`foaf:surName`,	"Jordan",	ϵ,	ϵ,	"Jordan",	"id")

ϵ denotes an empty string. Due to the overlap of o_1 with o_2 and o_3, sentence abstraction results in two abstracted sentences a_1 and a_2:

a_1 = "V1 is professor of Computer Science."
a_2 = "V1 V2 is professor of Computer Science."

The sentence s is abstracted to a_1 using o_1 and to a_2 using o_2 and o_2 and the graph is abstracted to a graph pattern. The graph pattern abstracts from concrete entities to groups of entities where entities within a group share certain similarities. For example, imagine the sentence *Paris is the capital of France* where the entities `:Paris` and `:France` were identified. Imagine further, that the hypothesis graph contains the triples expressing i)

Paris is a city, ii) France is a country, and iii) Paris is the capital of France, the hypothesis graph pattern contains the triple patterns i) ?V1 is a city, ii) ?V2 is a country, and iii) ?V1 is the capital of ?V2.

7.3.4 Grouping

Given a set of (sp, gp) tuples, for each language we build groups of tuples where in each group the sentence patterns are pairwise equivalent when ignoring modifiers. Sentence patterns sp_i and sp_j are equivalent if either they are identical ($sp_i = sp_j$), or if an injective function $m : Vars_{SP}(sp_i) \rightarrow Vars_{SP}(sp_j)$ exists such that when each variable v in sp_i is replaced with $m(v)$, the resulting string sp'_i is identical to $sp_j : sp'_i = sp_j$.

From each group, tuples (sp_i, gp_i) are removed if another tuple (sp_j, gp_j) exists within the group where the original sentences from which the sentence patterns sp_i and sp_j have been abstracted are identical.

For example, regard the following three sentence patterns:

(1) `{M(V1|id)M} University is a university in {M(V2|id)M}, {M(V3|id)M}.`

(2) `{M(V2|rm())M} University is a university in {M(V3|id)M}, {M(V6|id)M}.`

(3) `{M(V2|rm())M} University is a university in {M(V2|id)M}, {M(V4|id)M}.`

(1) and (2) are equivalent (with $m = \{(V1, V2), (V2, V3), (V3, V6)\}$), but neither (1) nor (2) is equivalent to (3) since equivalence could only be established by applying a non-injective function (with $m = \{(V1, V2), (V2, V2), (V3, V4)\}$ or $m = \{(V2, V2), (V3, V2), (V6, V4)\}$).

For each group the set of graph patterns is used as input for the algorithm presented in the following section.

Given the sentences *Paris is the capital of France*, *Berlin is the capital of Germany*, and *Oslo is the capital of Norway*, where for each sentence the city and the country have been identified; given also that all sentences have been abstracted to the sentence pattern *?V1 is the capital of ?V2*; due to their equivalent sentence patterns, the (sp, gp) tuples related to these sentences are grouped. Commonalities among sentence patterns in a group are explained using commonalities in the hypothesis graph patterns. Therefore, the next step identifies commonalities among hypothesis graph patterns where triple patterns that are specific to a certain sentence are removed. For example, unless all cities have the same population value, all triple patterns expressing a city's population value are removed.

7.3.5 Frequent Maximal Subgraph Pattern Extraction

Before we describe the *fmSpan* algorithm (fmSpan: Frequent Maximal Subgraph PAttern extractioN) we need to introduce our notation:

Two graph patterns gp_i and gp_j are *equivalent* ($gp_i = gp_j$) if an injective function $m : Var_{GP}(gp_i) \rightarrow Var_{GP}(gp_j)$ exists such that when each variable v in gp_i is replaced with $m(v)$, the resulting graph pattern gp_i' is identical to $gp_j : gp_i' = gp_j$. A graph pattern gp_i is *subgraph pattern* to another graph pattern gp_j, denoted by $gp_i \subseteq^p gp_j$, if an injective function $m : Var_{GP}(gp_i) \rightarrow Var_{GP}(gp_j)$ exists such that when each variable v in gp_i is replaced with $m(v)$, resulting in gp_i', each triple pattern in gp_i' is also a triple pattern in gp_j. Given a set of graph patterns $GP = \{gp_1, ..., gp_n\}$ and given a graph pattern x, the *coverage* of x regarding GP is the number of graph patterns in GP to which x is a subgraph pattern: $c(x, GP) := |\{gp_i \in GP | x \subseteq^p gp_i\}|$.

Given a set of graph patterns $I = \{gp_1, ..., gp_n\}$, from the set of all subgraph patterns $P = 2^{gp_1} \cup ... \cup 2^{gp_n}$ a set of graph patterns $K = \{gp_i, ..., gp_j\} \subseteq P$ is selected where:

1. for each $gp_k \in K$:
   a) $c(gp_k, I) \geqslant min\_coverage$
   b) $\neg\exists gp_l \in P : gp_k \neq gp_l \wedge gp_k \subseteq^p gp_l \wedge c(gp_l, I) \geqslant min\_coverage$
2. $\forall gp_l \in P \backslash K : c(gp_l, I) \geqslant min\_coverage \rightarrow \exists gp_k \in K : gp_l \subseteq^p gp_k$

Each member of K is (1a) sufficiently frequent and (1b) maximal (gp_k cannot be extended to gp_l such that gp_l is sufficiently frequent) and (2) every maximal graph pattern is contained in K (each sufficiently frequent graph pattern that is not member of K is not maximal).

Since a naive realization of an algorithm that satisfies these constraints and iterates over a set of power sets would be of high computational complexity, we developed an algorithm that is based on the following two principles:

1. A triple pattern t can be rare, which means that the coverage of the graph pattern, $c(\{t\}, I)$, is insufficient: $c(\{t\}, I) < min\_coverage$. In a preprocessing step we iterate over all graph patterns in I, count the coverage of each single triple pattern and then remove the rare triple patterns from all graph patterns.
2. If a graph pattern gp_i with a sufficiently high coverage is extended with a triple pattern $t \notin gp_i$ to gp_i', then $c(gp_i', I) \leqslant c(gp_i, I)$. A graph pattern with an insufficient coverage cannot be extended by any triple pattern such that its coverage becomes sufficient. Therefore, we realized a non-approximate (i.e., complete) algorithm based on the pattern-growth (a.k.a. edge extension) principle. A similar strategy is followed by the frequent subgraph mining algorithm gSpan [YH02].

7.3.6 Template Creation

For each (sentence pattern, graph patterns) tuple, frequent maximal subgraph pattern mining is performed on the group of graph patterns which results in a set K of subgraph patterns. Each $k \in K$ is pruned with Algorithm 7.7. Thereby, if a variable appears in a high number of triples that do not contain any other variable, then these triples are removed. For example, if in a set of equivalent sentence patterns a variable in a certain position is always related to the same entity e, then all triples about e in G will exist in every graph pattern. Consider, for example, the sentence `Gmina Nysa is a gmina in Poland.` where `Gmina Nysa` and `Poland` have been identified – thus resulting in the sentence pattern `?V1 is a gmina in ?V2.` Since the term `gmina`, a principal unit of administrative division of Poland, is specific to Poland, all sentences that are abstracted to this form are specific to Poland. Therefore, the entity bound to the variable `V2` is always Poland – thus the hypothesis graphs for all sentences contain all triples about Poland and the resulting graph pattern also contains all triples about Poland. After the pruning each $k \in K$ is then rejected if it is either not safe, not connected, or, when queried against G returns no results.

Algorithm 7.7 Graph-pattern pruning

procedure PRUNEGRAPHPATTERN(k)
  for each $v \in Var_{GP}(k)$ **do**
    $T \leftarrow \{(s, p, o) \in k \mid (s = v \wedge o \notin Var_{GP}(k)) \vee (o = v \wedge s \notin Var_{GP}(k))\}$
    if $|T| > max_t$ **then**
      $k \leftarrow k \setminus T$

7.4 Experiments

We created a multilingual (English, German) parallel text-data corpus using data from DBpedia[8] and documents from Wikipedia.[9] The graph G consists of $88,708,622$ triples, the set of documents D consists of $4,004,478$ English documents and $716,049$ German documents.

[8] See http://wiki.dbpedia.org/Downloads39
We used the files long_abstracts_en, long_abstracts_en_uris_de, mappingbased_properties_en, raw_infobox_properties_en, article_categories_en, instance_types_en, labels_en, labels_en_uris_de, category_labels_en, and category_labels_en_uris_de.

[9] The experiments continuously ran in parallel for two weeks on ten virtual machines (8 vCPUs, 8GB RAM, 40GB Disk) generously provided by Thorsten Tüllmann at the Steinbuch Centre for Computing (SCC) (http://www.scc.kit.edu).

Table 7.1: List of modifiers per datatype.

Datatype	Modifier	Description
xsd:string	id	Does not change the string.
	lcfirst	Sets the first char to lower case if that char is upper case.
	ucfirst	Sets the first char to upper case if that char is lower case.
	case-i	Case-insensitive match
	rm()	If a string ends with a string in round braces, e.g. "Dublin (Ohio)", that part is cut off.
	-1r	Removes the rightmost char.
xsd:gYear	YYYY	Transforms a year value into a four-digit representation.
xsd:integer	integer_id	Does not change the integer.
	enInt_sep	Adds English thousands separators, e.g., *10,000*.
	deInt_sep	Adds German thousands separators, e.g., *10.000*.
xsd:date	enM,_D_Y	Result, e.g., *March, 22 2014*
	enD_M_Y	Result, e.g., *22 March 2014*
	deM_D,_Y	Result, e.g., *März 22, 2014*
	deD_M_Y	Result, e.g., *22. März 2014*

The corpus relations and functions are defined as follows:

- $document(e,l) := \{d \mid (e, \text{dbo:abstract}, "d"@l) \in G\}$. The property `dbo:abstract` relates an entity to the abstract[10] of Wikipedia article describing the entity.
- $\lambda(e,l) := \{v \mid (e, \text{rdfs:label}, "v"@l) \in G\}$
- The *datatype* of a literal `"r^^t"` is t.
- The language l_l of a literal `"d"@l` is l.

The modifiers we used in the experiment are given in Table 7.1.[11] Application of date and integer modifiers may also depend on the language of a sentence. On a value a list of modifiers can be applied. The list of string modifier lists is shown in Table 7.2. The table also shows how often each list of modifiers was applied during the abstraction of English and German sentences.

We created two sets of entities E_{en} (E_{de}): those for which an English (German) document exist that consists of at least 100 characters. E_{en} and E_{de} contain $3,587,146$ and $613,027$

[10]The abstract of a Wikipedia article is the article's first section. These texts are part of the DBpedia dataset.
[11]Modifiers are only applied if their application to a literal modifies that literal. For example, if a string begins with a lower case character, then the *lcfirst* modifier is inapplicable.

Table 7.2: List of lists of string modifiers and their number of applications.

Modifier list	en	de	Modifier list	en	de	Modifier list	en	de
id	10,619,509	1,349,922	-1r	42,754	15,025	-1r, -1r, lcfirst	8430	90
lcfirst	141,865	868	-1r, lcfirst	7513	99	-1r, -1r, ucfirst	1020	5
ucfirst	11,018	8	-1r, ucfirst	875	4	-1r, -1r, case-i	733	92
case-i	295,593	16,351	-1r, case-i	863	50	rm(), -1r, -1r, lcfirst	0	0
rm()	2705	762	rm(), -1r, lcfirst	0	0	rm(), -1r, -1r, ucfirst	0	0
rm(), lcfirst	13	0	rm(), -1r, ucfirst	0	0	rm(), -1r, -1r, case-i	66	1
rm(), ucfirst	0	0	rm(), -1r, case-i	55	6			
rm(), case-i	50	0	-1r, -1r	39,113	11,632			

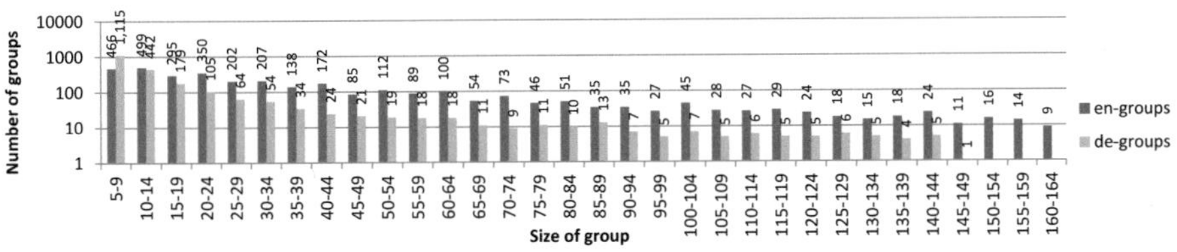

Figure 7.2: Histogram depicting how often sentence groups occurred with a particular size.

entities, respectively. For each entity for each document we split the text into sentences using the Perl module *Lingua::Sentence*[12] and discarded sentences that do not end with a full stop, an exclamation mark, or a question mark or that were shorter (longer) than 50 (200) characters. We used the set of string modifiers presented in Table 7.1 to identify entities via occurrence of a modified version of their labels in a sentence. The results are $3,811,992$ ($794,040$) English (German) sentences.

Abstraction resulted in 3,434,108 (530,766) abstracted English (German) sentences where at least two entities are identified per sentence.

The group size histogram is displayed in Figure 7.2.[13] The majority (90%) of all groups of English (German) sentences contain between 5 and 164 (5 and 39) sentences.

Table 7.3: Number of groups with a cardinality $\geqslant 5$, the number of induced templates, and the number of all groups.

	groups $\geqslant 5$	templates	all groups
en	4569	3816	686,687
de	2130	1250	269,551

[12]See http://search.cpan.org/~achimru/Lingua-Sentence-1.05

[13]We cut off the long tail. The largest group of English sentences (`V1 is a moth of the V4 family`) has 9716 members, the largest group of German sentences (`V1 ist eine V5 im französischen V2 in der V4 V6`) has 1719 members.

Table 7.3 gives, for each language, the number of groups that contain more than 5 graph patterns, the number of templates we induced, and the number of all groups. Results of the coverage evaluation $cov_t(G)$ are shown as a histogram in Figure 7.8. It shows that for the majority of the templates a high number of subgraphs of G can be verbalized, which means that the templates are not fitted to only a small number of subgraphs: for example 221 English templates verbalize between 10^5 and 10^6 subgraphs, each.

Figure 7.3 shows a list of sentence patterns and an example sentence the sentence pattern was abstracted from. It can be seen, that in some cases (e.g. in the first example) entities or literals remain in a sentence pattern where it would make sense to replace them by variables. Further abstraction was not possible since no modifier was used that could transform the string `Scotland` into `Scottish`. Entities remaining in a sentence pattern do not render a template incorrect but limit its applicability. This template may only be applied for Scottish people. Since unidentified entities may remain within a sentence pattern it is relevant that unidentified entities are added to the hypothesis graph. Thereby, from a set of sentences that can all be abstracted to the sentence pattern in the first example, all hypothesis graphs may have in common the fact that the person is of Scottish nationality.

Further, in the second example a sentence containing a birth date as well as a death date is written in past tense – the template decides the applicable tense based on the availability of certain facts. In the fourth example, identifying a number with a thousands separator as well as a number without thousands separators was possible. Some interesting templates are presented in Figure 7.4, Figure 7.5, Figure 7.6, and Figure 7.7.[14]

Example template #1 (Fig. 7.4) An entity bound to the variable `V2` is the only entity that is expressed in the sentence via its `rdfs:label`. The other entities, bound to `V4` and `V5` are expressed using non-labeling proerties. It is interesting to see that `V2` has an indirect relation to `V5`: `V2` is a subdivision of a subdivision of `V5` where `V2` is directly related to `V5` via `dbo:country`. Also, while `V2` is related to `V4` via both `dbp:subdivision` and `dbo:isPartOf` where it might seem that these properties express the same relation, `V4` is related to `V5` via both `dbp:subdivisionName` and `dbo:country`, where `dbo:isPartOf` is not used.

Example sentences this template has been learned from:
1) *Al Istiqlal District is a district of the Baghdad Governorate, Iraq.*
2) *Al Qatn District is a district of the Hadhramaut Governorate, Yemen.*

Example template #2 (Fig. 7.5) One can assume that the two properties `dbp:placeOfBirth` and `dbp:birthPlace` are redundant. However, this redundancy does not render the template incorrect. Besides that, what is interesting is that template #2

[14]Note that unlike in Figure 7.1, where variables have names such as `?book_label` or `?author_label`, here the variables have names such as `V1` or `V2`. This is the case since we manually named the variables in Figure 7.1 whereas for the induced templates the variables are named automatically and have therefore less meaningful names.

1. `{M(V1|id)M} is a novel by the Scottish {M(V5|id)M} {M(V6|id)M}, published in {M(V2|integer_id)M}.`
   Dead Air is a novel by the Scottish writer Iain Banks, published in 2002.

2. `{M(V1|id)M} ({M(V3|integer_id)M} February 1900 - {M(V5|id)M}) was a French poet and {M(V8|id)M}.`
   Jacques Prévert (4 February 1900 - 11 April 1977) was a French poet and screenwriter.

3. `{M(V1|id)M} (born {M(V3|id)M}; {M(V2|id)M}) is an American {M(V7|id)M} {M(V6|id)M} and actor.`
   Meat Loaf (born Marvin Lee Aday; September 27, 1947) is an American hard rock musician and actor.

4. `The population of {M(V1|id)M} {M(V4|id)M} was {M(V2|integer_id)M} in {M(V3|integer_id)M}.`
   The population of the Maritime provinces was 1,813,102 in 2011.

5. `{M(V1|id)M} is a rock band that originated in {M(V2|id)M}, {M(V6|id)M}.`
   Cold Chisel is a rock band that originated in Adelaide, Australia.

6. `{M(V1|id)M} is a {M(V3|id)M} and the {M(V11|id)M} of {M(V2|id)M} {M(V13|id)M}, {M(V8|id)M}, located on the {M(V5|id)M}.`
   Krasnoyarsk is a city and the administrative center of Krasnoyarsk Krai, Russia, located on the Yenisei River.

7. `{M(V2|id)M} is the principal town in the {M(V1|id)M}.`
   Bromley is the principal town in the London Borough of Bromley.

8. `{M(V1|id)M} is the highest mountain in the {M(V3|id)M}.`
   Ben Nevis is the highest mountain in the British Isles.

Figure 7.3: An example list of sentence patterns and example sentences.

is too restrictive due to the triple pattern ?V1 dbp:latm 30 . This means that this template is only applicable for entities that have a birth place located at geographic positions that have a latitude minute value of 30. Removing this triple pattern would increase the applicability of this template. Moreover, the sentence pattern does not explicitly express this fact.

Example sentences this template has been learned from:
1) *Michael Schmidt (born 6 August 1962 in Berlin) is a retired German football player.*
2) *Kinan Azmeh (born June 10, 1976 in Damascus) is a Syrian clarinet player.*

Example template #3 (Fig. 7.6) The sentence pattern uses past tense (`was a`) which makes sense since the graph pattern requires a death date to be known. Also, note that the variable `V2` has multiple types: `schema:Person`, `dbo:Agent`, `owl:Thing`, `dbo:Person`, and `foaf:Person`. The list contains redundancies that could be removed from the template: `schema:Person` is redundant since it is equivalentClass of `dbo:Person`. `dbo:Agent` is redundant since `dbo:Person` is subClassOf `dbo:Agent`. `owl:Thing` is redundant since `dbo:Agent` is subClassOf `owl:Thing`. `foaf:Person` is redundant since `dbo:Person` equivalentClass `foaf:Person`. Thus, the list of types could be reduced to `dbo:Person`. However, removing redundancies is not realized in the current approach.

Example sentences this template has been learned from:
1) *May Agnes Fleming (November 15, 1840 - March 24, 1880) was a Canadian novelist.*
2) *William Lutley Sclater (23 September 1863 - 4 July 1944) was a British zoologist and museum director.*

Example template #4 (Fig. 7.7) This template is similar to the first example template in Figure 7.4. However, template #4 is more complex. Also, template #4 is not correct since the graph pattern does not express the fact that the commune is located in the center of the country. This fact is expressed in the sentence pattern as `in central`. Incorrect templates cannot be identified automatically with our current approach.

Example sentences this template has been learned from:
1) *Bongheat is a commune in the Puy-de-Dôme department in Auvergne in central France.*
2) *Saint-Martin-d'Ollières is a commune in the Puy-de-Dôme department in Auvergne in central France.*

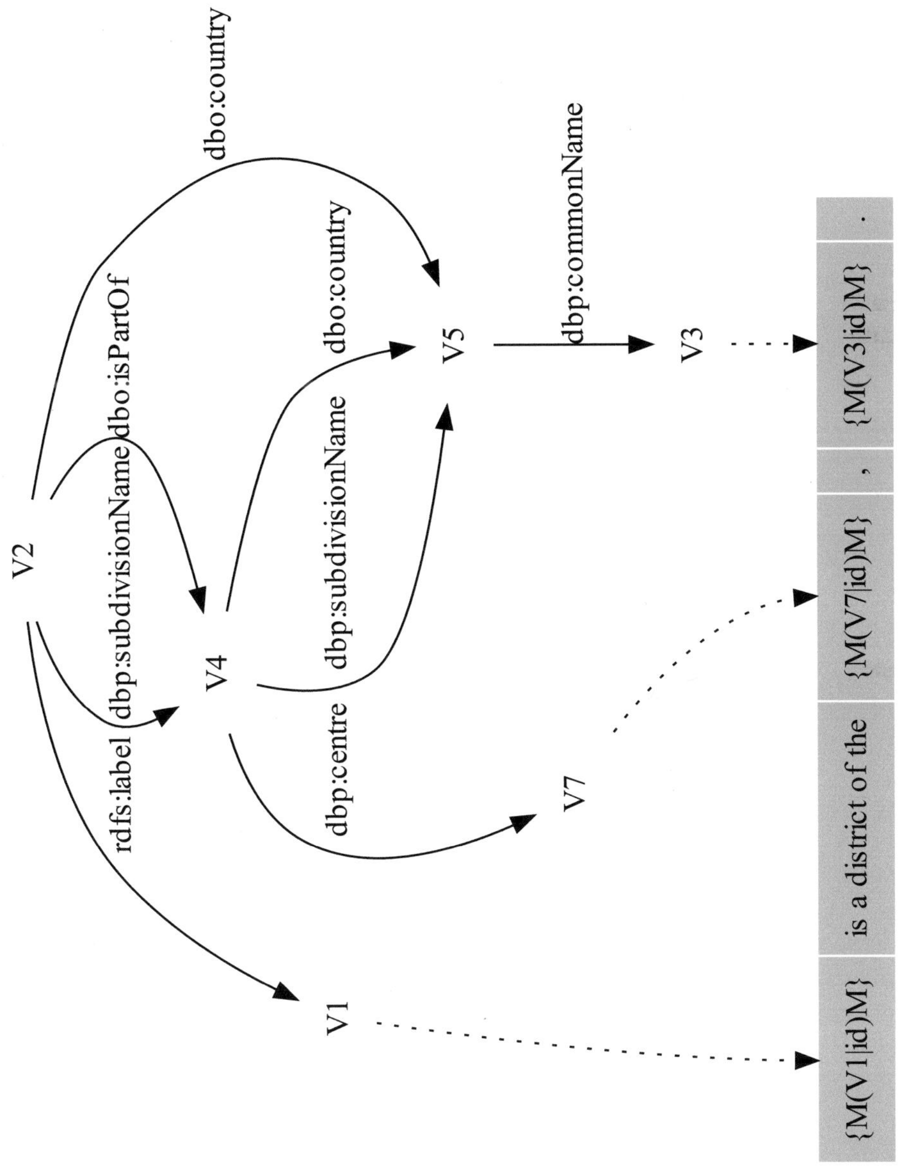

Figure 7.4: Example template #1

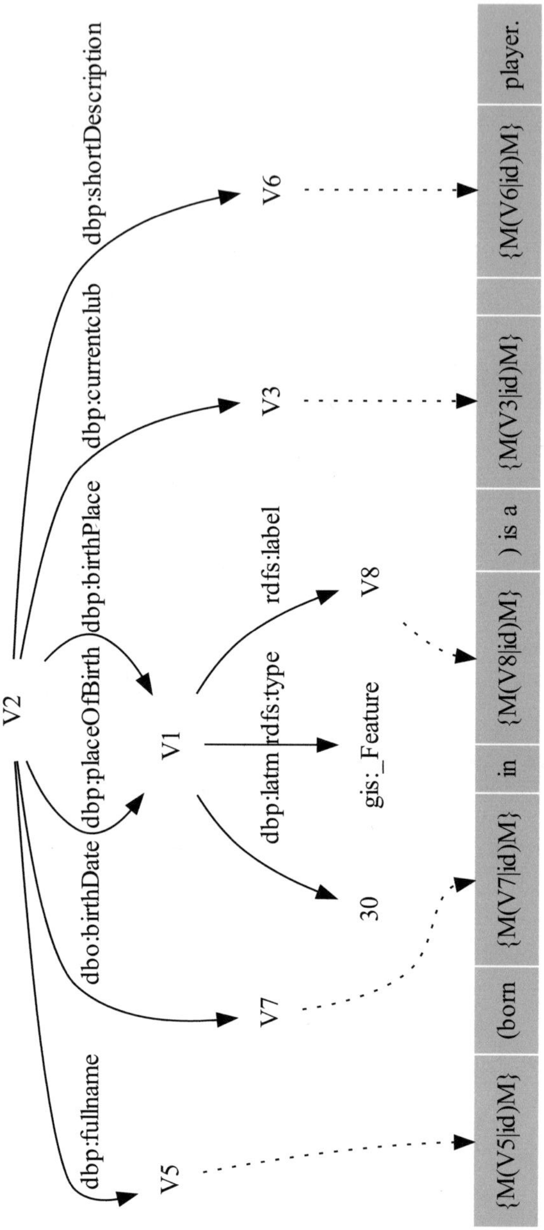

Figure 7.5: Example template #2

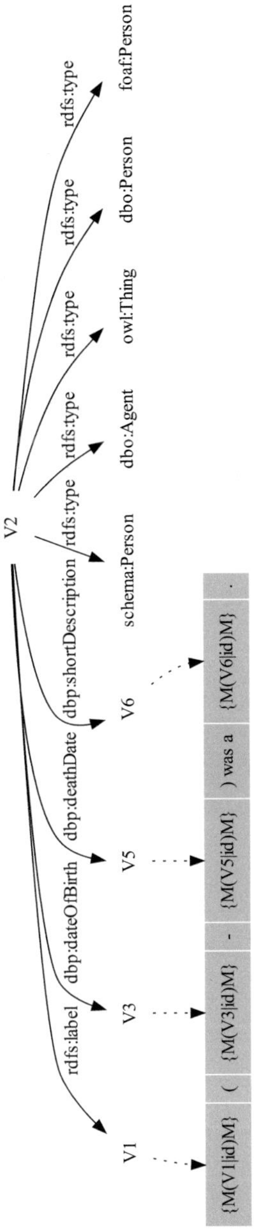

Figure 7.6: Example template #3

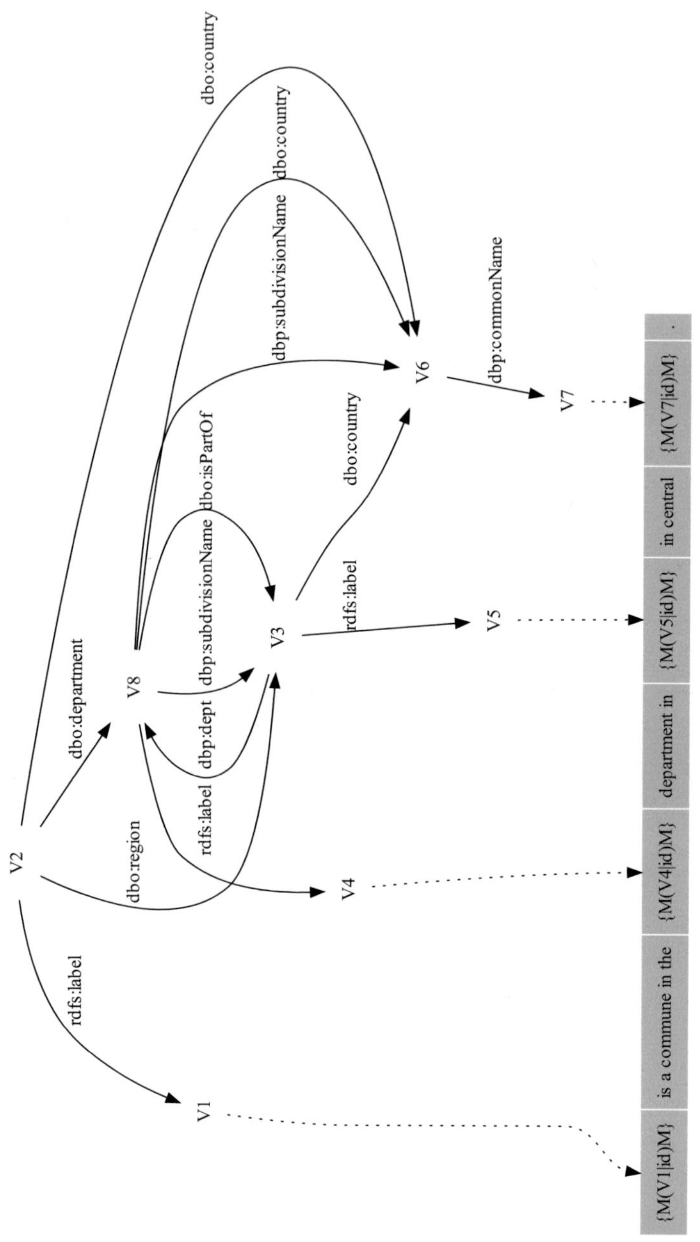

Figure 7.7: Example template #4

7.5 Evaluation

We evaluate the results from the experiment described in the previous section along the dimensions *coverage*, *accuracy*, *syntactic correctness*, and *understandability* where the latter three are inspired by [LP97; MD98; RB09].

Coverage: we define $cov(t,G)$ of a template $t = (sp, gp)$ regarding a data graph G as the number of subgraphs of G that can be verbalized with that template, i.e., match gp.

Furthermore, we define the coverage $cov_T(T,G)$ of a set T of templates regarding a data graph G. For each template $t = (sp, gp)$ we execute a SPARQL query `CONSTRUCT WHERE { gp }` thus retrieving a list of triples that occur in subgraphs of G that match the graph pattern gp. We combine these lists into a set of triples. The set consists of all triples that are contained in verbalizable subgraphs of G. $cov_T(T,G)$ is then calculated as the set's cardinality divided by the number of triples in G.

Accuracy: is measured in two parts:

1. The extent to which everything that is expressed in gp is also expressed in sp is measured for each triple pattern within the graph pattern on a 4-point scale: (1) *The triple pattern is explicitly expressed*, (2) *The triple pattern is implied*, (3) *The triple pattern is not expressed*, and (4) *Unsure*.

2. The extent to which the sp expresses information that is expressed in gp is measured on a 4-point scale: (1) *Everything is expressed*, (2) *Most things are expressed*, (3) *Some things are expressed*, and (4) *Nothing is expressed.*

Syntactic correctness: the degree to which the verbalization is syntactically correct, in particular whether it adheres to English or German grammar: (1) The verbalization is completely syntactically correct. (2) The verbalization is almost syntactically correct. (3) The verbalization presents some syntactical errors. (4) The verbalization is highly syntactically incorrect.

Understandability: The level of understandability of the verbalization, adapted from [NTN85]: (1) The meaning of the verbalization is clear. (2) The meaning of the verbalization is clear, but there are some problems in word usage, and/or style. (3) The basic thrust of the verbalization is clear, but the evaluator is not sure of some detailed parts because of word usage problems. (4) The verbalization contains many word usage problems, and the evaluator can only guess at the meaning. (5) The verbalization cannot be understood at all.

Given a set T, consisting of the 4569 English templates, we measured a $cov_T(T,G)$ value of $16,728,808$ / $88,708,622 = 18.86$ %. Ignoring whether each template is

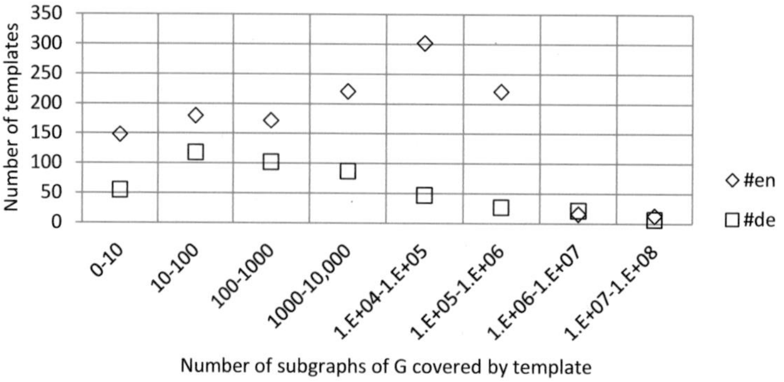

Figure 7.8: Histogram of the coverage $cov(t,G)$.

correct and explicitly verbalized each triple, the set of templates covers a considerable percentage of the DBpedia data graph.

We evaluated a random sample of 10 English and 10 German templates using a group of 6 evaluators which are experts in the fields of RDF and SPARQL (thus they understand RDF triple patterns) and that are proficient in both English and German. Each template was evaluated by 3 experts, each expert evaluated 10 templates. For each template we retrieved a maximum of 100 subgraphs that matched the graph pattern, randomly selected 10 subgraphs and verbalized them. For each template an evaluator was asked to evaluate accuracy given the graph pattern, the sentence pattern, and the list of 10 verbalizations, to evaluate each sentence regarding syntactic correctness and understandability.

$cov(t,G)$ of all 5066 templates is shown in Figure 7.8. For example, it shows that there are about 300 templates where each template can be used to verbalize between 10^4 and 10^5 subgraphs of G. Accuracy evaluation results are shown in Figure 7.9 and Figure 7.10, results of evaluating syntactical correctness and understandability are shown in Figure 7.11 and Figure 7.12, respectively. The majority of the triple patterns are either explicitly or implicitly expressed in the sentence pattern. However, some triple patterns are not expressed in the sentence pattern. Syntactical correctness and understandability are mostly high.

7.6 Related Work

Welty et al. [Wel+10] present *a technique for reading sentences and producing sets of hypothetical relations that the sentence may be expressing*. Given a parallel text-data corpus, entities identified as proper nouns in parsed sentences are replaced with variables. For each (pattern, set of relations) tuple for each sentence that matches this pattern, Welty et al. count in how many of said sentences a certain relation exists between the

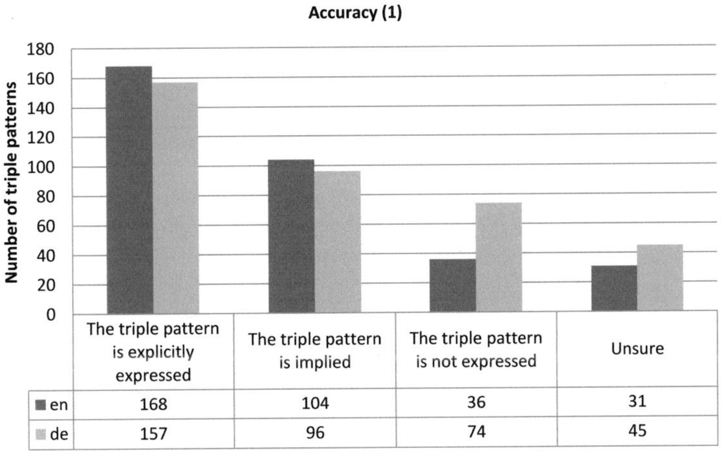

Figure 7.9: Evaluation results regarding accuracy (1).

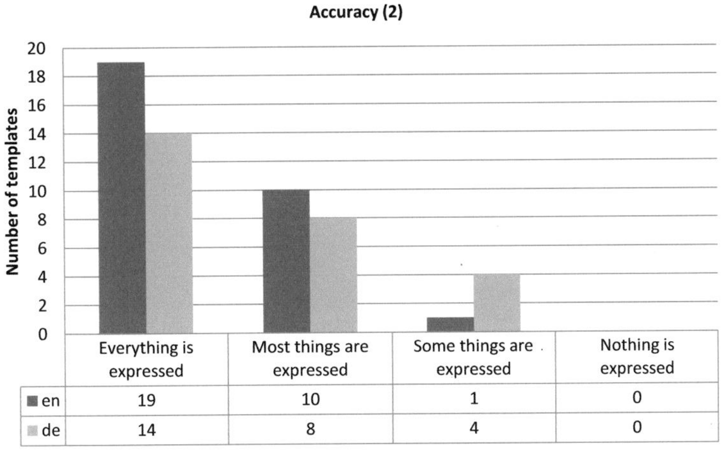

Figure 7.10: Evaluation results regarding accuracy (2).

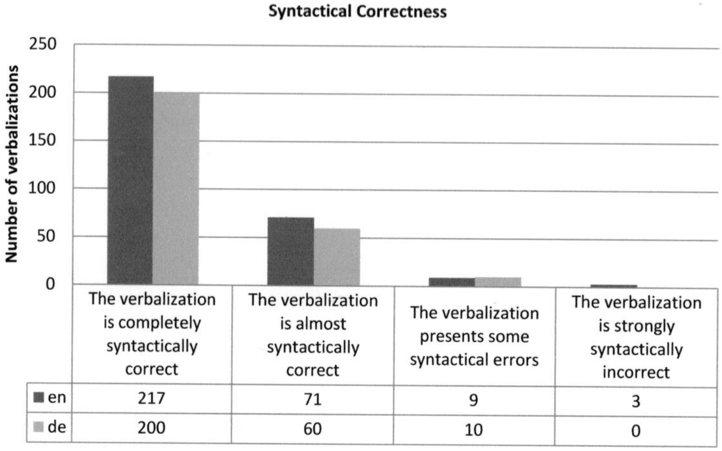

	The verbalization is completely syntactically correct	The verbalization is almost syntactically correct	The verbalization presents some syntactical errors	The verbalization is strongly syntactically incorrect
en	217	71	9	3
de	200	60	10	0

Figure 7.11: Evaluation results regarding syntactical correctness.

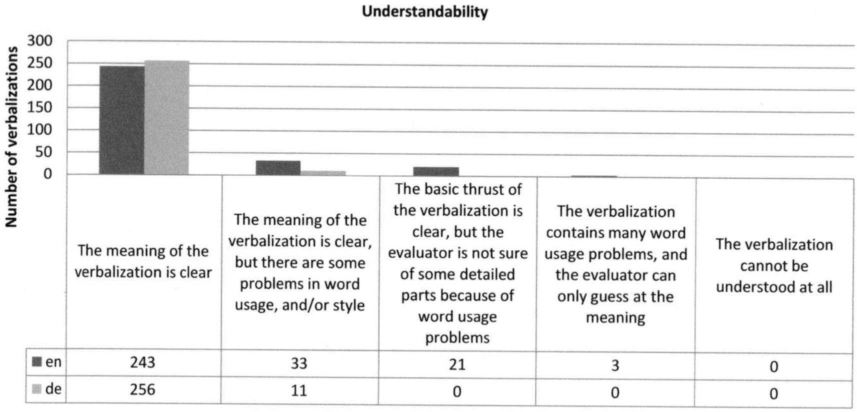

	The meaning of the verbalization is clear	The meaning of the verbalization is clear, but there are some problems in word usage, and/or style	The basic thrust of the verbalization is clear, but the evaluator is not sure of some detailed parts because of word usage problems	The verbalization contains many word usage problems, and the evaluator can only guess at the meaning	The verbalization cannot be understood at all
en	243	33	21	3	0
de	256	11	0	0	0

Figure 7.12: Evaluation results regarding understandability.

two entities identified in that sentence. This leads to positive weights being assigned to patterns. In a second phase, negative weights are assigned by applying patterns to sentences, identifying the entities and assigning a negative weight to the relation if the relation expressed by the pattern is not expressed in the data.

In contrast to their approach, our approach 1) does not require to parse input sentences 2) does not only regard relations between proper nouns, and 3) constrains candidate entities to the vicinity of already identified entities. Moreover, 4) our approach takes into account the graph of entities identified in a sentence (hypothesis graphs) compared to sets of relations and can thus express multiple relations between entities. The two approaches differ in their main goal. While their approach is targeted towards identifying patterns of relation expression that can be applied for information extraction, we need to understand all relations expressed in a sentence so that we can use this pattern for communicating knowledge in a NLG system.

Duma and Klein [DK13] present an unsupervised approach to NLG template extraction and statistical document planning from a parallel text-data corpus consisting of DBpedia data and text from Wikipedia. Similarly to our approach, text and data are aligned by identifying labels of entities in sentences. The search space is limited by only allowing entities to be matched that are directly linked to the entity a text is about. Sentences are abstracted by replacing the entity with the name of the property that links the entity with the entity the text is about, thus limiting the depth of the graph to one (1). Abstracted sentences are parsed and pruned by removing constituents that could not be aligned to the database and by removing constituents of certain classes and then post-processed using manually created rules.

In contrast to their approach, we do not limit the search space and, by creating templates consisting of sentence patterns and graph patterns, have a more expressive representation. Furthermore, our approach does not rely on parsing and manually created post-processing rules for pruning sentence patterns.

Gerber and Ngonga Ngomo [GNN11] present an approach to learning natural language representations of predicates from a parallel text-data corpus. For each predicate where a tuple of entities is identified in a sentence, the predicate's natural language representation is the string between the two entities, e.g. `'s acquisition of` for the predicate `subsidiary` and the sentence *Google's acquisition of Youtube comes as online video is really starting to hit its stride.* The main differences to our approach are: 1) that we do not focus on learning how a single predicate is expressed but rather how a graph, consisting of multiple related entities, can be expressed in natural language; and 2) that a relation between two entities is not only expressed by the string between two entities.

Summing up the main differences to the related approaches discussed, our approach 1) makes no use of linguistic resources such as parsers and is thus language-independent, 2) uses modifiers to increase the matching capabilities, 3) builds for each sentence a hypothesis graph and builds hypothesis graph patterns for a sentence pattern by applying *'has' + [unit]* +[noun] → 'has' + det* + units + noun*

Figure 7.13: A rule from the *Triple-Text* system that constructs a verb phrase from a property such as `hasEmail`.

frequent maximal subgraph pattern mining, and 4) represents a template using a sentence pattern and a graph pattern of unrestricted size.

The approach of the *Triple-Text* system by Sun and Mellish [SM07; SM06] is based on the observation that RDF representations contain linguistic information. Property names can be tokenized (e.g. `hasEmail` into *has* and *email*) and then classified into 6 categories: properties that start with *has*, that start with *is*, that end with a preposition, that are single words, that have two words, and those that have more than two words. The tokens' part of speech are recognized using QTAG [Mas03]. Given a single RDF triple a sentence is generated by applying the rule that corresponds to one of the 23 patterns in order to create a VP. Subject and object of the triple are seen as proper nouns. One rule that constructs a VP from a property is shown in Figure 7.13.[15]

Applied to the triple (*Peter, hasEmail, X@Y.com*) the pattern leads to the generation of the sentence *Peter has an email X@Y.com.*

In total the paper shows three patterns and property names matched by these patterns: 1) *'has'+...+noun* as for *hasColor* and *hasName*, 2) *'has'+...+preposition* as for *hasExposureTo* and *hasShapeAnalogousTo*, and 3) *'has'+...+adj* as for *hasTimeClose* and *hasTimeOpen*. Out of the set of 23 rules mentioned, the rule in Figure 7.13 is the only rule shown in their publication.

The *W-Ray toolkit* [Fur+10; Pic+10; Pic+11b] by Piccinini et al. evolved into a form where RDF data is verbalized [Pic+11a]. In a first step entity-relationship models of relational database views are described using RDF schema based on the approaches by Noy et al. [Noy+06] and by Bizer and Cyganiak [BC06].[16] In a second step verbalization templates are then either manually created, automatically generated according to the RDF schema or a mixture thereof. The method for the verbalization of RDF data is based on the approaches by Fliedl et al. [FKV10] and Kalyanpur [Hew+05]. Templates are represented in Prolog as lists whose items are either constant character strings or variables. See Figure 7.14 for an example. Given this template and the system's data, the system generates the sentence *The State of Amazonas is crossed by the Amazon River, which is permanent and navigable.* with the command *?- show((political_division(P), crosses(R, P), flow(R, S), navigability(R, V))).*

[15] We slightly deviate from the original presentation i) by removing the superfluous quotes in the right hand side of the rule and ii) removing the comma in the generated sentence since this is not covered by the rule.

[16] According to [Pic+10] this approach is based on [BC06] whereas according to [Pic+11b] it is based on [Noy+06].

utemplate(political_division(A), ['The State of ', A])
utemplate(crosses(A, _), ['is crossed by the ', A ,',')
utemplate(flow(_ , A), ['which is ', A])
utemplate(navigability(_ , A), ['and ', A , '.'])

Figure 7.14: A subset of the verbalization templates in W-Ray.

s(equivalentClasses(Class1,Class2), Lexicon) →
np(a, Class1, Lexicon),
[is], [defined], [as],
np(a, Class2, Lexicon).

Figure 7.15: The SWAT ontology verbaliser rule for the *equivalentClasses* expression.

The SWAT ontology verbalizer by Stevens et al. [Ste+11] verbalizes OWL ontologies in 5 steps: 1) transcoding from OWL to Prolog, 2) constructing a lexicon for atomic entities, 3) selecting the axioms relevant for describing each class, 4) aggregating axioms with a similar structure, and 5) generating sentences from (possibly aggregated) axioms. Axioms (or aggregated axioms) are realized using a Definite Clause Grammar with rules for (nearly) every logical pattern in OWL-DL. An OWL statement such as *equivalentClass(C,D)* can be realized with the rule shown in Figure 7.15. The result is a sentence where the first constituent, the noun phrase, expresses the class C using the indefinite article *a*. The noun phrase is followed by the three words *is defined as* and a noun phrase expressing the class D using the indefinite article *a*.

The main difference between our approach and the approach by Stevens et al. as well as other approaches to the verbalization of OWL ontologies (e.g., [ALG13; AOK07; Bao+09; Bon05; BA+11; FKV10; Gal+09; GA07; GNS10; KF07; PT10; Sch09; Ste+11; TWP11; Wil11; Wil03]) is that OWL provides a small vocabulary of terminological elements. Providing a verbalization template for each type of axiom can be achieved manually – verbalization templates are not learned from example texts.

7.7 Conclusion

The feasibility of our approach is validated for English and German given a large parallel text-data corpus consisting of texts from Wikipedia and data from DBpedia. We have shown that verbalization templates can be extracted from a parallel text-data corpus in a distant-supervised manner – without the need for pre-existing language resources such as parsers, grammars or dictionaries – and that applying these templates for NLG leads to promising results. Furthermore, it was observed that there are plenty of groups of sentences that share an equivalent sentence abstraction. The more such groups exist, the more templates can potentially be induced. In total, we derived 5066 templates. Coverage evaluation showed that: 1) given this set of templates a considerable fraction of the DBpedia data can be verbalized, and 2) most templates are applicable to a large number of subgraphs of DBpedia. Even though the approach is linguistically shallow, verbalization results are mostly syntactically correct and understandable. The main novelties are the definition of RDF verbalization templates as well as the application of frequent maximal subgraph pattern mining for the purpose of analyzing commonalities in sets of hypotheses graphs.

7.8 Contributions

The main contributions of this chapter are as follows:

- We formally introduced RDF verbalization templates consisting of a sentence pattern which includes modifiers and a graph pattern of unrestricted size. These templates allow RDF data to be verbalized as sentences, thus addressing RQ5.1 *How can RDF graphs be verbalized as a single sentence using a template?*
- We discussed how RDF verbalization templates can support the NLG tasks *content determination*, *lexicalization*, *referring expression generation*, *aggregation*, *linguistic realization*, and *structure realization*.
- For the purpose of answering RQ5.2 *How can RDF verbalization templates be learned from a parallel text-data corpus?* we devised an approach that induces RDF verbalization templates from a parallel corpus. This is relevant since manual creation of templates is tedious work. Furthermore, automatically inducing templates from examples has the benefit that the templates generate sentences that are similar in style to the sentences found in the example texts. Furthermore, due to the variability of natural language, there are multiple ways to express a set of facts. By learning from examples, these variabilities can be captured within the set of induced templates, which offers an NLG system the potential to exploit this variability by having available multiple templates to express the same set of facts.
- The approach is based on the distant supervision principle: training data is generated automatically by aligning a database of facts with text; therefore, no hand-labeled data is required. We apply simultaneous multi-relation learning for text-data alignment. Hypotheses about a sentence's content are represented as an RDF graph pattern. For the purpose of observing commonalities among hypothesis graphs frequent maximal subgraph pattern mining is applied. The approach does not use language resources such as parsers or dictionaries and is thus language independent. Furthermore, it does not depend on a certain ontology.

8 Conclusions

In the introduction I discussed how the Semantic Web vision led to the publication of large amounts of machine-processable RDF data on the Web. A core part of this vision is that machines can support humans in information retrieval tasks on the Web without necessarily understanding natural language text. However, RDF data should be related to natural language (e.g., English). If it was not, how would humans that do not understand machine-processable data communicate their information needs to machines, that do not understand natural language? And how would machines, once they retrieved machine-processable data that address human users' information needs, communicate these data to humans, that do not understand machine-processable data? Hence, a gap between these two worlds would impede applicability of the Web of Data.

The principal research question of this thesis concerns **interfaces enabling human users to interact with the Web of Data**. This question is broken down into ten individual research questions for which our findings are summarized in the next section. An outlook on future research opportunities is presented in Section 8.2.

8.1 Summary

The summary is structured according to the core chapters of this thesis and the individual research questions, repeated in the following list:

RQ1.1 *How can capabilities of researchers be enhanced by a semantically-enhanced Virtual Research Environment?*
RQ1.2 *How can research interactions be enabled by a semantically-enhanced Virtual Research Environment?*
RQ2.1 *Which properties are used for the purpose of labeling?*
RQ2.2 *Which metrics help study the properties of labeling within a dataset?*
RQ2.3 *What is the state of labeling in the Web of Data according to these metrics?*
RQ3.1 *How can human-readable labels be derived from variable names in SPARQL queries?*
RQ3.2 *Which SPARQL graph patterns are common?*
RQ4 *How can SPARQL queries be verbalized in a mostly schema-agnostic manner?*
RQ5.1 *How can RDF graphs be verbalized as a single sentence using a template?*
RQ5.2 *How can RDF verbalization templates be learned from a parallel text-data corpus?*

In the context of a Virtual Research Environment (VRE) that is based on Semantic Web technologies and where research objects are described in RDF, I described in Chapter 3 how certain interactions with research data in various stages of corpus-based analysis may be enabled or enhanced (RQ1.1). I give an example of a concrete research practice: the qualitative and quantitative analysis of a large digital corpus of educational lexica in the field of History of Education. Furthermore, I detailed in my discussion of the potential of Semantic Web technologies how previously unsupported interactions between life-cycles can now be enabled, thus addressing (RQ1.2).

The research tasks are supported via a set of tools developed for this purpose as extensions to MediaWiki that require Semantic MediaWiki: *OfflineImport*, *SemanticImageAnnotator*, *SemanticTextAnnotator*, *SemanticWebBrowser* (co-developed), and *AnalysisTool*. The extensions are made publicly available. Furthermore, a data import tool, various visualizations such as the visualization of reference types in annotated lemmata, the snippet table, and a data cleansing facility were developed.

A lightweight collaborative and adaptive VRE was designed. Since the VRE is based on a flexible Open Source platform it can be tailored by the researchers towards their specific needs. Therefore, this lightweight environment may serve as a starting point for further re-uses and re-configurations in unforeseen research settings and required functionalities in the future.

In Chapter 4 I analyzed the gap between RDF data and natural language in terms of the availability of human-readable labels of entities in the Web of Data. Taking the Billion Triples Challenge (BTC) corpus as a large snapshot of the Web of Data, we identified properties that are used for the task of labeling (RQ2.1), introduced four label-related metrics (*Completeness*, *Efficient accessibility*, *Unambiguity*, and *Multilinguality*) that help studying the properties of labeling within a dataset (RQ2.2), and applied these metrics on the BTC corpus (RQ2.3). We found that, regarding completeness, only 38.2% of all non-information resources have a label, regarding efficient accessibility labels for non-vocabulary URIs are only provided within a dataset in 33.82% cases, regarding unambiguity most labels (98.0%) are unambiguous, and multilinguality is a highly underexploited feature.

The finding that many entities lack human-readable labels lead to the development of an approach, presented in Chapter 5, that automatically generates human-readable labels for entities. In a context where expert users interact with entities, they leave traces of their knowledge about these entities in the form of meaningful variable names in SPARQL queries. I presented an approach to derive human-readable labels from variable names in SPARQL queries from a large set of SPARQL queries which we extracted from the DBpedia and Semantic Web Dog Food (SWDF) query logs. The evaluation shows that the approach is applicable for deriving human-readable labels (RQ3.1). Furthermore, again given this large set of SPARQL queries, we analyzed frequent graph patterns in

SPARQL queries, developed a hypergraph-based visualization of the most frequently occurring graph patterns, and applied it to visualize our measurement results (RQ3.2).

In the context of search interfaces to RDF data a class of SPARQL query-generating systems exists where users signify their information needs in the form of keywords or questions. For the purpose of enabling a user to observe a potential discrepancy between the user's information need and the system-generated query I presented an approach to SPARQL query verbalization in Chapter 6. The approach is mostly schema-agnostic because, besides being tied to a set of properties known to be labeling properties (e.g., the property `rdfs:label`) and the property `rdf:type`, all other elements are treated only based on linguistic cues found in their labels or their local name (RQ4). For the evaluation we created a query dataset using the QALD (Question Answering over Linked Data) challenges datasets.

In a comparative evaluation the approach outperformed the state of the art approach SPARQL2NL [NN+13] by obtaining higher or equal accuracy (43 cases (37.72%) and 66 cases (57.89%) respectively); higher or equal syntactical correctness (52 cases (45.61%) and 45 cases (39.47%) respectively); and higher or equal understandability (74 cases (64.91%) and 16 cases (14.04%) respectively). In a non-comparative evaluation our system successfully verbalized 98.6% (287/291) of our query dataset. In 70 out of 120 cases the evaluators attested the best score for syntactical correctness (58.33%), in 47 out of 120 cases the evaluators attested the best understandability score (39.16%).

The different syntaxes of RDF are not suitable for presentation to casual users. However, information encoded in RDF can be of interest to them, e.g., when RDF data is returned by a search interface. In Chapter 7 I introduced the notion of RDF verbalization templates which allow RDF graphs to be verbalized as sentences (RQ5.1). I discussed how RDF verbalization templates can support the NLG tasks *content determination*, *lexicalization*, *referring expression generation*, *aggregation*, *linguistic realization*, and *structure realization*.

Since manual creation of these templates is tedious work, we developed a language-independent approach for automatically inducing RDF verbalization templates from a parallel text-data corpus (RQ5.2). Automatically inducing templates from examples has the benefit that generated sentences are similar in style to sentences found in the example texts. The approach is based on the distant supervision principle: training data is generated automatically by aligning a database of facts with text; therefore, no hand-labeled data is required. We apply simultaneous multi-relation learning for text-data alignment. Hypotheses about a sentence's content are represented as an RDF graph pattern. For the purpose of observing commonalities among hypothesis graphs of similar sentences, frequent maximal subgraph pattern mining is applied. The feasibility of the approach is validated for English and German given a large parallel text-data corpus consisting of texts from Wikipedia and data from DBpedia. We showed that there are plenty of groups of sentences sharing equivalent abstractions. The more such groups exist, the more templates can potentially be induced. In total, we derived 5066 templates. Coverage evaluation showed, that: 1) given this set of templates a considerable percentage of DBpedia can be verbalized, and 2) most templates are applicable to a large number of subgraphs of DBpedia. Verbalization results are mostly syntactically correct and understandable.

8.2 Outlook

In the introduction I argued that: i) machines currently have limited Natural Language Understanding (NLU) capabilities, therefore NLU remains an active area of research; ii) a vast source of humanity's knowledge is available in textual form; and iii) humans with specific information needs need to have tools available for the purpose of searching and retrieving relevant information. As part of pursuing the Semantic Web vision, the knowledge representation formalism RDF was developed and a wealth of RDF data has been published in the Web constituting a Web of Data.

Now that this data is available, it can be leveraged for language learning. In Chapter 7 I presented an approach that exploits a parallel text-data corpus for the purpose of learning how to express information encoded in RDF as natural language sentences. RDF verbalization templates could probably also be applied for Natural Language Understanding: to represent the meaning of a natural language sentence in RDF.

Given a sentence and a template (a template consists of a sentence pattern and an RDF graph pattern) where the sentence pattern matches the sentence, the RDF graph pattern can be transformed into an RDF graph by replacing the graph pattern's variables either with literals extracted from the sentence, with newly created URIs, with existing URIs, or with blank nodes. Comparable to a bridge which can be crossed in both directions, these templates can be regarded as *bridge patterns* since they enable the gap between natural language and a formal knowledge representation to be bridged via Natural Language Generation (from RDF to text) as well as via Natural Language Understanding (from text to RDF).

If we combine the induction of bridge patterns (BPs) with the application of BPs for NLU, then we could realize a system that induces BPs from an initial parallel corpus (consisting of a set of documents and an RDF database) and applies the induced BPs for NLU, thereby enriching the RDF database. In a subsequent BP induction phase, given the extended database, new BPs could be derived or BPs derived in the previous phase could be refined. The iterative approach would realize a form of *Never-Ending Language Learning* [Car+10] but without the need for a grammar for parsing input sentences – thus being able to process input data that does not follow strict grammatical rules which is common for social media content. Application of the approach would result in a large knowledge graph and a large set of BPs. Moreover, since the approach is language-independent, BPs can be learned for multiple languages and information extracted from sentences in one language can help inducing BPs for another language

Several challenges need to be addressed in future work in this direction, of which the two most relevant challenges are, briefly:

- An iterative system such as the one described here is prone to *semantic drift*. Applying incorrectly induced BPs for NLU leads to incorrect data added to the RDF database. An incorrect database will lead to incorrectly induced BPs in subsequent iterations, thus the overall data quality decreases with subsequent iterations. Crowdsourcing might be one approach to tackle the problem: having humans in the loop that assess the correctness of induced BPs. Crowdsourcing is especially interesting since the system may have BPs available that were assessed as being correct and thus can be applied for NLG. Where non-experts would not easily understand extracted RDF, they would more easily understand the text generated from the extracted RDF data.
- The system is limited by its initial ontology. BPs applied for NLU would populate the database only in terms of entities and triples using existing properties. What is missing is the ability to learn new properties. When trying to induce BPs for sentences that contain information which cannot be expressed by the ontology, the system could never construct hypothesis graphs that explain the sentence and thus never learn a BP that explains the sentence.

Given i) the data available in the Web of Data, ii) the natural language texts available on the Web, iii) the approach to induce bridge patterns, and iv) the approach to applying bridge patterns for Natural Language Understanding, the Web of Data could be iteratively populated with knowledge extracted from texts available on the Web – thus transforming unstructured content into structured, machine-processable data and thereby improving the accessibility of knowledge on the Web.

List of Figures

List of Tables

Bibliography

[ABG00] Paul Atkinson, Martin W. Bauer, and George Gaskell. "Constructing a research corpus". In: *Qualitative Researching with Text, Image and Sound: A Practical Handbook for Social Research*. Sage Publications, 2000. ISBN: 9780761964810.

[Agu+98] G. Aguado, A. Bañón, John A. Bateman, Socorro Bernardos, Mariano G. Fernández, Asunción Gómez-Pérez, Elena Nieto, A. Olalla, Ramon G. Plaza, and Antonio Sánchez. "ONTOGENERATION: Reusing domain and linguistic ontologies for Spanish text generation". In: *Workshop on Applications of Ontologies and Problem Solving Methods, ECAI'98*. 1998.

[Ala06] Harith Alani. "Position paper: ontology construction from online ontologies". In: *Proceedings of the 15th International Conference on World Wide Web*. Ed. by Les Carr, David De Roure, Arun Iyengar, Carole A. Goble, and Michael Dahlin. WWW 2006. Edinburgh, Scotland: ACM, May 2006, pp. 491–495. ISBN: 1-59593-323-9.

[ALG13] Ion Androutsopoulos, Gerasimos Lampouras, and Dimitrios Galanis. "Generating Natural Language Descriptions from OWL Ontologies: The Natural OWL System". In: *Journal of Artificial Intelligence Research* 48.1 (Oct. 2013), pp. 671–715. ISSN: 1076-9757.

[AOK07] Ion Androutsopoulos, Jon Oberlander, and Vangelis Karkaletsis. "Source authoring for multilingual generation of personalised object descriptions". In: *Natural Language Engineering* 13.3 (2007), pp. 191–233.

[ASB09] Samur Araujo, Daniel Schwabe, and Simone Barbosa. "Experimenting with Explorator: a Direct Manipulation Generic RDF Browser and Querying Tool". In: *Proceedings of the Workshop on Visual interfaces to the social and the semantic web (VISSW 2009)*. Ed. by Siegfried Handschuh, Tom Heath, and VinhTuan Thai. Vol. 443. CEUR Workshop Proceedings. CEUR-WS.org, 2009.

[Aue+07] Sören Auer, Chris Bizer, Georgi Kobilarov, Jens Lehmann, Richard Cyganiak, and Zachary Ives. "DBpedia: A Nucleus for a Web of Open Data". In: *Proceedings of the 6th International Semantic Web Conference and 2nd Asian Semantic Web Conference.* ISWC 2007/ASWC 2007. Busan, Korea: Springer, 2007, pp. 722–735. ISBN: 3-540-76297-3, 978-3-540-76297-3.

[Aue+12] Sören Auer, Lorenz Bühmann, Christian Dirschl, Orri Erling, Michael Hausenblas, Robert Isele, Jens Lehmann, Michael Martin, Pablo N. Mendes, Bert van Nuffelen, Claus Stadler, Sebastian Tramp, and Hugh Williams. "Managing the Life-cycle of Linked Data with the LOD2 Stack". In: *Proceedings of the 11th International Semantic Web Conference.* ISWC 2012. Boston, MA: Springer, 2012, pp. 1–16. ISBN: 978-3-642-35172-3.

[BA+11] Nadjet Bouayad-Agha, Gerard Casamayor, Leo Wanner, Fernando Díez, and Sergio López Hernández. "FootbOWL: Using a generic ontology of football competition for planning match summaries". In: *Proceedings of the 8th Extended Semantic Web Conference.* ESWC 2011. Heraklion, Crete, Greece: Springer, 2011, pp. 230–244. ISBN: 978-3-642-21033-4.

[BACW14] Nadjet Bouayad-Agha, Gerard Casamayor, and Leo Wanner. "Natural Language Generation in the context of the Semantic Web". In: *Semantic Web* 5.6 (2014), pp. 493–513.

[Bao+09] Jie Bao, Paul Smart, Dave Braines, and Nigel Shadbolt. "A Controlled Natural Language Interface for Semantic Media Wiki Using the Rabbit Language". In: *Workshop on Controlled Natural Language (CNL'09).* June 2009.

[BB09] Christian Becker and Chris Bizer. *Marbles.* http://marbles.sourceforge.net/. 2009.

[BC06] Christian Bizer and Richard Cyganiak. "D2R server–publishing relational databases on the web as SPARQL Endpoints". In: *Proceedings of the 15th International Conference on World Wide Web.* WWW 2006. Edinburgh, Scotland: ACM, 2006. ISBN: 1-59593-323-9.

[BCH07] Christian Bizer, Richard Cyganiak, and Tom Heath. *How to publish linked data on the web.* http://www4.wiwiss.fu-berlin.de/bizer/pub/LinkedDataTutorial/. 2007.

[BG04] Dan Brickley and Ramanathan V. Guha. *RDF Vocabulary Description Language 1.0: RDF Schema.* W3C Recommendation, http://www.w3.org/TR/rdf-schema/. Feb. 2004.

[BG07] Chris Bizer and Tobias Gauß. *Disco – Hyperdata Browser.* http://www4.wiwiss.fu-berlin.de/bizer/ng4j/disco/. Jan. 2007.

[Bib93] Douglas Biber. “Representativeness in corpus design”. In: *Literary and Linguistic Computing* 8.4 (1993), pp. 243–257.

[BK06] Abraham Bernstein and Esther Kaufmann. “GINO – A Guided Input Natural Language Ontology Editor”. In: *Proceedings of the 5th International Semantic Web Conference*. ISWC 2006. Athens, Georgia (US): Springer, 2006. ISBN: 3-540-49029-9, 978-3-540-49029-6.

[BL+06] Tim Berners-Lee, Yuhsin Chen, Lydia Chilton, Dan Connolly, Ruth Dhanaraj, James Hollenbach, Adam Lerer, and David Sheets. “Tabulator: Exploring and Analyzing linked data on the Semantic Web”. In: *Proceedings of the 3rd International Semantic Web User Interaction Workshop (SWUI2006) at the International Semantic Web Conference (ISWC2006)*. Ed. by Lloyd Rutledge, m.c. schraefel, Abraham Bernstein, and Duane Degler. 2006.

[BL06] Tim Berners-Lee. *Linked Data*. http://www.w3.org/DesignIssues/LinkedData.html. July 2006.

[BLFM05] Tim Berners-Lee, Roy Fielding, and Larry Masinter. *Uniform Resource Identifier (URI): Generic Syntax*. RFC 3986, http://www.ietf.org/rfc/rfc3986.txt. June 2005.

[BLHL+01] Tim Berners-Lee, James Hendler, Ora Lassila, et al. “The semantic web”. In: *Scientific American* 284.5 (May 2001), pp. 29–37.

[BM05] Dan Brickley and Libby Miller. *The Friend Of A Friend (FOAF) Vocabulary Specification*. http://xmlns.com/foaf/0.1/. July 2005.

[BM07] Razvan Bunescu and Raymond Mooney. “Learning to Extract Relations from the Web using Minimal Supervision”. In: *Proceedings of the 45th Annual Meeting of the Association for Computational Linguistics*. Ed. by John A. Carroll, Antal van den Bosch, and Annie Zaenen. Vol. 45. 1. The Association for Computational Linguistics, 2007, p. 576.

[Boa12] DCMI Usage Board. *DC (DCMI Metadata Term)*. http://dublincore.org/documents/dcmi-terms/. June 2012.

[Bon05] Kalina Bontcheva. “Generating tailored textual summaries from ontologies”. In: *Proceedings of the Second European Conference on The Semantic Web: Research and Applications*. ESWC 2005. Heraklion, Greece: Springer, 2005, pp. 531–545.

[Bor09] Christine L. Borgman. “The Digital Future is Now: A Call to Action for the Humanities”. In: *Digital Humanities Quarterly* 3.4 (2009), pp. 1–30.

[Bor12] Christine L. Borgman. “The conundrum of sharing research data”. In: *Journal of the American Society for Information Science and Technology* 63.6 (Apr. 2012), pp. 1059–1078.

[BS07] Sheridan Brown and Alma Swan. *Researchers' use of academic libraries and their services: a report commissioned by the Research Information Network and the Consortium of Research Libraries*. Tech. rep. 2007. URL: http://eprints.soton.ac.uk/263868/.

[Bui+09] Paul Buitelaar, Philipp Cimiano, Peter Haase, and Michael Sintek. "Towards linguistically grounded ontologies". In: *Proceedings of the 6th Extended Semantic Web Conference*. ESWC 2009. Heraklion, Crete, Greece: Springer, 2009, pp. 111–125. ISBN: 978-3-642-02120-6. DOI: 10.1007/978-3-642-02121-3_12.

[BW04] Kalina Bontcheva and Yorick Wilks. "Automatic Report Generation from Ontologies: The MIAKT Approach". In: *Proceedings of the 9th International Conference on the Application of Natural Language to Information Systems*. Ed. by Farid Meziane and Elisabeth Métais. NLDB 2004. Salford, UK: Springer, 2004, pp. 324–335. ISBN: 978-3-540-27779-8.

[Böh+12] Christoph Böhm, Gerard de Melo, Felix Naumann, and Gerhard Weikum. "LINDA: Distributed Web-of-data-scale Entity Matching". In: *Proceedings of the 21st ACM International Conference on Information and Knowledge Management*. CIKM 2012. Maui, Hawaii, USA: ACM, 2012, pp. 2104–2108. ISBN: 978-1-4503-1156-4. DOI: 10.1145/2396761.2398582.

[Car+09] Andrew Carlson, Justin Betteridge, Estevam R. Hruschka Jr., and Tom M. Mitchell. "Coupling semi-supervised learning of categories and relations". In: *Proceedings of the NAACL HLT 2009 Workshop on Semi-Supervised Learning for Natural Language Processing*. SemiSupLearn 2009. Boulder, Colorado: Association for Computational Linguistics, 2009, pp. 1–9. ISBN: 978-1-932432-38-1.

[Car+10] Andrew Carlson, Justin Betteridge, Bryan Kisiel, Burr Settles, Estevam R. Hruschka Jr., and Tom M. Mitchell. "Toward an Architecture for Never-Ending Language Learning". In: *Proceedings of the 24th Conference on Artificial Intelligence*. AAAI 2010. 2010.

[CG11] Louise Corti and Arofan Gregory. "CAQDAS Comparability. What about CAQDAS Data Exchange?" In: *Forum Qualitative Sozialforschung/Forum: Qualitative Social Research*. Vol. 12. 1. 2011.

[CGQ08] Gong Cheng, Weiyi Ge, and Yuzhong Qu. "Falcons: Searching and Browsing Entities on the Semantic Web". In: *Proceedings of the 17th International Conference on World Wide Web*. WWW 2008. Beijing, China: ACM, 2008, pp. 1101–1102. ISBN: 978-1-60558-085-2. DOI: 10.1145/1367497.1367676.

[Cha+13] Vinay K Chaudhri, Britte Cheng, Adam Overtholtzer, Jeremy Roschelle, Aaron Spaulding, Peter Clark, Mark Greaves, and Dave Gunning. "Inquire Biology: A Textbook that Answers Questions". In: *AI Magazine* 34.3 (2013), pp. 55–72.

[Cim+07] Philipp Cimiano, Peter Haase, Matthias Herold, Matthias Mantel, and Paul Buitelaar. "LexOnto: A Model for Ontology Lexicons for Ontology-based NLP". In: *Proceedings of the OntoLex07 Workshop held in conjunction with 6th International Semantic Web Conference (ISWC 2007)*. 2007.

[Cim+08] P. Cimiano, P. Haase, J. Heizmann, M. Mantel, and R. Studer. "Towards portable natural language interfaces to knowledge bases – The case of the ORAKEL system". In: *Data & Knowledge Engineering* 65.2 (2008), pp. 325–354.

[Cim+13] Philipp Cimiano, Janna Lüker, David Nagel, and Christina Unger. "Exploiting ontology lexica for generating natural language texts from RDF data". In: *Proceedings of the 14th European Workshop on Natural Language Generation*. ENLG 2013. 2013.

[CK99] Mark Craven and Johan Kumlien. "Constructing Biological Knowledge Bases by Extracting Information from Text Sources". In: *Proceedings of the 7th International Conference on Intelligent Systems for Molecular Biology (ISMB 1999)*. Ed. by Thomas Lengauer, Reinhard Schneider, Peer Bork, Douglas L. Brutlag, Janice I. Glasgow, Hans-Werner Mewes, and Ralf Zimmer. AAAI, 1999, pp. 77–86.

[CR10] Annamaria Carusi and Torsten Reimer. *Virtual Research Environment Collaborative Landscape Study*. Tech. rep. Joint Information Systems Committee, Bristol, Jan. 2010, p. 106. URL: http://www.jisc.ac.uk/publications/reports/2010/vrelandscapestudy.aspx.

[CSM07] Anne Cregan, Rolf Schwitter, and Thomas Meyer. "Sydney OWL Syntax – towards a Controlled Natural Language Syntax for OWL 1.1." In: *Proceedings of the OWLED 2007 Workshop on OWL: Experiences and Directions*. Ed. by Christine Golbreich, Aditya Kalyanpur, and Bijan Parsia. Vol. 258. CEUR Workshop Proceedings. CEUR-WS.org, 2007.

[CW14] Richard Cyganiak and Markus Wood David Lanthaler. *RDF 1.1 Concepts and Abstract Syntax*. W3C Recommendation, http://www.w3.org/TR/rdf11-concepts/ (URL last accessed 2015-01-02). Feb. 2014.

[d'A+07a] Mathieu d'Aquin, Claudio Baldassarre, Laurian Gridinoc, Sofia Angeletou, Marta Sabou, and Enrico Motta. "Characterizing Knowledge on the Semantic Web with Watson". In: *Proceedings of 5th International Workshop on Evaluation of Ontologies and Ontology-Based Tools (EON2007) at the 6th International Semantic Web Conference (ISWC 2007)*. Ed. by

Raul Garcia-Castro, Denny Vrandečić, Asunción Gómez-Pérez, York Sure, and Zhisheng Huang. Vol. 329. CEUR Workshop Proceedings. CEUR-WS.org, Nov. 2007, pp. 1–10.

[d'A+07b] Mathieu d'Aquin, Claudio Baldassarre, Laurian Gridinoc, Marta Sabou, Sofia Angeletou, and Enrico Motta. "Watson: Supporting next generation semantic web applications". In: *Proceedings of the 16st International Conference on World Wide Web*. WWW 2007. ACM, 2007.

[DAC12] Danica Damljanovic, Milan Agatonovic, and Hamish Cunningham. "FREyA: An interactive way of querying Linked Data using natural language". In: *Proceedings of the 8th Extended Semantic Web Conference*. ESWC 2011. Heraklion, Crete, Greece: Springer, 2012, pp. 125–138. ISBN: 978-3-642-25952-4. DOI: 10.1007/978-3-642-25953-1_11.

[Dal89] Robert Dale. "Cooking up referring expressions". In: *Proceedings of the 27th Annual Meeting on Association for Computational Linguistics*. ACL 1989. Vancouver, British Columbia, Canada: Association for Computational Linguistics, 1989, pp. 68–75. DOI: 10.3115/981623.981632.

[Dav+08] Brian Davis, Ahmad Iqbal, Adam Funk, Valentin Tablan, Kalina Bontcheva, Hamish Cunningham, and Siegfried Handschuh. "RoundTrip Ontology Authoring". In: *Proceedings of the 7th International Semantic Web Conference*. ISWC 2008. Karlsruhe, Germany: Springer, 2008, pp. 50–65. ISBN: 978-3-540-88563-4. DOI: 10.1007/978-3-540-88564-1_4.

[DF06] Li Ding and Tim Finin. "Characterizing the Semantic Web on the Web". In: *Proceedings of the 5th International Semantic Web Conference*. ISWC 2006. Athens, GA: Springer, 2006, pp. 242–257. ISBN: 3-540-49029-9, 978-3-540-49029-6. DOI: 10.1007/11926078_18.

[DG09] Bruce D'Arcus and Frédérick Giasson. *BIBO (The Bibliographic Ontology)*. http://purl.org/ontology/bibo/. Nov. 2009.

[Din+04] Li Ding, Tim Finin, Anupam Joshi, Rong Pan, R Scott Cost, Yun Peng, Pavan Reddivari, Vishal Doshi, and Joel Sachs. "Swoogle: A Search and Metadata Engine for the Semantic Web". In: *Proceedings of the 13th ACM International Conference on Information and Knowledge Management*. CIKM 2004. Washington, D.C., USA: ACM, 2004, pp. 652–659. ISBN: 1-58113-874-1. DOI: 10.1145/1031171.1031289.

[DK13] Daniel Duma and Ewan Klein. "Generating Natural Language from Linked Data: Unsupervised template extraction". In: *Proceedings of the 10th International Conference on Computational Semantics – Long Papers*. IWCS 2013. Association for Computational Linguistics, 2013, pp. 83–94.

[DKT05] Kees van Deemter, Emiel Krahmer, and Mariët Theune. "Real vs. template-based natural language generation: a false opposition?" In: *Computational Linguistics* 31.1 (2005), pp. 15–23.

[DP06] Florian Deissenboeck and Markus Pizka. "Concise and Consistent Naming". In: *Software Quality Journal* 14.3 (Sept. 2006), pp. 261–282.

[DRGS09] David De Roure, Carole Goble, and Robert Stevens. "The design and realisation of the Virtual Research Environment for social sharing of workflows". In: *Future Generation Computer Systems* 25.5 (2009), pp. 561–567.

[Dun09] Stuart Dunn. "Dealing with the complexity deluge: VREs in the arts and humanities". In: *Library Hi Tech* 27.2 (2009), pp. 205–216.

[Edw+11] Paul N. Edwards, Matthew S. Mayernik, Archer L. Batcheller, Geoffrey C. Bowker, and Christine L. Borgman. "Science friction: Data, metadata, and collaboration". In: *Social Studies of Science* 41.5 (Oct. 2011), pp. 667–690.

[Edw+12] Peter Edwards, Edoardo Pignotti, Alan Eckhardt, Kapila Ponnamperuma, Chris Mellish, and Thomas Bouttaz. "ourSpaces – Design and Deployment of a Semantic Virtual Research Environment". In: *Proceedings of the 11th International Semantic Web Conference*. ISWC 2012. Boston, MA: Springer, 2012, pp. 50–65. ISBN: 978-3-642-35172-3. DOI: 10.1007/978-3-642-35173-0_4.

[EH14] Basil Ell and Andreas Harth. "A language-independent method for the extraction of RDF verbalization templates". In: *Proceedings of the 8th International Natural Language Generation Conference (INLG 2014)*. The Association for Computer Linguistics, June 2014, pp. 26–34.

[EHS14] Basil Ell, Andreas Harth, and Elena Simperl. "SPARQL Query Verbalization for Explaining Semantic Search Engine Queries". In: *Proceedings of the 11th Extended Semantic Web Conference*. ESWC 2014. Heidelberg: Springer, 2014, pp. 426–441.

[EP09] Vyvyan Evans and Stephanie Pourcel. *New directions in cognitive linguistics*. Vol. 24. John Benjamins Publishing, 2009. ISBN: 9789027289445.

[ESR13] Basil Ell, Christoph Schindler, and Marc Rittberger. "Semantically Enhanced Interactions between Heterogeneous Data Life-Cycles. Analyzing Educational Lexica in a Virtual Research Environment". In: *Proceedings of the 7th Metadata and Semantics Research Conference (MTSR 2013)*. Ed. by Emmanouel Garoufallou and Jane Greenberg. Communications in Computer and Information Science Vol. 390. Thessaloniki: Springer, Nov. 2013, pp. 277–288.

[EVS11a] Basil Ell, Denny Vrandečić, and Elena Simperl. "Deriving Human-readable Labels from SPARQL Queries". In: *Proceedings of the 7th International Conference on Semantic Systems (I-SEMANTICS 2011)*. ACM, Sept. 2011, pp. 126–133.

[EVS11b] Basil Ell, Denny Vrandečić, and Elena Simperl. "Labels in the Web of Data". In: *Proceedings of the 10th International Semantic Web Conference*. Ed. by Lora Aroyo, Chris Welty, Harith Alani, Jamie Taylor, Abraham Bernstein, Lalana Kagal, Natasha Noy, and Eva Blomqvist. ISWC 2011. Springer, Oct. 2011, pp. 162–176.

[EVS12] Basil Ell, Denny Vrandečić, and Elena Simperl. "SPARTIQULATION: Verbalizing SPARQL queries". In: *Proceedings of the Interacting with Linked Data Workshop, co-located with the 9th Extended Semantic Web Conference*. Vol. 913. ILD 2012. Heraklion, Greece: CEUR-WS.org, May 2012, pp. 50–60.

[EVS15] Basil Ell, Denny Vrandečić, and Elena Simperl. "SPARTIQULATION: Verbalizing SPARQL queries". In: *The Semantic Web: ESWC 2012 Satellite Events*. Ed. by Elena Simperl, Barry Norton, Dunja Mladenic, Emanuele Della Valle, Irene Fundulaki, Alexandre Passant, and Raphaël Troncy. LNCS 7540. Springer, 2015, pp. 426–441.

[Fel98] Christine Fellbaum. *WordNet – An Electronic Lexical Database*. MIT Press, 1998. ISBN: 978-0262061971.

[Fie+99] Roy Fielding, James Gettys, Jeffrey Mogul, Henrik Frystyk, Larry Masinter, Paul Leach, and Tim Berners-Lee. *Hypertext Transfer Protocol – HTTP/1.1*. RFC 2616, http://www.ietf.org/rfc/rfc2616.txt. June 1999.

[FKV10] Günther Fliedl, Christian Kop, and Jürgen Vöhringer. "Guideline based evaluation and verbalization of OWL class and property labels". In: *Data & Knowledge Engineering* 69.4 (Apr. 2010), pp. 331–342.

[Fra05] Michael Fraser. "Virtual research environments: overview and activity". In: *Ariadne* 44 (2005), pp. 31–40.

[FS69] Ivan P. Fellegi and Alan B. Sunter. "A Theory for Record Linkage". In: *Journal of the American Statistical Association* 64.328 (1969), pp. 1183–1210.

[Fur+10] Antonio L. Furtado, Simone D. J. Barbosa, Marco A. Casanova, and Helena Piccinini. *First version of a Prototype for Publishing Deep Web Data*. Tech. rep. Departamento de Informática, PUC-Rio, July 2010.

[GA07] Dimitrios Galanis and Ion Androutsopoulos. "Generating multilingual descriptions from linguistically annotated OWL ontologies: the NaturalOWL system". In: *Proceedings of the 11th European Workshop on Natural Language Generation*. ENLG 2007. Stroudsburg, PA, USA: Association for Computational Linguistics, 2007, pp. 143–146.

[Gal+09] Dimitrios Galanis, George Karakatsiotis, Gerasimos Lampouras, and Ion Androutsopoulos. "An open-source natural language generator for OWL ontologies and its use in Protégé and Second Life". In: *Proceedings of the 12th Conference of the European Chapter of the Association for Computational Linguistics: Demonstrations Session.* EACL 2009. Athens, Greece: Association for Computational Linguistics, 2009, pp. 17–20.

[Gal+11] Mario Arias Gallego, Javier D. Fernández, Miguel A. Martínez-Prieto, and Pablo de la Fuente. *An Empirical Study of Real-World SPARQL Queries.* Tech. rep. arXiv:1103.5043. 1st International Workshop on Usage Analysis and the Web of Data (USEWOD2011) at the 20th International Conference on World Wide Web (WWW2011), Hyderabad, India. Mar. 2011.

[GDK94] Eli Goldberg, Norbert Driedger, and Richard I Kittredge. "Using natural-language processing to produce weather forecasts". In: *IEEE Expert* 9.2 (1994), pp. 45–53.

[GMM03] R. Guha, Rob McCool, and Eric Miller. "Semantic Search". In: *Proceedings of the 12th International Conference on World Wide Web.* WWW 2003. Budapest, Hungary: ACM, 2003, pp. 700–709. ISBN: 1-58113-680-3. DOI: 10.1145/775152.775250.

[GNN11] Daniel Gerber and Axel-Cyrille Ngonga Ngomo. "Bootstrapping the linked data web". In: *Proceedings of the 1st Workshop on Web Scale Knowledge Extraction at the 10th International Semantic Web Conference (ISWC 2011).* 2011.

[GNS10] Normunds Grūzītis, Gunta Nešpore, and Baiba Saulīte. "Verbalizing Ontologies in Controlled Baltic Languages". In: *Proceedings of the 4th International Conference on Baltic Human Language Technologies.* Amsterdam, The Netherlands: IOS Press, 2010, pp. 187–194. ISBN: 978-1-60750-640-9.

[Gra+08] Bernardo Cuenca Grau, Ian Horrocks, Boris Motik, Bijan Parsia, Peter Patel-Schneider, and Ulrike Sattler. "OWL 2: The next step for OWL". In: *Web Semantics: Science, Services and Agents on the World Wide Web* 6.4 (2008), pp. 309–322.

[GTS09] Ljubinka Gareva-Takasmanov and Ilias Sakellariou. "OWL for the Masses: From Structured OWL to Unstructured Technically-Neutral Natural Language". In: *Proceedings of the 2009 Fourth Balkan Conference in Informatics.* Ed. by Petros Kefalas, Demosthenes Stamatis, and Christos Douligeris. BCI 2009. Washington, DC, USA: IEEE Computer Society, 2009, pp. 260–265. ISBN: 978-0-7695-3783-2. DOI: 10.1109/BCI.2009.32.

[Har10] Andreas Harth. "VisiNav: A System for Visual Search and Navigation on Web Data". In: *Web Semantics: Science, Services and Agents on the World Wide Web* 8.4 (Nov. 2010), pp. 348–354. ISSN: 1570-8268. DOI: 10.1016/j.websem.2010.08.001.

[HB11] Tom Heath and Chris Bizer. *Linked Data: Evolving the Web into a Global Data Space*. Synthesis Lectures on the Semantic Web: Theory and Technology. Morgan & Claypool, Feb. 2011.

[HCB08] Tuukka Hastrup, Richard Cyganiak, and Uldis Bojars. "Browsing Linked Data with Fenfire". In: *Proceedings of the Workshop on Linked Data on the Web*. LDOW 2008. 2008.

[HD05] Andreas Harth and Stefan Decker. "Optimized Index Structures for Querying RDF from the Web". In: *Proceedings of the Third Latin American Web Congress*. LA-WEB 2005. Washington, DC, USA: IEEE Computer Society, 2005, pp. 71–80. ISBN: 0-7695-2471-0. DOI: 10.1109/LAWEB. 2005.25.

[He+07] Hao He, Haixun Wang, Jun Yang, and Philip S. Yu. "BLINKS: ranked keyword searches on graphs". In: *Proceedings of the 2007 ACM SIGMOD International Conference on Management of Data*. Ed. by Chee Yong Chan, Beng Chin Ooi, and Aoying Zhou. SIGMOD 2007. Beijing, China: ACM, 2007, pp. 305–316. ISBN: 978-1-59593-686-8. DOI: 10.1145/1247480.1247516.

[Hea08] Tom Heath. "How Will We Interact with the Web of Data?" In: *IEEE Internet Computing* 12.5 (Sept. 2008), pp. 88–91.

[Hep08] Martin Hepp. "GoodRelations: An Ontology for Describing Products and Services Offers on the Web". In: *Proceedings of the 16th International Conference on Knowledge Engineering: Practice and Patterns*. Ed. by Aldo Gangemi and Jérôme Euzenat. Vol. 5268. EKAW 2008. Acitrezza, Italy: Springer, 2008, pp. 329–346. ISBN: 978-3-540-87695-3. DOI: 10. 1007/978-3-540-87696-0_29.

[Hew+05] Daniel Hewlett, Aditya Kalyanpur, Vladimir Kolovski, and Christian Halaschek-Wiener. "Effective NL Paraphrasing of Ontologies on the Semantic Web". In: *Proceedings of the Workshop on End User Semantic Web Interaction at the 4th International Semantic Web Conference*. ISWC 2005. 2005.

[HHS14] Andreas Harth, Katja Hose, and Ralf Schenkel. *Linked Data Management*. CRC Press, 2014. ISBN: 9781466582408.

[Hig08] Sarah Higgins. "The DCC curation lifecycle model". In: *Proceedings of the 8th ACM/IEEE-CS Joint Conference on Digital Libraries*. JCDL 2008. Pittsburgh, PA, USA: ACM, 2008, pp. 453–453. ISBN: 978-1-59593-998-2. DOI: 10.1145/1378889.1378998.

[HK07] Andrew F. Hayes and Klaus Krippendorff. "Answering the call for a standard reliability measure for coding data". In: *Communication methods and measures* 1.1 (2007), pp. 77–89.

[HKR09] Pascal Hitzler, Markus Krötzsch, and Sebastian Rudolph. *Foundations of Semantic Web Technologies*. CRC Press, 2009. ISBN: 142009050X, 9781420090505.

[HO11] Jane Hunter and Suleiman Odat. "Building a Semantic Knowledge-base for Painting Conservators". In: *Proceedings of the IEEE 7th International Conference on E-Science*. e-science 2011. IEEE. Dec. 2011, pp. 173–180.

[Hof+11] Raphael Hoffmann, Congle Zhang, Xiao Ling, Luke Zettlemoyer, and Daniel S. Weld. "Knowledge-based weak supervision for information extraction of overlapping relations". In: *Proceedings of the 49th Annual Meeting of the Association for Computational Linguistics: Human Language Technologies*. HLT 2011. Portland, Oregon: Association for Computational Linguistics, 2011, pp. 541–550. ISBN: 978-1-932432-87-9.

[Hog+11] Aidan Hogan, Andreas Harth, Jürgen Umbrich, Sheila Kinsella, Axel Polleres, and Stefan Decker. "Searching and Browsing Linked Data with SWSE: the Semantic Web Search Engine". In: *Web Semantics: Science, Services and Agents on the World Wide Web* 9.4 (2011), pp. 365–401.

[HS10] Steve Harris and Andy Seaborne. *SPARQL 1.1 Query Language*. W3C Recommendation, http://www.w3.org/TR/sparql11-query/ (URL last accessed 2015-01-02). Oct. 2010.

[HT03] Anthony J. G. Hey and Anne E. Trefethen. "The Data Deluge: An e-Science Perspective". In: *Grid Computing – Making the Global Infrastructure a Reality*. Ed. by Fran Berman, Anthony J. G. Hey, and Geoffrey C. Fox. Chapter: 36. Wiley and Sons, 2003, pp. 809–824.

[Huv08] Isto Huvila. "Participatory archive: towards decentralised curation, radical user orientation, and broader contextualisation of records management". In: *Archival Science* 8.1 (Sept. 2008), pp. 15–36.

[Huv12] Isto Huvila. "Being Formal and Flexible: Semantic Wiki as an Archaeological e-Science Infrastructure". In: *Revive the Past: Proceeding of the 39th Conference on Computer Applications and Quantitative Methods in Archaeology*. 2012, pp. 186–197.

[IDE12] IDEAlliance. *PRISM (Publishing Requirements for Industry Standard Metadata)*. http://www.idealliance.org/specifications/prism-metadata-initiative/prism. Oct. 2012.

[Juo08] Patrick Juola. "Killer applications in digital humanities". In: *Literary and Linguistic Computing* 23.1 (2008), pp. 73–83.

[JW14] Ian Jacobs and Norman Walsh. *Architecture of the World Wide Web Vol. 1*. W3C Recommendation, 15 December 2014 http://www.w3.org/TR/webarch/. 2014.

[KBF07] Esther Kaufmann, Abraham Bernstein, and Lorenz Fischer. "NLP-Reduce: A "naïve" but Domain-independent Natural Language Interface for Querying Ontologies". In: *Proceedings of the 4th European Semantic Web Conference*. ESWC 2007. Springer, 2007.

[KBZ06] Esther Kaufmann, Abraham Bernstein, and Renato Zumstein. "Querix: A natural language interface to query ontologies based on clarification dialogs". In: *Proceedings of the 5th International Semantic Web Conference*. ISWC 2006. Athens, GA: Springer, 2006, pp. 980–981. ISBN: 3-540-49029-9, 978-3-540-49029-6.

[KD08] Georgi Kobilarov and Ian Dickinson. "Humboldt: Exploring linked data". In: *Proceedings of the Workshop on Linked Data on the Web*. LDOW 2008. 2008.

[KF07] Kaarel Kaljurand and Norbert E. Fuchs. "Verbalizing OWL in Attempto Controlled English". In: *Proceedings of the OWLED 2007 Workshop on OWL: Experiences and Directions*. Ed. by Christine Golbreich, Aditya Kalyanpur, and Bijan Parsia. Vol. 258. CEUR Workshop Proceedings. CEUR-WS.org, 2007.

[KM03] Dan Klein and Christopher D. Manning. "Accurate Unlexicalized Parsing". In: *Proceedings of the 41st Annual Meeting of the Association for Computational Linguistics*. Ed. by Erhard Hinrichs and Dan Roth. ACL 2003. Sapporo, Japan: Association for Computational Linguistics, 2003, pp. 423–430. DOI: 10.3115/1075096.1075150.

[Kri04] Klaus Krippendorff. "Reliability in Content Analysis". In: *Human Communication Research* 30.3 (2004), pp. 411–433.

[KSI10] Georgia Koutrika, Alkis Simitsis, and Yannis E Ioannidis. "Explaining Structured Queries in Natural Language". In: *Data Engineering (ICDE), 2010 IEEE 26th International Conference on*. IEEE. 2010, pp. 333–344.

[KZC07] Anastasia Karanastasi, Alexandros Zotos, and Stavros Christodoulakis. "The OntoNL framework for natural language interface generation and a domain-specific application". In: *Digital Libraries: Research and Development*. Springer, 2007, pp. 228–237.

[Leh+12] Jens Lehmann, Tim Furche, Giovanni Grasso, Axel-Cyrille Ngonga Ngomo, Christian Schallhart, Andrew Sellers, Christina Unger, Lorenz Bühmann, Daniel Gerber, Konrad Höffner, David Liu, and Sören Auer. "DEQA: Deep Web Extraction for Question Answering". In: *Proceedings of the 11th International Semantic Web Conference*. ISWC 2012.

Boston, MA: Springer, 2012, pp. 131–147. ISBN: 978-3-642-35172-3. DOI: 10.1007/978-3-642-35173-0_9.

[Leh03] Meir M. Lehman. "Software evolution threat and challenge". In: *Proceedings of the International Conference on Software Maintenance (ICSM)*. ICSM 2003. Washington, DC, USA: IEEE Computer Society, 2003. ISBN: 0-7695-1905-9.

[LP97] James C. Lester and Bruce W. Porter. "Developing and Empirically Evaluating Robust Explanation Generators: The KNIGHT Experiments". In: *Computational Linguistics* 23.1 (1997), pp. 65–101.

[LRR00] Benoit Lavoie, Owen Rambow, and Ehud Reiter. "Customizable descriptions of object-oriented models". In: *Proceedings of the 6th Conference on Applied Natural Language Processing*. ANLC 2000. Seattle, Washington: Association for Computational Linguistics, 2000, pp. 253–256. DOI: 10.3115/974147.974178.

[LS10] Éric Leclercq and Marinette Savonnet. "Access and Annotation of Archaeological Corpus via a Semantic Wiki". In: *Proceedings of the 5th Workshop on Semantic Wikis (Semwiki) at the 5th European Semantic Web Conference (ESWC 2008)*. Ed. by Christoph Lange, Jochen Reutelshoefer, Sebastian Schaffert, and Hala Skaf-Molli. Vol. 632. CEUR Workshop Proceedings. CEUR-WS.org, May 2010.

[LSR11] Shao Fen Liang, Robert Stevens, and Alan Rector. "OntoVerbal-M: a Multilingual Verbaliser for SNOMED CT". In: *Proceedings of the 2nd International Workshop on the Multilingual Semantic Web*. Ed. by Elena Montiel-Ponsoda, John McCrae, Paul Buitelaar, and Philipp Cimiano. Vol. 775. CEUR Workshop Proceedings. CEUR-WS.org, 2011, pp. 13–24.

[LUM06] Yuangui Lei, Victoria Uren, and Enrico Motta. "SemSearch: A Search Engine for the Semantic Web". In: *Managing Knowledge in a World of Networks*. Springer, 2006, pp. 238–245.

[Mas03] Oliver Mason. *Qtag 3.1*. Department of English, School of Humanities, University of Birmingham. 2003.

[MB09] Alistair Miles and Sean Bechhofer. *SKOS Simple Knowledge Organization System Reference*. W3C Recommendation, 18 August 2009, http://www.w3.org/TR/skos-reference/. 2009.

[MBS10] Nor Azlinayati Abdul Manaf, Sean Bechhofer, and Robert Stevens. "A Survey of Identifiers and Labels in OWL Ontologies". In: *Proceedings of the OWLED 2007 Workshop on OWL: Experiences and Directions*. Ed. by Christine Golbreich, Aditya Kalyanpur, and Bijan Parsia. Vol. 258. CEUR Workshop Proceedings. CEUR-WS.org, 2010.

[McD92] David D. McDonald. "Natural-Language Generation". In: *Encyclopedia of Artificial Intelligence*. Ed. by Stuart C. Shapiro. 2nd. New York: John Wiley, 1992, pp. 642–655.

[MD98] Chris Mellish and Robert Dale. "Evaluation in the context of natural language generation". In: *Computer Speech & Language* 12.4 (1998), pp. 349–373.

[Men+08] Pablo N. Mendes, Bobby McKnight, Amit P. Sheth, and Jessica C. Kissinger. "TcruziKB: Enabling Complex Queries for Genomic Data Exploration". In: *Proceedings of the 2008 IEEE International Conference on Semantic Computing*. ICSC 2008. Washington, DC, USA: IEEE Computer Society, 2008, pp. 432–439. ISBN: 978-0-7695-3279-0. DOI: 10.1109/ICSC.2008.93.

[Mik08] Peter Mika. "Microsearch: An Interface for Semantic Search". In: *Proceedings of the Workshop on Semantic Search (SemSearch 2008) at the 5th European Semantic Web Conference (ESWC 2008)*. Ed. by Stephan Bloehdorn, Marko Grobelnik, and Duc Thanh Tran. Vol. 334. CEUR Workshop Proceedings. CEUR-WS.org, June 2008, pp. 79–88.

[Min+09] Mike Mintz, Steven Bills, Rion Snow, and Dan Jurafsky. "Distant Supervision for Relation Extraction Without Labeled Data". In: *Proceedings of the Joint Conference of the 47th Annual Meeting of the ACL and the 4th International Joint Conference on Natural Language Processing of the AFNLP*. ACL 2009. Suntec, Singapore: Association for Computational Linguistics, 2009, pp. 1003–1011. ISBN: 978-1-932432-46-6.

[Min05] Michael Minock. "A Phrasal Approach to Natural Language Interfaces over Databases". In: *Proceedings of the 10th International Conference on Natural Language Processing and Information Systems*. Ed. by Andrés Montoyo, Rafael Muñoz, and Elisabeth Métais. NLDB 2005. Alicante, Spain: Springer, 2005, pp. 333–336. ISBN: 3-540-26031-5, 978-3-540-26031-8. DOI: 10.1007/11428817_30.

[Min10] Michael Minock. "C-Phrase: A system for building robust natural language interfaces to databases". In: *Data & Knowledge Engineering* 69.3 (Mar. 2010), pp. 290–302.

[MMZ09] Peter Mika, Edgar Meij, and Hugo Zaragoza. "Investigating the Semantic Gap through Query Log Analysis". In: *Proceedings of the 8th International Semantic Web Conference*. ISWC 2009. Berlin, Heidelberg: Springer, 2009, pp. 441–455.

[Mor+08] Luc Moreau, Juliana Freire, Joe Futrelle, Robert E McGrath, Jim Myers, and Patrick Paulson. "The open provenance model: An overview". In: *Provenance and Annotation of Data and Processes*. Springer, 2008, pp. 323–326.

[MS06] Chris Mellish and Xiantang Sun. "The Semantic Web as a Linguistic Resource: Opportunities for Natural Language Generation". In: *Knowledge-Based Systems* 19.5 (2006), pp. 298–303.

[MSC12] John McCrae, Dennis Spohr, and Philipp Cimiano. "Linking Lexical Resources and Ontologies on the Semantic Web with Lemon". In: *Proceedings of the 8th Extended Semantic Web Conference*. ESWC 2011. Heraklion, Crete, Greece: Springer, 2012, pp. 245–259. ISBN: 978-3-642-25952-4.

[MTD96] Maria Milosavljevic, Adrian Tulloch, and Robert Dale. "Text generation in a dynamic hypertext environment". In: *Australian Computer Science Communications* 18 (1996), pp. 417–426.

[Möl+07] Knud Möller, Tom Heath, Siegfried Handschuh, and John Domingue. "Recipes for Semantic Web Dog Food – The ESWC and ISWC Metadata Projects". In: *Proceedings of the 6th International Semantic Web Conference and the 2nd Asian Semantic Web Conference*. ISWC 2007/ASWC 2007. Busan, Korea: Springer, 2007, pp. 802–815. ISBN: 3-540-76297-3, 978-3-540-76297-3. DOI: 10.1007/978-3-540-76298-0_58.

[Möl+10] Knud Möller, Michael Hausenblas, Richard Cyganiak, and Gunnar Aastrand Grimnes. "Learning from Linked Open Data Usage: Patterns & Metrics". In: *Proceedings of the 2nd Annual Web Science Conference*. WebSci 2010. Raleigh, North Carolina, USA, 2010.

[Neu+09] Heike Neuroth, Fotis Jannidis, Andrea Rapp, and Felix Lohmeier. "Virtuelle Forschungsumgebungen für e-Humanities. Maßnahmen zur optimalen Unterstützung von Forschungsprozessen in den Geisteswissenschaften". In: *BIBLIOTHEK Forschung und Praxis* 33.2 (2009), pp. 161–169.

[New+59] Howard B. Newcombe, James M. Kennedy, S. J. Axford, and Allison P. James. "Automatic Linkage of Vital Records Computers can be used to extract follow-up statistics of families from files of routine records". In: *Science* 130.3381 (1959), pp. 954–959.

[NN+13] Axel-Cyrille Ngonga Ngomo, Lorenz Bühmann, Christina Unger, Jens Lehmann, and Daniel Gerber. "SPARQL2NL: Verbalizing Sparql Queries". In: *Proceedings of the 22st International Conference on World Wide Web*. WWW 2013. New York, NY, USA: ACM, 2013, pp. 329–332.

[Noy+06] Natasha Noy, Alan Rector, Pat Hayes, and Chris Welty. *Defining N-ary Relations on the Semantic Web*. W3C Working Group Note, http://www.w3.org/TR/swbp-n-aryRelations/. Apr. 2006.

[NTN85] Makoto Nagao, Jun-ichi Tsujii, and Jun-ichi Nakamura. "The Japanese government project for machine translation". In: *Computational Linguistics* 11.2-3 (Apr. 1985), pp. 91–110.

[Ovc12] Ekaterina Ovchinnikova. *Integration of World Knowledge for Natural Language Understanding*. Vol. 3. Springer, 2012. ISBN: 978-94-91216-53-4.

[PAG08] Jorge Pérez, Marcelo Arenas, and Claudio Gutierrez. *Semantics of SPARQL*. http://dcc.uchile.cl/~jperez/papers/sparql_semantics.pdf. 2008.

[PHH12] Camille Pradel, Ollivier Haemmerlé, and Nathalie Hernandez. "A semantic web interface using patterns: the SWIP system". In: *Graph Structures for Knowledge Representation and Reasoning*. Springer, 2012, pp. 172–187.

[Pic+10] Helena Piccinini, Melissa Lemos, Marco A. Casanova, and Antonio L. Furtado. "W-Ray: A strategy to publish deep web geographic data". In: *Proceedings of the 2010 International Conference on Advances in Conceptual Modeling: Applications and Challenges*. ER 2010. Vancouver, BC, Canada: Springer, 2010, pp. 2–11. ISBN: 978-3-642-16384-5.

[Pic+11a] Helena Piccinini, Luiz A. G. A. Figueredo, Marco A. Casanova, and Antonio L. Furtado. *Publishing Deep Web Data with the W-Ray Toolkit*. 2011.

[Pic+11b] Helena Piccinini, Marco A. Casanova, Antonio L. Furtado, and Bernardo P. Nunes. "Verbalization of RDF Triples with Applications". In: *Proceedings of the 10th International Semantic Web Conference*. ISWC 2011. Springer, Oct. 2011.

[Pig96] Thomas M. Pigoski. *Practical Software Maintenance: Best Practices for Managing Your Software Investment*. Ed. by Marjorie Spencer. 1st edition. New York, NY, USA: John Wiley & Sons, Inc., 1996, p. 400.

[Pro10] The Protégé Project. *Protégé*. http://protege.stanford.edu. 2010.

[PS08] Eric Prud'hommeaux and Andy Seaborne. *SPARQL Query Language for RDF*. W3C Recommendation, http://www.w3.org/TR/rdf-sparql-query/. Jan. 2008.

[PT10] Richard Power and Allan Third. "Expressing OWL axioms by English sentences: dubious in theory, feasible in practice". In: *Proceedings of the 23rd International Conference on Computational Linguistics: Posters*. COLING 2010. Beijing, China: Association for Computational Linguistics, 2010, pp. 1006–1013.

[RB09] Ehud Reiter and Anja Belz. "An investigation into the validity of some metrics for automatically evaluating natural language generation systems". In: *Computational Linguistics* 35.4 (2009), pp. 529–558.

[RD00] Ehud Reiter and Robert Dale. *Building Natural Language Generation Systems*. Natural Language Processing. Cambridge University Press, 2000. ISBN: 0-521-62036-8.

[Rit03] Christian Ritzi. "Scripta Paedagogica Online". In: Göttingen: Duehrkohp und Radicke, 2003, pp. 115–119. ISBN: 978-3897442214.

[RK09] Vivek Anandan Ramachandran and Ilango Krishnamurthi. "NLION: Natural Language Interface for querying Ontologies". In: *Proceedings of the 2nd Bangalore Annual Compute Conference*. ACM. 2009, p. 17.

[Row+11] Ian Rowlands, David Nicholas, Bill Russell, Nicholas Canty, and Anthony Watkinson. "Social media use in the research workflow". In: *Learned Publishing* 24.3 (2011), pp. 183–195.

[SC08] Leo Sauermann and Richard Cyganiak. *Cool URIs for the Semantic Web*. W3C Note, http://www.w3.org/TR/2008/NOTE-cooluris-20081203/. Dec. 2008.

[Sch+11] Christoph Schindler, Cornelia Veja, Marc Rittberger, and Denny Vrandečić. "How to teach digital library data to swim into research". In: *Proceedings of the 7th International Conference on Semantic Systems (I-SEMANTICS 2011)*. New York, NY, USA: ACM, 2011, pp. 142–149.

[Sch09] Niels Schütte. "Generating natural language descriptions of ontology concepts". In: *Proceedings of the 12th European Workshop on Natural Language Generation*. ENLG 2009. Athens, Greece: Association for Computational Linguistics, 2009, pp. 106–109.

[SE12] Christoph Schindler and Basil Ell. *Semantic MediaWiki for Collaborative Corpora Analysis: Analyzing Educational Reference Books in a Virtual Research Environment*. Peer-reviewed abstract. ECER 2012. Sept. 2012.

[SE13] Christoph Schindler and Basil Ell. "Kollaborative Analyse von historischen Netzwerken: Virtuelle Forschungsumgebung für die Historische Bildungsforschung". In: *Netzwerke in bildungshistorischer Perspektive*. Ed. by Andreas Hoffmann und Peter Metz Hans-Ulrich Grunder. Bad Heilbrunn: Verlag Julius Klinkhardt, Oct. 2013, pp. 142–148.

[SER12] Christoph Schindler, Basil Ell, and Marc Rittberger. "Intra-linking the Research Corpus: Using Semantic MediaWiki as a lightweight Virtual Research Environment". In: *Digital Humanities 2012*. Ed. by Jan Christoph Meister, Katrin Schönert, Bastian Lomsché, Wilhelm Schernus, Lena Schüch, and Meike Stegkemper. Hamburg: Hamburg University Press, 2012, pp. 359–362.

[SER13] Christoph Schindler, Basil Ell, and Marc Rittberger. "Virtual Research Environment SMW-CorA and its Capacities for Interaction in Social Science and Humanities Research – Using the Example of History of Education". In: *Informationswissenschaft zwischen virtueller Infrastruktur und materiellen Lebenswelten. Tagungsband des 13. Internationalen Symposiums der Informationswissenschaft*. Ed. by H.-C. Hobohm. Glückstadt: vwh, Mar. 2013, pp. 254–266.

[She+11] Saeedeh Shekarpour, Sören Auer, Axel-Cyrille Ngonga Ngomo, Daniel Gerber, Sebastian Hellmann, and Claus Stadler. "Keyword-driven SPARQL Query Generation Leveraging Background Knowledge". In: *Proceedings of the 2011 IEEE/WIC/ACM International Conferences on Web Intelligence and Intelligent Agent Technology – Volume 01*. WI-IAT 2011. Washington, DC, USA: IEEE Computer Society, 2011, pp. 203–210. ISBN: 978-0-7695-4513-4. DOI: 10.1109/WI-IAT.2011.70.

[SHR08] Nicholas Smith, Sebastian Hoffmann, and Paul Rayson. "Corpus tools and methods, today and tomorrow: Incorporating linguists' manual annotations". In: *Literary and Linguistic Computing* 23.2 (2008), pp. 163–180.

[Sid+05] Amandeep S. Sidhu, Tharam S. Dillon, Elizabeth Chang, and Baldev S. Sidhu. "OWL, proteins and data integration". In: *Proceedings of the 18th Australian Joint Conference on Advances in Artificial Intelligence*. AI 2005. Sydney, Australia: Springer, 2005, pp. 1158–1161. ISBN: 3-540-30462-2, 978-3-540-30462-3. DOI: 10.1007/11589990_161.

[SM06] Xiantang Sun and Chris Mellish. "Domain Independent Sentence Generation from RDF Representations for the Semantic Web". In: *Proceedings of Combined Workshop on Language-Enabled Educational Technology and Development and Evaluation of Robust Spoken Dialogue Systems (part of ECAI 2006)*. Ed. by Charles Callaway, Andrea Corradini, Jörn Kreutel, Johanna Moore, and Manfred Stede. 2006.

[SM07] Xiantang Sun and Chris Mellish. "An experiment on "free generation" from single RDF triples". In: *Proceedings of the 11th European Workshop on Natural Language Generation*. ENLG 2007. Stroudsburg, PA, USA: Association for Computational Linguistics, 2007, pp. 105–108.

[Ste+10] Robert Stevens, James Malone, Sandra Williams, and Richard Power. "Automating class definitions from OWL to English". In: *Proceedings of Bio-Ontologies 2010: Semantic Applications in Life Sciences SIG at the 18th Annual International Conference on Intelligent Systems for Molecular Biology*. ISMB 2010. July 2010.

[Ste+11] Robert Stevens, James Malone, Sandra Williams, Richard Power, and Allan Third. "Automating generation of textual class definitions from OWL to English". In: *Journal of Biomedical Semantics* 2.Suppl 2 (2011). DOI: 10.1186/2041-1480-2-S2-S5.

[Sti+14] Anna Stisser, Anne Hild, Basil Ell, and Christoph Schindler. "Neue Forschungswerkzeuge in der Historischen Bildungsforschung. Die virtuelle Forschungsumgebung SMW-CorA für die kollaborative Analyse und Aus-wertung umfangreicher digitalisierter Quellen". In: *Jahrbuch für Historische Bildungsforschung 2013*. Vol. 19 Avantgarden. Bad Heilbrunn: Julius Klinkhardt, 2014, pp. 305–324. ISBN: 978-3-7815-1960-2.

[Sur+05] York Sure, Stephan Bloehdorn, Peter Haase, Jens Hartmann, and Daniel Oberle. "The SWRC Ontology – Semantic Web for Research Communities". In: *Proceedings of the 12th Portuguese Conference on Artificial Intelligence – Progress in Artificial Intelligence (EPIA 2005)*. Ed. by Gael Dias Carlos Bento Amilcar Cardoso. Vol. 3803. LNCS. Covilha, Portugal: Springer, Dec. 2005, pp. 218–231.

[Sur+12] Mihai Surdeanu, Julie Tibshirani, Ramesh Nallapati, and Christopher D. Manning. "Multi-instance multi-label learning for relation extraction". In: *Proceedings of the 2012 Joint Conference on Empirical Methods in Natural Language Processing and Computational Natural Language Learning*. EMNLP-CoNLL 2012. Jeju Island, Korea: Association for Computational Linguistics, 2012, pp. 455–465.

[SWM04] Michael K. Smith, Chris Welty, and Deborah McGuinness. *OWL Web Ontology Language Guide*. W3C Recommendation, 10 February 2004, http://www.w3.org/TR/owl-guide/. Feb. 2004.

[TAN10] Samir Tartir, Ismailcem Arpinar, and Mustafa Nural. "Question answering in linked data for scientific exploration". In: *Proceedings of the 2nd Annual Web Science Conference*. WebSci 2010. Raleigh, North Carolina, USA, Apr. 2010.

[TDO07] Giovanni Tummarello, Renaud Delbru, and Eyal Oren. "Sindice.com: Weaving the open linked data". In: *Proceedings of the 6th International Semantic Web Conference and 2nd Asian Semantic Web Conference*. ISWC 2007/ASWC 2007. Busan, Korea: Springer, 2007, pp. 552–565. ISBN: 3-540-76297-3, 978-3-540-76297-3.

[TPS07] Edward Thomas, Jeff Z. Pan, and Derek Sleeman. "ONTOSEARCH2: Searching ontologies semantically". In: *Proceedings of the OWLED 2007 Workshop on OWL: Experiences and Directions*. Ed. by Christine Golbreich, Aditya Kalyanpur, and Bijan Parsia. Vol. 258. CEUR Workshop Proceedings. CEUR-WS.org, 2007, pp. 70–72.

[Tra+09] Duc Thanh Tran, Haofen Wang, Sebastian Rudolph, and Philipp Cimiano. "Top-k Exploration of Query Candidates for Efficient Keyword Search on Graph-Shaped (RDF) Data". In: *Proceedings of the 25th International Conference on Data Engineering (ICDE'09)*. Shanghai, China, Mar. 2009, pp. 405–416.

[Tum+10] Giovanni Tummarello, Richard Cyganiak, Michele Catasta, Szymon Danielczyk, Renaud Delbru, and Stefan Decker. "Sig.ma: Live views on the Web of Data". In: *Web Semantics: Science, Services and Agents on the World Wide Web* 8.4 (2010), pp. 355–364. ISSN: 1570-8268. DOI: http://dx.doi.org/10.1016/j.websem.2010.08.003.

[TWH09] Duc Thanh Tran, Haofen Wang, and Peter Haase. "Hermes: Data Web search on a pay-as-you-go integration infrastructure". In: *Journal of Web Semantics* 7.3 (2009), pp. 189–203.

[TWP11] Allan Third, Sandra Williams, and Richard Power. "OWL to English: a tool for generating organised easily-navigated hypertexts from ontologies". In: *Proceedings of the 10th International Semantic Web Conference*. ISWC 2011. Oct. 2011.

[Ung+12] Christina Unger, Lorenz Bühmann, Jens Lehmann, Axel-Cyrille Ngonga Ngomo, Daniel Gerber, and Philipp Cimiano. "Template-based question answering over RDF data". In: *Proceedings of the 21st International Conference on World Wide Web*. WWW 2012. Lyon, France: ACM, 2012, pp. 639–648. ISBN: 978-1-4503-1229-5. DOI: 10.1145/2187836.2187923.

[Vol+09] Julius Volz, Christian Bizer, Martin Gaedke, and Georgi Kobilarov. "Discovering and Maintaining Links on the Web of Data". In: *Proceedings of the 8th International Semantic Web Conference*. ISWC 2009. Springer, 2009, pp. 650–665.

[VP09] Alexander Voss and Rob Procter. "Virtual research environments in scholarly work and communications". In: *Library Hi Tech* 27.2 (June 2009), pp. 174–190.

[Vra+11] Denny Vrandečić, Varun Ratnakar, Markus Krötzsch, and Yolanda Gil. "Shortipedia: Aggregating and Curating Semantic Web Data". In: *Web Semantics: Science, Services and Agents on the World Wide Web* 9.3 (2011), pp. 334–338. ISSN: 1570-8268. DOI: http://dx.doi.org/10.1016/j.websem.2011.06.006.

[VSS11] Denny Vrandečić, Philipp Sorg, and Rudi Studer. "Language Resources extracted from Wikipedia". In: *Proceedings of the 6th International Conference on Knowledge Capture*. K-CAP 2011. Banff, Alberta, Canada: ACM, 2011, pp. 153–160. ISBN: 978-1-4503-0396-5. DOI: 10.1145/1999676.1999703.

[Wan+07] Chong Wang, Miao Xiong, Qi Zhou, and Yong Yu. "Panto: A portable natural language interface to ontologies". In: *Proceedings of the 4th European Semantic Web Conference*. ESWC 2007. Springer, 2007, pp. 473–487.

[Wan+08a] Haofen Wang, Kang Zhang, Qiaoling Liu, Thanh Tran, and Yong Yu. "Q2semantic: A lightweight keyword interface to semantic search". In: *Proceedings of the 5th European Semantic Web Conference*. ESWC 2008. 2008, pp. 584–598.

[Wan+08b] Haofen Wang, Thanh Tran, Peter Haase, Thomas Penin, Qiaoling Liu, Linyun Fu, and Yong Yu. "SearchWebDB: Searching the Billion Triples". In: *Proceedings of the Billion Triple Challenge at the 7th International Semantic Web Conference (ISWC 2008)*. 2008.

[Wel+10] Chris Welty, James Fan, David Gondek, and Andrew Schlaikjer. "Large scale relation detection". In: *Proceedings of the NAACL HLT 2010 First International Workshop on Formalisms and Methodology for Learning by Reading*. FAM-LbR 2010. Los Angeles, California: Association for Computational Linguistics, 2010, pp. 24–33.

[WGD12] Matthias Wendt, Martin Gerlach, and Holger Düwiger. "Linguistic Modeling of Linked Open Data for Question Answering". In: *Proceedings of the Interacting with Linked Data Workshop, co-located with the 9th Extended Semantic Web Conference*. Vol. 913. ILD 2012. Heraklion, Greece: CEUR-WS.org, May 2012, pp. 75–86.

[Wil03] Graham Wilcock. "Talking OWLs: Towards an Ontology Verbalizer". In: *Proceedings of 5th International Workshop on Human Language Technology for the Semantic Web and Web Services at the 2nd International Semantic Web Conference*. ISWC 2003. Sanibel Island, Florida, 2003, pp. 109–112.

[Wil11] Sandra Williams. "Generating mathematical word problems". In: *2011 Association for the Advancement of Artificial Intelligence (AAAI) Fall Symposium on Question Generation*. Nov. 2011, pp. 61–64.

[WJ03] Graham Wilcock and Kristiina Jokinen. "Generating responses and explanations from RDF/XML and DAML+OIL". In: *Proceedings of the 7th IJCAI workshop on Knowledge and Reasoning in Practical Dialogue Systems*. 2003, pp. 58–63.

[WPH06] Taowei David Wang, Bijang Parsia, and James Hendler. "A Survey of the Web Ontology Landscape". In: *Proceedings of the 5th International Semantic Web Conference*. ISWC 2006. Athens, GA: Springer, 2006, pp. 682–694. ISBN: 3-540-49029-9, 978-3-540-49029-6. DOI: 10.1007/11926078_49.

[WUC13] Sebastian Walter, Christina Unger, and Philipp Cimiano. "A Corpus-Based Approach for the Induction of Ontology Lexica". In: *Natural Language Processing and Information Systems*. Ed. by Elisabeth Métais, Farid Meziane, Mohamad Saraee, Vijayan Sugumaran, and Sunil Vadera. Vol. 7934. Lecture Notes in Computer Science. Springer Berlin Heidelberg, 2013, pp. 102–113. ISBN: 978-3-642-38823-1. DOI: 10.1007/978-3-642-38824-8_9.

[Yah+12] Mohamed Yahya, Klaus Berberich, Shady Elbassuoni, Maya Ramanath, Volker Tresp, and Gerhard Weikum. "Deep Answers for Naturally Asked Questions on the Web of Data". In: *Proceedings of the 21st International Conference on World Wide Web*. WWW 2012. Lyon, France: ACM, 2012, pp. 445–449. ISBN: 978-1-4503-1230-1. DOI: 10.1145/2187980.2188070.

[YH02] Xifeng Yan and Jiawei Han. "gSpan: Graph-Based Substructure Pattern Mining". In: *Proceedings of the 2002 IEEE International Conference on Data Mining*. ICDM 2002. Washington, DC, USA: IEEE Computer Society, 2002, pp. 721–724. ISBN: 0-7695-1754-4.

[Zho+07] Qi Zhou, Chong Wang, Miao Xiong, Haofen Wang, and Yong Yu. "SPARK: Adapting Keyword Query to Semantic Search". In: *Proceedings of the 6th International Semantic Web Conference and 2nd Asian Semantic Web Conference*. Ed. by Karl Aberer, Key-Sun Choi, Natasha Fridman Noy, Dean Allemang, Kyung-Il Lee, Lyndon J. B. Nixon, Jennifer Golbeck, Peter Mika, Diana Maynard, Riichiro Mizoguchi, Guus Schreiber, and Philippe Cudré-Mauroux. Vol. 4825. ISWC 2007/ASWC 2007. Busan, Korea: Springer, 2007, pp. 694–707. ISBN: 978-3-540-76297-3.

[Şen+10] Murat Şensoy, Timothy J. Norman, Wamberto W. Vasconcelos, and Katia Sycara. "OWL-POLAR: Semantic policies for agent reasoning". In: *Proceedings of the 9th International Semantic Web Conference*. ISWC 2010. Shanghai, China: Springer, 2010, pp. 679–695. ISBN: 3-642-17745-X, 978-3-642-17745-3.